East Timor, Australia and Regional Order

While humanitarian intervention was the major innovation in global governance in the 1990s, until the East Timor case it was always in the territory of a failing state. This book explains the exceptional nature of the East Timor intervention of 1999, and deals with the background to the trusteeship role of the UN in building the new polity. All of these developments had an important impact on regional order, not least testing the ASEAN norm of 'non-interference'.

Australian complicity in the Indonesian occupation of East Timor was a major factor in the persistence of Indonesian rule in the territory which was maintained for 25 years despite international censure and which required an unremitting campaign against the independence movement. This work reviews the reasons for that history of complicity, and explains the extraordinary change of policy that led ultimately to the occupation of the territory by the Australian-led INTERFET coalition.

This book will be essential reading for students of political science, Asian studies and international relations.

James Cotton is a highly respected Australian academic who has written extensively about Asian politics and political thought. A professor in the University of New South Wales at the Australian Defence Force Academy, he is the author of over 150 publications and currently acts as consulting editor of the *Australian Journal of International Affairs*.

Politics in Asia series
Formerly edited by Michael Leifer
London School of Economics

East Timor, Australia and Regional Order

Intervention and its aftermath in Southeast Asia

James Cotton

RoutledgeCurzon
Taylor & Francis Group
LONDON AND NEW YORK

First published 2004 by RoutledgeCurzon
11 New Fetter Lane, London EC4P 4EE

Simultaneously published in the USA and Canada
by RoutledgeCurzon
29 West 35th Street, New York, NY 10001

RoutledgeCurzon is an imprint of the Taylor & Francis Group

Typeset in Baskerville by
Keystroke, Jacaranda Lodge, Wolverhampton
Printed and bound in Great Britain by
Antony Rowe Ltd, Chippenham, Wiltshire

British Library Cataloguing in Publication Data
A catalogue record for this book is available from the British Library

Library of Congress Cataloging in Publication Data
A catalog record for this book has been requested

ISBN 0–415–33580–9

Contents

Acknowledgements

I am obliged to the following friends and scholars for their counsel and advice: Peter Bartu, Anthony Bergin, Jean Berlie, James Brew, Peter Carey, Jarat Chopra, Ross Cottrill, Antonio Barbedo de Magalhães, Peter Bartu, Des Ball, Derek da Cunha, Peter Edwards, Jim Fox, David Goodman, Paulo Gorjão, David Hicks, Robert King, Michael Leifer, Liem Sioe Liong, Michael Maley, William Maley, Anthony Milner, Gavin Mount, John Ravenhill, Leonard Sebastian, Anthony Smith, Mike Smith, Hadi Soesastro, Bong-Scuk Sohn, 'Max Stahl', John Taylor, Ramesh Thakur, Jusuf Wanandi, Hugh White, Phillip Winn, two anonymous referees acting for Routledge and especially Geoffrey Gunn; to Sue Moss and Susan Cowan for research assistance; and to the libraries of the Australian National University, the Institute of Southeast Asian Studies, Singapore, the Australian Defence Force Academy, the London School of Economics, and the School of Oriental and African Studies, London for their assistance in obtaining materials. Madeleine Davis prepared the index. I wish also to record my thanks to officials and politicians in East Timor, the United States, the United Kingdom, Indonesia, South Korea, Thailand, the Philippines, Singapore and Australia for finding time to answer my inquiries.

Parts of this book incorporate in revised form some material drawn from the following previous publications:

'East Timor and Australia – 25 years of the policy debate', in *East Timor and Australia. AIIA Contributions to the Policy Debate* (Canberra: ADSC/AIIA, 1999); '"Peacekeeping" in East Timor: an Australian Policy Departure', *Australian Journal of International Affairs*, 53 (1999), no. 3, 237–46, reproduced by permission of Taylor and Francis <www.tandf.co.uk/journals/carfax/10357718.html>; '"Part of the Indonesian world": lessons in East Timor policy making, 1974–76', *Australian Journal of International Affairs* 55 (2001), no. 1, 119–31; 'Against the grain: the East Timor intervention', *Survival* 43 (2001), no. 1, 127–42, reproduced by permission of Oxford University Press and the International Institute for Strategic Studies, © Oxford University Press <www.oup.com>; 'The emergence of an independent East Timor: national and regional challenges', *Contemporary Southeast Asia* 22 (2000), no. 1, 1–22; 'Australia's commitment in East Timor', *Contemporary Southeast Asia* 23 (2001), no. 3, 552–68, reproduced with the kind permission of the publisher, the Institute of Southeast Asian Studies, Singapore <http://bookshop.iseas.edu. sg>;

'The East Timor commitment and its consequences', in (edited with John Ravenhill) *The National Interest in a Global Era: Australia in World Affairs 1996–2000* (Melbourne: Oxford University Press, 2001), 213–34, by permission of Oxford University Press Australia, © Oxford University Press <www.oup.com.au>; 'Timor Gap to Timor Sea', *Australian Quarterly* 75 (2003) no. 2, 27–32, 40.

I am obliged to the editors and publishers for permission to use this material. The map in Chapter 5 is reproduced by permission of the Australian Senate, Foreign Affairs, Defence and Trade References Committee.

James Cotton
University of New South Wales
@The Australian Defence Force Academy,
Canberra

Acronyms

ABC	Australian Broadcasting Corporation
ABRI	*Angkatan Bersenjata Republik Indonesia* (Armed Forces of the Republic of Indonesia)
ADF	Australian Defence Force
AFP	Australian Federal Police
AMS	Australia–Indonesia Agreement on Maintaining Security
ANZUS	Australia-New Zealand-US alliance
Apodeti	*Associação Popular Democrática Timorense* (Timorese Association for Popular Democracy)
ARF	ASEAN Regional Forum
ASDT	*Associação Social Democrata Timorense* (Timorese Popular Democratic Association)
ASEAN	Association of Southeast Asian Nations
AusAID	Australian Agency for International Development
BAKIN	*Badan Koordinasi Intelijens Negara* (State Intelligence Coordinating Body)
CIVPOL	(UN) civilian police
CNRM	*Conselho Nacional da Resistência Maubere* (National Council of the Maubere Resistance)
CNRT	*Conselho Nacional Da Resistência Timorense* (National Council of the Timorese Resistance)
CPD-RDTL	*Conselho Popular pela Defesa da República Democrática de Timor Leste* (Popular Council for the Defence of the Democratic Republic of East Timor)
CRRN	*Conselho Revolucionária da Resistência Nacional* (Revolutionary Council of the National Resistance)
CSCE	Conference on Security and Cooperation in Europe
CSIS	Center for Strategic and International Studies
DCP	Defence Co-operation Program
DFAT	Department of Foreign Affairs and Trade (Australia)
DJFHQ	Deployable Joint Force Head Quarters
DPKO	(UN) Department of Peace Keeping Operations
ETDF	East Timor Defence Force

ETNC	East Timor National Council
ETTA	East Timor Transitional Administration
FALINTIL	*Forças Armadas de Libertação Nacional Timor Leste* (National Liberation Armed Forces of East Timor)
FRELIMO	*Frente de Libertaçao de Moçambique* (Liberation Front of Mozambique)
FRETILIN	*Frente Revolucionária do Timor-Leste Independente* (Revolutionary Front for an Independent East Timor)
GAM	*Gerakan Aceh Merdeka* (Movement for Independent Aceh)
GOLKAR	*Golongan Karya* (Functional Groups)
HANKAM	*Departemen Pertahanan Keamanan* (Department of Defence and Security)
ICJ	International Court of Justice
ICRC	International Committee of the Red Cross
IGGI	Inter-Governmental Group on Indonesia
IMET	International Military Education and Training
INTERFET	International Force East Timor
JI	*Jemaah Islamiyah* ('Islamic Community')
Komnas HAM	*Komisi Nasional Hak Asasi Manusia* (National Commission on Human Rights)
Kopassus	*Komando Pasukhan Khusus* (Special Forces Command)
KOPKAMTIB	*Komando Operasi Pemulihan Keamanan dan Ketertiban* (Operations Command for the Restoration of Order and Security)
KOTA	*Klibur Oan Timur Aswain* (Sons of the Mountain Warriors)
KPP HAM	*Komisi Penyelidik Pelanggaran Hak Asasi Manusia* (Commission of Inquiry into Human Rights Violations in East Timor)
MPR	*Majelis Permusyawaratan Rakyat* (People's Consultative Assembly)
NCC	National Consultative Council
OPM	*Organisasi Papua Merdeka* (Free Papua Movement)
OPSUS	*Operasi Khusus* (Special Operations group)
PD	*Partido Demokrático* (Democratic Party)
PKF	Peace-keeping Force
PKI	*Partai Komunis Indonesia* (Communist Party of Indonesia)
PST	*Partido Socialista de Timor* (East Timor Socialist Party)
SBS	Special Broadcasting Service
SFADTRC	Senate Foreign Affairs, Defence and Trade References Committee
SRSG	(UN) Special Representative of the Secretary-General
TNI	*Tentara Nasional Indonesia* (Indonesian National Army)
UDT	*União Democrática de Timor* (Timorese Democratic Union)
UNAMET	United Nations Mission to East Timor
UNAVEM III	United Nations Angola Verification Mission III
UNMISET	United Nations Mission of Support in East Timor
UNOSOM II	United Nations Operation in Somalia II
UNPROFOR	United Nations Protection Force (in former Yugoslavia)

UNTAC   United Nations Transitional Authority in Cambodia
UNTAET   United Nations Transitional Administration in East Timor
UNTEA   UN Temporary Executive Authority
ZOPFAN   Zone of Peace, Freedom and Neutrality

Introduction

Southeast Asia continues to be a region of incomplete and contested nationalisms. Muslim separatism in the southern Philippines as well as in southern Thailand, independence movements in various regions of Indonesia most notably at the extremities of the republic in Aceh and West Papua, even the incomplete incorporation of the Borneo territories of eastern Malaysia all indicate that the national project in the region is still under construction. And in the case of Myanmar/Burma it may be contended that the nation-state of 1948, composed of regions that were only loosely associated during the era of British rule, is only kept together by the exercise of military power.

Nevertheless, from the perspective of formal-legal sovereignty, those state entities that emerged on the demise of colonialism have proved surprisingly resilient. With the exception of Vietnam – the division of which between 1954 and 1975 can be variously interpreted as the temporary expression of external inter-vention or as the result of competing national visions – though severely tested, none of the post-colonial states have disintegrated into component nationalities. Singapore's expulsion from Malaysia after its brief incorporation between 1963 and 1965 in many ways reflects the continuity of the British decision in 1946 to re-constitute the island as a separate colony. Secessionist movements have thus not achieved their objectives. In the wider region, the creation of Bangladesh is an exception to this generalization, as is the continued persistence of a Chinese state on Taiwan, though without the powerful patronage, respectively, of India in 1971 and of the United States from 1950, it is doubtful whether either would have come into existence. Even in the Southwest Pacific, despite problematic state performance, none of the post-colonial states have dissolved or fractured, though many have suffered major turmoil. Consequently these state entities have been the enduring foundation of regional order.

The one striking exception to this resilience of post-colonial forms is the appearance in May 2002 of an independent state in East Timor, now officially Timor-Leste, in territory formerly occupied by Indonesia between 1975 and 1999. In many respects East Timor was an unpromising candidate for nationhood. Its tiny population, meager resources and considerable internal ethno-linguistic differences militated against post-colonial statehood, as did the apparently weak cultural and political impact of the Portuguese despite their long though often tenuous association with the island.

Against all the odds, for a brief period in 1999, East Timor became a major global issue. This book is concerned with explaining the contextual reasons why East Timor defied the regional pattern and achieved independent nationhood. It is not principally concerned with the dynamics of the independence movement which sustained, unbroken since 1975, a guerilla resistance and developed in the later 1980s into a broadly based urban movement with a sophisticated political and cultural agenda. Without the sacrifice and determination of the East Timorese resistance the territory would still be a province of Indonesia; but the existence of this resistance, though a necessary factor in the events of 1999, was not in itself determining. The reasons that are the focus of this study are regional and global. They include the rise in the international arena of the doctrine of humanitarian intervention, as well as the particular circumstances of the Indonesian invasion of 1975 which prevented the effective legitimation of Jakarta's annexation in 1976. This study is also concerned, equally, with Australian policy, given Australia's role in encouraging Indonesia to confront the unresolved issue of East Timor, and then in leading the intervention coalition, the actions of which effectively launched the territory on the path to nationhood.

If East Timor's nationhood has been an unlikely development, so was Australia's sponsorship of it. Despite a legacy of complicity in Indonesian rule, from 1998 the East Timor issue was reassessed. This reassessment entailed, in important respects, a reversal in a policy of regional 'engagement' that had been pursued since at least the middle 1980s. Successive Australian leaders had embraced Suharto as a statesman and an economic genius, and had ignored the deleterious aspects of his rule in the interests of national security and economic and diplomatic integration with the neighbourhood. This profound change in Australia's regional policy, and its continuing consequences and legacies, are the second focus of this book. It is argued that the East Timor experience has taught some important security lessons while also posing lasting problems.

Finally, the book reflects on the consequences for regional order of the events of 1999. Since its inception, the ASEAN organization has been dedicated to the creation of a regional order, sufficiently resilient and self-referencing as to avoid entanglements with the great powers. To achieve these ends, respect for sovereignty, non-interference in the affairs of other states and the pacific settlement of disputes have been the norms promoted by the organization. In the interests of group solidarity and in deference towards Indonesia's informal leadership role, the attempt to 'integrate' East Timor was overlooked, despite its violation of these norms. With Indonesia unable to sustain its rule in East Timor following the fallout from the financial crisis of 1997, ASEAN had become so closely associated with the former policy as to be unable to craft an effective regional response.

Given the paralysis of regional institutions, the way was opened for the internationalization of the issue, now the gravest security problem faced by the region since the Cambodia conflict of the 1980s. The international intervention of 1999 in East Timor was unlike those other examples of the decade, in that, far from it occurring in the territory of a failed or disintegrating state, it involved a disputed province of the world's fourth most populous country and largest Muslim nation.

These events have had a lasting impact on the long-standing project of Southeast Asian nations to regulate their own security environment with their own resources. Not least, they have left Australia intimately involved in that environment by virtue of its role as informal security guarantor for the newly independent Timor-Leste, while simultaneously estranged from prevailing regional security dynamics.

The plan of this work is as follows. The first chapter reviews the place of East Timor in Australian foreign policy from the beginnings of decolonization to the end of the 'New Order' and the consequent internationalization of the issue. The second chapter considers the record of Australia–Indonesia relations, focusing especially on the events of 1974–75 and Australia's support for Jakarta's policy of annexation. Chapter 3 analyzes the failure of that policy, dealing also with the retrospective assessment in Indonesia of the issue following the relinquishing of control over the territory in October 1999. In Chapter 4 the background to and reasons for the international intervention are discussed, especially in the context of regional norms. Chapter 5 offers an account of Australia's shift in policy towards East Timor, first to support the UNAMET mission in the territory and then to lead the INTERFET intervention. This chapter also reviews some of the consequences for Australia–East Timor relations. A chapter is then devoted to a critique of the Australian government's account of the events of 1999 as expounded in its study published in 2001. The various outcomes of the intervention are the subject of Chapter 7, including the lessons to be drawn from the peace-keeping exercise and the impact it has had on Australia's regional orientation and especially on bilateral relations with Indonesia. Finally, Chapter 8 sets East Timor's independence in its widest context, dealing particularly with the role of the United Nations and its impact upon emerging domestic political structures.

1 East Timor and Australia

The 25-year policy legacy

The fact that the issue of East Timor dominated the foreign and security policy debates in Australia in 1999 is the point of departure for this account. The social and political crisis which gripped Indonesia following the economic meltdown in Asia was justifiably a topic of major concern and prompted preparations for security contingencies as well as programmes of economic and political support. Yet it seemed that almost as much attention was devoted to a territory of some 14,874 km^2 with a population of around 800,000, a minor part (albeit unwillingly) of Indonesia since 1976. To understand why East Timor was the focus of such attention it is necessary to consider first the various Australian interests – and interested publics – that were involved.

Australian interests in East Timor

Although not a major issue in earlier times, economic interest in East Timor is as old as Australian federation. While it was far from a profitable business, the first oil concession sought by an Australian business dates from 1905 (Hastings 1999). In more recent times, seabed oil and gas reserves in the Timor Gap have proven sufficiently large to justify a programme of exploration and recovery. The bulk of the proven reserves are of gas, of which there is presently a global abundance, but longer term this will comprise a significant resource. Most of the fields are in the area of joint exploration as defined by the 1989 Timor Gap Treaty. With the change in its political status, new arrangements have had to be negotiated with independent East Timor.

Timor has been a concern to Australians for reasons of security for as long as it has been a subject of commercial interest. Rumours of Portuguese plans to abandon, or Japanese intentions to acquire, East Timor were recurrent in the decades before World War II. A small Australian expeditionary force was sent to pre-empt Japanese occupation in 1941, and a bloody guerilla campaign – in which many Timorese supporters of the Australians lost their lives – ensued. In 1975 – the year of communist victories in the Indochina states – a powerful factor conditioning some attitudes to the political forces emerging in East Timor was the conviction that they might seek to establish a communist-aligned regime, thus perhaps offering a foothold for a Russian or Chinese presence 500 kms from

Australia's shores. From 1998, the spectre of a disunited or 'Balkanized' Indonesia has similarly haunted policy makers. An independent East Timor might open the way to other regions seeking a separate political identity. The resulting disorder might generate refugee flows as well as military uncertainty. In May 1995, a boat carrying 18 East Timorese asylum seekers arrived in Darwin, the first 'boat people' to arrive from the territory.

East Timor has also functioned as something of a test for the notion of regional engagement and especially the long-standing policy of seeking closer relations with Indonesia. A stronger identification of Australia with the region means little without a comprehensive accord with Indonesia, and to this end aid, investment, security and political ties have all been sought by successive Australian governments. An influential Indonesia lobby long argued in favour of a realist acceptance of the 'New Order' as the only basis for fruitful cooperation. And yet Jakarta's policy in East Timor ran counter to so many of the fundamentals held by Australians regarding good governance and humanitarian values. The army was used as an instrument of rule, the human rights of those who contested Indonesian sovereignty were systematically violated, political and even cultural expression were constrained. Every crisis in the territory stirred debate on the desirability and morality of seeking systematic accord with such a regime. And the range of opinions expressed on the issue was exceedingly broad, with some alleging that critics of Indonesia were engaged in a 'vendetta', while others characterized Australian policy as nothing less than 'Finlandization' (Arndt 1979; Wheeldon 1984).

The question of East Timor, in the process, became a major item in domestic politics. Timor provided the substance for major differences that have been as much inter- as intra-party, differences which were as important in 1999 as they were in the 1970s. Even within the Labor Party, the Whitlam policy of 1975 was soon regarded as acquiescing in Indonesian occupation and was repudiated after a bitter internal debate, and from that time until the recognition by the Hawke government in 1985 of Indonesian sovereignty, differences between the party leadership and some members of the rank and file were pronounced. The Timor Gap Treaty, and the policy adopted towards East Timor refugees, who the Labor government insisted were citizens of Portugal and thus ineligible for refugee status, continued to keep the issue alive in the party. In opposition, Andrew Peacock was critical of Whitlam's policy, though as foreign minister (from November 1975) he rapidly accommodated to the control of the territory by Indonesia at a time (in 1978) when strategies of forcible resettlement and resultant famine were being used in an attempt to break the resistance led by the pro-independence FRETILIN (*Frente Revolucionária do Timor-Leste Independente*: Revolutionary Front for an Independent East Timor) movement. In the 1998 elections the emphasis accorded to human rights issues in the Labor Party platform, and especially the statement in support of 'self-determination' for the East Timorese, moved the party again towards potential disputation with Indonesia as well as with its own record.

There is a sense in which Foreign Minister Alexander Downer's energetic efforts to contribute to a settlement of the issue were in the 'activist' mould of his predecessor. This marked a continuation across administrations of differing party complexion of the strategy whereby Australia's interests, especially in matters of regional concern, are furthered by devoting exceptional resources to issues neglected by others, or where the country possesses some special expertise. At the same time they were in marked contrast since, while Downer similarly acknowledged the vital importance of the relationship with Indonesia, his recognition of the legitimate aspirations for self-determination on the part of the people of East Timor were strongly at variance with many of the policies pursued by Gareth Evans when foreign minister in the Hawke and Keating Labor governments.

Australia's concern with East Timor therefore also reflected unease and disquiet regarding past failures. From the first, Australian eye-witnesses and East Timor hands, including Jill Jolliffe, Roger East, Greg Shackleton, Michael Richardson and, most importantly, Jim Dunn, provided sophisticated and influential accounts of events in the territory (Dunn 1983; Jolliffe 1978). The presence of East Timorese refugees in the country served to remind Australians of those failures, just as it also focused attention on each new outrage by the Indonesian administration. The Balibo incident in 1975, and the widespread belief in the journalistic community that the Australian government knew almost immediately that Indonesian forces were directly involved in the deaths of the journalists there but withheld this information in the interests of better relations with Indonesia, undoubtedly encouraged interest in the Timor issue among the media.

In all, over a considerable period of time the Timor issue has been able to mobilize many interest groups and publics. For some in 1999, the focus was upon the security impact of the creation of a new and aid-dependent close neighbour, or upon the consequences that a new political status for East Timor would have for the regions of Indonesia as that country proceeded in its uncertain way to the reordering of its political system in the post-Suharto era. All of these matters are of the greatest importance for Australia, and the choice of policy to deal with them and their implications has been a major national priority. But for others, the Timor debate was not so much about the future but about the past. Its focus was on the record of successive governments in their handling of the Timor issue, but especially on the role then Prime Minister Gough Whitlam played – or did not play – in the events which led to the occupation of East Timor by Indonesian forces in December 1975. It was also, to that extent, focused not primarily upon Timor but upon Australia, and thus on the success and failure of leaderships and political institutions.

Debating Australia's past role

While the remarks of President Habibie in June 1998 that Indonesia was considering granting special status to East Timor, and the pro-independence demonstrations that ensued in the territory itself, stimulated this second debate about the past, it had proceeded almost from the time of Indonesian annexation. Like a water course that slows to a trickle but never quite disappears beneath the sands, the debate was kept alive through the 1980s by internal Labor Party disputation, the public reaction to the Timor Gap Treaty of 1989, the Santa Cruz Cemetery massacre of 1991, and the new testimony that appeared in 1999 on the fate of the five Australian-based newsmen killed in Balibo in October 1975. Internal party dynamics played their part. It received perhaps its greatest impetus from the statement of the Labor foreign affairs spokesman of the time, Laurie Brereton, who reflecting upon his party's record on the Timor issue, had the following judgement to offer:

> it is a matter of enduring regret that Whitlam did not speak more forcefully and clearly in support of an internationally supervised act of self-determination as the only real means of achieving a lasting and acceptable resolution of East Timor's status. At best Whitlam's approach was dangerously ambiguous, and by mid 1975 increasingly unsustainable.
>
> (Brereton 1999: 6)

Whitlam's response was an acerbic attack on an individual he described as 'a shallow, shabby, shonky foreign affairs spokesman' (Shanahan 1999). Whitlam maintained he had always been emphatic that, in one form or another, an act of self-determination would have to be effected in the territory. At the same time, documents appeared in the public domain providing further details of Whitlam's diplomatic dealings with Suharto, most notably a letter written to the president in February 1975, and the record of the Whitlam–Suharto exchange in Yogyakarta in September 1974 (Shanahan 1999; Whitlam Documents, *Sydney Morning Herald* 1999). Both were extensively analyzed, though this historical chapter is by no means closed.

To some degree, there is room for differences of opinion on the pragmatics of these exchanges. When, for example, Whitlam says in February 1975 that 'no Australian Government could allow it to be thought . . . that it supported' Indonesian 'military action against Portuguese Timor', it could be alleged that this referred to the appearance of the matter as opposed to its reality, which could be different, an issue which has moved many Australian columnists to comment (Sheridan 1999: 17; McDonald 1999; Juddery 1999: 9). This interpretation is supported when the likely extent of Whitlam's knowledge of Indonesia's campaign to orchestrate integration is taken into account. But setting these matters aside at this stage, what is readily apparent in these and the other records like them is that Whitlam's preferences were clearly stated and evidently grounded in principles of national policy he regarded as important and which he believed or hoped would be understood by his interlocutors (Viviani 1997: 99–109).

Whitlam made it clear that he believed the best course for Timor after Portuguese control was relinquished was to become part of Indonesia. At the same time he held that the future of Timor should be a matter for the people themselves to decide through an act of self-determination. The principles in question were, respectively, the recognition of Indonesia's national aspirations and claims in a manner consistent with a post-colonial approach to regional policy on the part of Australia, and an affirmation of the importance of self-determination.

Both of these principles were advanced because they were desirable as general rules. Self-determination accorded with the egalitarian inheritance of the Labor Party as well as comprising one of those yardsticks which External Affairs Minister Dr H. V. Evatt had sought to apply in the 1940s to the workings of the United Nations, thereby defending the role of smaller countries and populations against the claims of the major powers (Lee 1997: 48–61). But self-determination was a difficult principle to apply in a territory so poorly prepared for independence. Moreover, Whitlam's critical if not disparaging remarks on the predominant role of *mestiço* political leaders in East Timor suggested that he believed that an act of self-determination would hardly lead to a result that truly reflected the opinions of the majority.

Anti-colonialism, on the other hand, provided a much clearer standard for Australian policy. Indonesia was a state formed after a long and bitter struggle against colonialism during which Australia (under a Labor government) played a positive role in pressuring the Netherlands to relinquish its claims. Indonesia was an important actor in the non-aligned world, and whatever shape the Southeast Asian region would assume in the future would depend significantly upon choices made in Jakarta. Friendship with Indonesia – however favourable to Australia's material interests – was therefore also an affirmation of Australia's determination to support a post-colonial regional order. Moreover it was Whitlam's personal assessment, an assessment he repeated in his statement on the UDT (*União Democrática de Timor*: Timorese Democratic Union) coup of 11 August 1975, that East Timor was 'in many ways part of the Indonesian world' (Parliament of the Commonwealth of Australia, *Debates, House of Representatives* 1975: 493). Though this assessment had some historical basis, what was of greater significance was that it was held by an individual with a keen historical sense who was inclined to pay especial attention to historical claims.

Lest this position not appear as one of principle, it should be seen in the context of the contemporary alternative. For a long period the Australian government supported the presence of the Netherlands in Irian Jaya because it was considered that this was of strategic advantage to Australia. The claims of the inhabitants for self-determination were not stressed, and Indonesia's assertion that it represented the decolonized successor state to all the territories of the Netherlands East Indies was rejected (Verrier 1976). Whitlam criticized this view as a perpetuation of a colonial arrangement, and supported the acquisition of Irian Jaya by Indonesia. He seems to have seen East Timor in the same light. As early as 1963 he referred to Portuguese East Timor as 'an anachronism' and warned that 'we would not have a worthy supporter in the world if we backed the Portuguese' (Whitlam 1963: 13).

In 1974, both of these preferences could be stated without any apparent contradiction between them. With the emergence of indigenous political movements in the territory, and especially the rise of FRETILIN, along with a hardening of Indonesian resolve to influence the outcome in East Timor, a choice presented itself. Sufficient material was available in 1999 to show that the government was very well informed on Indonesian military operations inside Indonesia. Material from the highly classified US *National Intelligence Daily*, the sources of which were conveyed to Australia under the UK/USA intelligence sharing agreement (and which indeed depended in part on Australian intelligence assets) showed that by the end of August 1975 Indonesian determination to invade East Timor was clear, and all that was wanting was an appropriate pretext (Toohey and Wilkinson 1987: 146–54). Knowing that an Indonesian campaign of de-stabilization was underway, and that an attempt to assess East Timorese opinion on the issue of integration with Indonesia would be unlikely to produce a positive result, the principle of self-determination was abandoned. These issues are discussed in greater detail in the following chapter, especially in relation to foreign affairs documents de-classified in 2000.

There were differences between Whitlam, Foreign Minister Willesee and Ambassador Woolcott on the equanimity with which these developments should be received; there was also the fact that with regard to this aspect of national policy, if not others, the prime minister was determined to have his head. But the drift of policy was clear enough. It must nevertheless have come as a great surprise to the Indonesian leadership that the deaths of the journalists at Balibo in October 1975 did not elicit a stronger reaction (Sherman 1999: 95–7). Although the surviving documentation now available does not, apparently, support their recollections, two of the former intelligence officers interviewed by Tom Sherman in 1998 stated that intelligence sources had reported the arrival of the journalists in Balibo, their subsequent capture, and within 'a day and a half' the fact that they were 'executed' (Sherman 1999: 95–7). By this stage, however, Australia was immired in a domestic political crisis so grave as to unseat the government in the following month.

In the framing of policy towards Indonesia, Richard Woolcott, who became Australian ambassador in March 1975, played a major role. Woolcott penned Whitlam's first remarks, after he had won the 1972 election, on the subject of the intended reform of foreign policy (Freudenberg 1993: 201), and his advice from Jakarta was a powerful influence upon the prime minister's policy. Woolcott's views, as he unashamedly admitted, were based upon a pragmatic or realist approach to international affairs. By August 1975, if not before, he had formed the view that 'it is Indonesia's policy to incorporate Timor', a point he repeated in many of his cables to Canberra. That being so, he advocated a policy of 'disengagement' and allowing 'events to take their course'. And this would have a payoff, as he noted, in the form of presenting an opportunity then to negotiate Australia's territorial claims to the seabed resources of the Timor Sea. The closing thus of the 'Timor Gap' could be expected to reap a reward in the form of energy supplies. The basis of the policy advice he was offering was therefore clear. As he candidly admits: 'I know I am recommending a pragmatic rather than a principled stand but that is what national interest and foreign policy is all about' (Walsh and Munster 1980: 200, 197, 217). So strongly held was Woolcott's view that nothing should be done to deter the Indonesian invasion since this would provoke a rift with Jakarta that, when transmitting to the Indonesian government the Ministerial Statement to the Senate by Willesee on 30 October 1975 (on the eve of the Indonesian landing at Dili) which referred to 'widespread reports that Indonesia is involved in military intervention in Portuguese Timor', he deleted this passage (Willesee 1999: 15; Parliament of the Commonwealth of Australia, *Debates, House of Representatives* 1975: 1609–10).

In the diplomacy of states it is rare for realism and idealism to be mutually supportive. But in this instance, the advice that Woolcott was proffering on pragmatic grounds and the principles which caused Whitlam to prefer the outcome of an Indonesian East Timor happened to coincide.

If Australia was never in a position to assert a claim to be a 'party principal' in the resolution of the Timor issue, why did self-determination loom so large in Australian diplomacy? This raises the question of the assumptions that Whitlam brought to the discussion with Suharto of the question of 'self-determination' for East Timor. Here, perhaps, Whitlam's chosen principle was seriously at odds with the realities of power in Jakarta. It should be recalled that Indonesia's own record on self-determination was not impressive. Australian forces were committed to the defence of the Borneo states of Malaysia in 1964 as a result of Indonesia's rejection of the consultative processes of the Cobbold Commission which had been used to determine that the inhabitants of Sabah and Sarawak wished to join the federation. As well as the direct infiltration of Indonesian forces into Sarawak, Jakarta, in an operation masterminded by the military, also used money and other inducements to create a fifth column, the task of which was to de-stabilize the political order. The fall of Sukarno led to an improvement in Indonesia's relations with its Southeast Asian neighbours and the end of 'confrontation' with Malaysia, but the realization of another of Sukarno's projects, the incorporation of Irian Jaya through an extremely dubious 'Act of Free Choice' conducted in 1969, demonstrated that his successor was committed to many of the same methods and instruments.

Indeed, there was a direct connection between the Irian Jaya and East Timor cases, a connection of which Whitlam was surely aware by the end of October 1974 (McDonald 1980: 189–211; Richardson 1976: 9–15; Department of Foreign Affairs, Republic of Indonesia 1977: 17). The engineering of the 'Act of Free Choice' had been the task of General Ali Moertopo, of Kostrad's Special Operations (OPSUS). So successful had Moertopo been in inducing and pressuring the Irianese representatives that in the 1969 *musjawarah* (consultation), all 1,025 delegates voted unanimously for integration, a result of North Korean finality. Even Cobbold in Borneo had conceded that 20 per cent of the populations of Sabah and Sarawak were not in favour of membership of Malaysia under any circumstances. Moertopo went on to organize the GOLKAR victory in the national 'elections' of 1971, a further instance of the importance accorded to public opinion in the 'New Order'. In October 1974, Moertopo was given the responsibility of negotiating with Portugal on Timor's future status, and in secret talks in Lisbon seems to have succeeded in convincing the then government of the rationale for integration.

Australia was briefed on these developments through the Australian Embassy in Lisbon. By December that year OPSUS had launched a campaign of propaganda and intimidation against anti-integrationist groups in East Timor, the details of which were freely discussed in the Australian press, where the first public warnings of the possibility of a direct Indonesian military invasion were published. Moertopo's plans suffered a setback when, during a second meeting with the Portuguese in March 1975 and in the context of an alliance of UDT and FRETILIN, Lisbon stated its preference for a three-year transition to possible independence under Portuguese auspices. The OPSUS response was to attempt to win over some members of the UDT leadership, and this seems ultimately to have been successful. The UDT coup of August was intended as a further installment in the campaign of de-stabilization, though Suharto hesitated when the resultant disorder seemed to offer an excuse for direct intervention. These details were well known to the Australian government and its advisers.

Even setting these specifics aside, Whitlam knew only too well that Suharto presided over a military regime that had come to power during an orgy of blood letting which had claimed the lives of at least 500,000 civilians. The political *modus operandi* of the 'New Order' was far from consultative, and it cannot be supposed that the incorporation of a lightly inhabited portion of an island at the extremity of the nation – however, in practice, it was achieved – would have led to its inhabitants being treated with any greater attention to their wishes than was the case in hydrocarbon-rich Aceh or timber-rich East Kalimantan. Albeit with the advantage of hindsight, the modern reader of the Whitlam–Suharto exchanges cannot but be struck by the fantastical element in proceedings that saw the Australian prime minister taking the time to extract a solemn undertaking from the Indonesian leader regarding the latter's observance of a policy far removed from his experience and inclinations. Suharto's thought processes at this time can only be the subject of speculation, but he might well have drawn the conclusion that given Whitlam's familiarity with his record what was being asked of him was to have Indonesia act with the appearance of conformity with the principle of self-determination. The fact that Indonesia bothered to stage an 'act of integration' of 31 May 1976 whereby East Timor's leaders agreed to Indonesian sovereignty may be seen in this light. It is noteworthy that Australia refused to dispatch an envoy to attend on the grounds that as the UN was not involved its status was doubtful, though a representative from New Zealand was present. Whatever the reservations the Australian government had regarding this charade, Prime Minister Malcolm Fraser on an official visit to Jakarta in October of that year acknowledged that a merger had taken place, though de facto recognition of East Timor's status as Indonesia's twenty-seventh province was to wait until January 1978.

Accommodating to integration

Timor remained an issue for successive Australian governments for several inter-related reasons, and the remembrance of what was and was not achieved in this period later become an element in the debate of 1999. Though the precise dimensions of the tragedy are still disputed, the early impact of Indonesian rule was a disaster for the inhabitants. A combination of deliberate policy, whereby the military occupation sought to separate the FRETILIN guerillas (now under the command of their military wing, FALINTIL: *Forças Armadas de Libertação Nacional Timor Leste*) from food supplies, as well as neglect, saw many East Timorese die of hunger and disease. In 1979, the Indonesian foreign minister, Mochtar Kusumaatmadja, estimated the number of dead as a result of the war at 120,000. Journalists who were permitted to travel in some parts of the island in October 1979 published photographs depicting widespread malnutrition. The refugee East Timorese community helped publicize these events, and a number of human rights and relief organizations kept the issue of Indonesian mis-rule before the Australian public. The Australian Campaign for Independent East Timor, for example, under an energetic leadership including communist Denis Freney, helped maintain a radio link based near Darwin which was the sole means by which FRETILIN made its point of view known to the outside world in 1976 (Freney 1991: 357–73).

Within the Labor Party, accommodating to the invasion generated a debate so intense and bitter that it was a contributing factor to Whitlam's inability to lead the party to victory in the elections of 1977 and to his subsequent decision to vacate the leadership. Very shortly after the election defeat of December 1975, the Labor Party Federal Caucus adopted a resolution affirming what was described as the policy from April 1974 of the (then) foreign minister, Don Willesee, on East Timor, namely that of 'self-determination' (Cameron 1990: 102). Until an act of self-determination had taken place, military aid to Indonesia should be suspended. This formulation conveniently avoided the issue of the extent to which this policy was ignored in practice (a question considered in more detail in the following chapter). Despite reaffirmations of this policy, Whitlam was never content to abide by it, given the implied repudiation of his own role, criticizing the policy in public and in comments to the media. Exasperated Labor parliamentarians finally took the step of passing a censure motion in the party Caucus which was adopted overwhelmingly (Cameron 1990: 643–50).

In the Australian parliament Whitlam's attempted defence of his record elicited searing condemnation from the government. In an exchange on 29 April 1976, he raised the issue of a conversation that Andrew Peacock had in Bali in 1975 with members of the Jakarta CSIS (Centre for Strategic and International Studies), the think-tank maintained by General Ali Moertopo. In this conversation, a record of which was later leaked in Jakarta, he was alleged to have stated that a future coalition government would acquiesce in an Indonesian annexation of East Timor. In rebuttal, Peacock, at this time foreign minister, was devastating in his critique. Referring to Whitlam's pleas that the issue of the confidentiality of the record of the then Prime Minister's exchanges with Suharto prevented him from mounting a full defence of his policies, he said:

> It is not merely a matter of [these] discussions . . . It is the lack of action by your government in the international forum, on a government to government basis and in this parliament itself. You stand condemned by the lack of activity during your own period in government.
>
> (Parliament of the Commonwealth of Australia,
> *Debates, House of Representatives* 1976: 1746)

A backbench member of the coalition, Maurice Neil, even threatened to initiate an official enquiry into the extent to which the Labor government knew of Indonesian armed infiltration into the territory and how much this knowledge was at variance both with its policy towards Indonesia and its advice to the newsmen killed at Balibo (Parliament of the Commonwealth of Australia, *Debates, House of Representatives* 1976: 1750–1). East Timor was a liability in 1976–77, not least because there were Labor parliamentarians who were sufficiently concerned by contemporary events in the territory as to raise them in the parliament despite thus giving the government repeated opportunities to refer to the debacle of 1975.

Whitlam, having retired from the Labor leadership, continued to take a personal interest in the issue. In February 1982, he spent four days in the territory on a tour organized by CSIS, publishing an account of his experiences which presented a generally positive image of the improvements that had been made under Indonesian administration. Indeed, he went so far as to chastise the Apostolic Administrator of Dili, Mgr. Costa Lopes, for warning of the danger of renewed famine if Indonesian policies were not altered, lest this prejudice future Indonesian funding. Later in the year, Whitlam appeared at the UN General Assembly Fourth (Decolonization) Committee, arguing the case for withdrawing the issue from the business of the United Nations. He received a very critical reception from some African delegations, and was cross-questioned in a notable exchange by José Ramos-Horta, then FRETILIN representative. Each year until 1982, the UN General Assembly had voted (albeit with a diminishing majority on each occasion) to support the claims of the East Timorese for self-determination; in 1983, a further vote on this question was deferred to allow the Secretary-General the opportunity to convene negotiations between Indonesia and Portugal. Meanwhile, a series of leaked papers revealed more of the inside record of the government's dealings with Indonesia prior to December 1975.

Despite the preponderance of Indonesian military force, FRETILIN-led guerilla resistance continued into the 1980s (Taylor 1991; Budiardjo and Liem 1984). During the election of 1983, 'self-determination' for East Timor and the specific condemnation of the policy of recognition of Indonesian sovereignty by the Fraser government were explicit Labor Party commitments. Prominent members of the party, including Tom Uren, who had become deputy parliamentary leader after the 1975 elections, had argued the case for taking this view, and it had been adopted by Bill Hayden when he became opposition leader after Whitlam's failure to win office in the elections of December 1977. On his first visit to Jakarta as foreign minister, however, Hayden signaled his intention to abandon this position on the grounds that a more constructive relationship with the Indonesian leadership would give the government more leverage to raise human rights and other issues of concern. As a means to reconcile party opinion, the dispatch of a study group to visit the territory was negotiated with Indonesia. In July, former defence minister, Bill Morrison, led a delegation to East Timor which concluded positively on Indonesia's record. Though the tour was conducted during a cease-fire arranged the previous month, the itinerary of Morrison's group was entirely controlled by the military, and the members did not visit any FRETILIN-held areas, despite being invited to do so (Ramos-Horta 1987: 83). The cease-fire lasted until the following month, when a new offensive was launched. The leaders of the government then addressed the variance between Labor Party official policy and their own diplomatic practice. At their party's 1984 Federal Conference, a resolution was adopted expressing 'concern' that East Timor was annexed in the absence of an act of self-determination.

Despite the continuing violence, in August 1985 Prime Minister Bob Hawke explicitly stated, in an interview conducted to mark Indonesia's National Day, that Australia recognized unequivocally Indonesian sovereignty over East Timor. This is perhaps an instance of the phenomenon whereby parties in opposition can afford to be more outspoken than when faced with the responsibilities of government. While opposition foreign affairs spokesman in 1974–75, Andrew Peacock was critical of Whitlam's concessions to Indonesia, but as a member of the Fraser cabinet he accepted the fact of Indonesian control.

In 1979, following Australia's acceptance of the Indonesian occupation, negotiations had begun on the question of closing the Timor Gap. Under the Hawke government, these negotiations reached the point where joint exploration for hydrocarbon deposits was considered as a way of bridging the different views the two nations took of their respective rights to the resources of the seabed (Bergin 1990: 383–93). Indeed, this approach was first proposed by Australian negotiators within months of the change in Labor Party policy in 1984, and it immediately received a favourable response (King 2002: 20). Upon assuming the position of foreign minister in 1988, Gareth Evans expressed the determination to add 'ballast' to the relationship between Australia and Indonesia. To this end, he concluded the 'Timor Gap "Zone of Co-operation" Agreement' which was gazetted in February 1991 after a highly publicized signing ceremony held in an aircraft flying over the area in question.

This latter step underlined Australia's acceptance of Indonesia's sovereignty over East Timor, and further stimulated criticism from domestic critics who continued to dispute that policy. Within weeks it also induced Portugal to initiate proceedings against the legality of the Agreement before the International Court of Justice (ICJ). Portugal argued that it violated Portugal's rights as administering power, and also infringed upon the rights of the East Timorese to self-determination. The Australian counter to this claim was to assert that if there was a dispute about the status of the Agreement, it was between Portugal and Indonesia and not with Australia. After a lengthy case the Court found that there was in fact a dispute between Australia and Portugal, but judgement on this dispute could not be given since it depended upon a prior assessment of the legality of Indonesia's role as a party to the Agreement. As Indonesia had not consented to such a role for the ICJ, no decision could be offered. However, the ICJ took the opportunity to observe that Portugal's contention that the right of peoples to self-determination was 'irreproachable' in international law and usage, and consequently 'the Territory of East Timor remains a non-self-governing territory and its people has the right to self-determination' (International Court of Justice

1995). Given the ostensible commitment of the government to the international rule of law this finding was nothing less than a profound embarrassment.

Meanwhile, a further event had contrived to keep the Timor issue before the Australian public. On 12 November 1991, a memorial procession at the Santa Cruz Cemetery was attacked by Indonesian troops after independence banners were unfurled. On that day Dili was hosting a visit by the UN Special Rapporteur on Torture, Pieter Koojimans, who was holding talks with the local military leadership. The official death toll was first placed at 19, and later revised to 50, but local activists claimed that there were as many as 273 deaths with hundreds injured, and 255 subsequently disappeared in large-scale arrests. Not only were a number of foreign journalists witness to the event – two US journalists were beaten by the military at the scene – but an Australian-based human rights activist, Kamal Bamadhaj, was killed (Gunn 1994; McMillan 1992). The findings of the 'National Commission of Inquiry' established by President Suharto after an international outcry was a public relations disaster for Jakarta, and tough talking from the military command in Dili on future manifestations of dissent added to Indonesia's problems. The Santa Cruz killings also stimulated a further review of past Labor Party policy on East Timor, with Prime Minister Hawke agreeing to meet a FRETILIN delegation, and Gough Whitlam criticizing the government's handling of Indonesia while defending his own record (Bowers 1991).

These events, which were captured on a widely-screened film by a visiting British journalist, Max Stahl, brought to international attention the extent to which the resistance to Indonesian rule had moved from a guerilla to a civil focus. This change was identified with the rise to leadership of José Alexandre 'Xanana' Gusmão (Pinto and Jardine 1997), who had founded the CNRM (*Conselho Nacional da Resistência Maubere*: National Council for Maubere Resistance) in 1989 as an umbrella organization for all anti-integrationist groups. Gusmão's meeting with Australian journalist Robert Domm in September 1990 was the first such contact in 15 years, and did much to maintain Australian interest in the question (Aarons and Domm 1992). Similarly, his arrest in November 1992 and later sentencing demonstrated that the resistance was still active. An influential documentary on conditions in East Timor by John Pilger (in part incorporating Max Stahl's material) struck a particular chord in Australia (Pilger 1998: 153–76).

At this time the efforts of the United Nations to convene an all-inclusive dialogue in East Timor, which was first initiated in 1983, began to bear fruit. As a result of this diplomacy, not only did Indonesia agree to improve the human rights situation in the territory and facilitate visits by human rights representatives, but Indonesian Foreign Minister Ali Alatas held direct talks with East Timorese spokesman José Ramos-Horta in early 1995. A meeting of East Timorese groups from across the political spectrum was convened at Burg Schlaining in Austria in June 1995, producing an accord on steps to improve material and spiritual conditions in East Timor and to facilitate greater contact between members of the diaspora (Gunn 1997). The following year, the former chairman of the Australian National Crime Authority, Tom Sherman, reviewing the record of the Balibo incident at government behest found that the death of the journalists in October

1975 was most likely the result of their being caught in cross-fire during a firefight. Though Sherman considered some new evidence, his findings did not satisfy those who held that the full record was still not available. Furthermore, the joint award in October 1996 of the Nobel Peace Prize to the Bishop of East Timor, Carlos Filipe Ximenes Belo and José Ramos-Horta demonstrated that influential elements of international opinion were still unconvinced of Indonesia's insistence that the troubles in Timor were no more significant than, in the phrase used by Ali Alatas, 'a pebble in Indonesia's shoe' (Anderson 1998: 131–8).

Though all these developments continued to remind Australians that most East Timorese remained unreconciled to Indonesian rule, the decisive shift in Australian opinion and policy was occasioned by the regional economic crisis which broke in 1997 and which issued in the demise of the Suharto regime.

The 'New Order' collapse and the internationalization of the East Timor issue

The collapse of the Suharto regime in Indonesia prompted a wholesale reassess-ment of the policies and institutions of the 'New Order'. By the middle of 1998 this reassessment had extended not merely to a questioning of the central role of the armed forces in the state, but also to the consequences in some of the more far-flung regions of the nation of using the military as a vehicle for rule from the centre. Regarding Aceh and East Timor especially, there developed an awareness among more sophisticated leaders that the methods of the past could not be sustained but indeed constituted a very sorry legacy to be overcome. Thus President Habibie, after little more than a month in office, offered East Timor 'special status' with wide autonomy though still within Indonesia. Since July 1976 East Timor had been officially the nation's twenty-seventh province, though in practice largely a fiefdom of the armed forces.

On the one hand, East Timorese campaigners for independence were embold-ened and this development was followed closely in the Australian media. At the same time, facing dissention and civil disorder from Aceh to Ambon, and no longer guaranteed a political role in the emerging post-Suharto political order, the Indonesian armed forces were forced to reassess their role and the extent to which they could rely upon old methods. The relaxation in the political atmosphere and the emergence of independent political movements raised the prospect that such developments might also be seen in East Timor.

The demise of Suharto also led many Australians to question the modalities that had been chosen to cultivate closer relations with Indonesia. It should be recalled that as late as December 1995 the Australia–Indonesia Agreement on Maintaining Security (AMS) was hailed by some specialists as marking a new era in which Australia was seen to be accepted as an equal player through participating as a partner in the weaving of the highly personalized and vague web which seemed to characterize the Asian way of security. And there was some substance to this position, given Indonesia's central role in ASEAN as well as its strategic location. Emblematic of these modalities was Australia's acceptance of the occupation of

East Timor. Successive Australian leaders and politicians had been prepared to acquiesce in Indonesia's occupation and annexation of the territory. While some adopted the pragmatic and realist position expounded by former ambassador to Jakarta, Richard Woolcott, others were reluctant to ignore the tragic record of ABRI activity in East Timor but did so for the greater good of maintaining harmonious relations with Australia's major northern neighbour.

In keeping with a new emphasis upon human rights, the Labor Party platform for the federal elections in October 1998, repudiating the Hawke–Evans–Keating legacy, incorporated once again a statement in support of 'self-determination' for East Timor. The espousal of this policy was more than electoral expediency, since it marked the revisiting of an issue of great sensitivity that had divided the party and dogged successive leaderships. Though the Labor Party did not win office, it was instrumental in a decision by the Senate at the end of November to convene a wide-ranging inquiry into all aspects of the Timor issue.

The approach taken by the Coalition government, both before and after the election, also demonstrated a preparedness to take a new approach. In June, Australian ambassador to Jakarta John McCarthy undertook a visit to Dili, and in the following month he met Xanana Gusmão in Cipinang gaol. Here the government had been anticipated by the private sector. BHP, the largest Australian participant in the exploitation of Timor Gap oil and gas, had already made contact with Gusmão, their representative in Jakarta being relocated when this initiative was censured by the Indonesian authorities. In August, Foreign Minister Alexander Downer appealed publicly for Indonesia to release Gusmão so that he could play a direct role in addressing the Timor problem. For their part, Indonesia announced that all combat troops had been 'withdrawn' from the territory, though leaked military documents later demonstrated that troop levels had not been reduced.

Following the 1998 elections, Downer took the lead in re-evaluating Australia's approach to Timor. Downer's activism invites comparison with that of his predecessor, Gareth Evans, in the region. Where Evans was determined that Australia would make a difference in Cambodia, Downer had grasped the importance of the Timor issue. This was a strategy with many merits, and also accorded with Australia's other interests, as well as constituting something of a break with the policies of the previous Liberal–National coalition government of Malcolm Fraser. And yet it was also a strong practical repudiation of the Evans record given that the Hawke–Keating governments negotiated the two major instruments through which Australia identified its national interests closely with the Suharto regime – the Timor Gap Treaty and the 1995 'Agreement on Maintaining Security'. The contrast with Evans was all the more evident when it is recalled that he had been a strong advocate of a world order based upon common security and on the United Nations and its regimes. Although it predated his stewardship of foreign policy, on each of the occasions between 1975 and 1982 when the UN General Assembly voted on the Timor question, Indonesia was condemned. And most analyses concede that in incorporating the territory forcibly and without regard to a test of the opinions of the population, Indonesia violated fundamental principles of international law as well as the obligations of nations as defined in the United Nations Charter.

In late November, in the context of growing disorder and uncertainty in Dili, Downer stated that a resolution of the issue must involve the leaders of the East Timorese themselves. The Australian military attaché in Jakarta made the first visit to East Timor since 1984, on this occasion to investigate claims that villagers had been massacred at Alas. The appearance of armed militias led to charges – later admitted as correct by military commanders – that ABRI was distributing weapons to anti-secessionist elements.

At this time Australian Department of Foreign Affairs officers embarked on a review of possible outcomes in East Timor. After consulting East Timorese political figures they formed the view that the great majority of the population in the territory would only be satisfied with complete independence. Accordingly, they recommended a direct approach to Jakarta. Meanwhile, in the Department of Defence, contingency plans were formulated for a possible relief delivery or international peace-keeping role for Australian personnel.

In December 1998, the National Security Committee of the Cabinet considered the many security, economic and political issues involved and the extent to which Australian interests would best be served by a new intervention. The prime minister undertook to write to President Habibie to suggest that a new formula be found to permit eventual Indonesian dis-engagement from the territory if such a choice was popularly approved. While praising Habibie's commitment to reform, Mr Howard suggested that a possible model for a resolution of the problem was to be found in the Matignon accords, which provided for a future referendum among the population of New Caledonia but only after the realization of a lengthy programme of development of local political institutions and confidence building (Henningham 1993). This letter was delivered to the president by Ambassador McCarthy on 21 December.

At the time President Habibie rejected the parallel with New Caledonia, a reaction which was hardly surprising given that it implicitly equated Indonesian conduct in East Timor with French occupation of territory on the other side of the globe from the metropole. It should be recalled that each school day children across Indonesia read passages from the national constitution which identifies colonialism as the most reprehensible political practice.

Not discouraged, Downer pursued this initiative, proposing on 12 January 1999 that the East Timorese should be permitted an act of self-determination after a substantial period of autonomy. The timetable thus enunciated was consistent with that proposed by the CNRT in East Timor. Though other influences were clearly at work, this 'historic shift' in Australian policy helped prompt a change of mind in Jakarta. On 27 January, Foreign Minister Ali Alatas made the first public reference to the possibility of complete independence for the territory if autonomy proved unwelcome or unworkable. In keeping with this trend, United Nations brokered talks involving Indonesia and Portugal produced a draft settlement plan. However, disagreement on provisions for a referendum, a future constitution and an interim UN presence prevented assent to the document. In an extraordinary personal intervention, Habibie, while rejecting a referendum, announced that whatever the result Indonesia wished to be free of the Timor problem by the year 2000. He was to realize this project, though in a fashion unimagined at the time.

What factors did Australian policy makers weigh as they contemplated this new attempt to contribute to the shaping of regional order? Relations with Indonesia continued to comprise the most important context. Here the internal situation in the country appeared more and more uncertain as campaigning began for the first free elections in 40 years. But the internal situation in East Timor also comprised a major focus. Inside the territory civil order was in a precarious state. The appearance of armed 'militias', including Halilinitar led by João Tavares (former *bupati* of Bobonaro), Mahidi led by Cançio Lopes de Carvalho, as well as Besi Merah Putih, and Pana led to a sharp deterioration in the security of the territory (Murphy 1999: 24–5; van Klinken 1999; Martinkus 1999: 1). The use of militias, raised by the Interior Ministry but attached to territorial or combat military groups, had been a long-standing practice in East Timor. Now these and other groups declared themselves in favour of integration, and were provided with additional arms so that they might terrorize the populations in their areas. Through February 1999 attacks on civilians emptied whole villages, and roadblocks staged by armed gangs led to beatings and murders. The background to these tragic developments was complex. It is evident that some groups who had cooperated with Indonesia during the 'New Order' era were seeking to maintain their hold over their regions, yet others were hoping to create personal fiefdoms or exploit the climate of disorder for gain. And some analysts considered that while the government in Jakarta was talking as though East Timor was a problem to be discarded, not all in the armed forces were so committed to abandoning (or abandoning in an orderly fashion) an adventure which had been so costly in treasure, lives and prestige. Indeed, prominent militia leaders were dispatched to Jakarta by the military as part of a pro-integrationist delegation for talks with President Habibie in February, thus giving them a measure of respectability.

On 15 March 1999, the ABC's television documentary series 'Four Corners' screened an influential programme on the terror that had accompanied the emergence of the militias, especially in the western border regions but also in Dili. The message of this and other reports seemed to be that the pro-independence movement was taking great pains to remain unprovoked by the beatings and killings that had accompanied the rise of the militias, but there were clearly limits beyond which the population would abandon restraint. At the same time, media reports from Ambon particularly, indicated that in parts of Indonesia, society had seriously fragmented to the point where something akin to tribal warfare was emerging. The inference from the Timor evidence, however, was quite different. Whereas in so much of Indonesia civil society was at the point of breakdown, in East Timor it seemed extraordinarily strong and resilient in that it could deliver such a concerted and relatively successful campaign of non-violence.

In this outcome, it was generally held that the role of the Roman Catholic Church was crucial (Archer 1995: 120–33). Ironically, Indonesian promotion of *panca sila* – which requires all Indonesian citizens to profess a recognized faith – as much as the brutality of the military administration, seems to have had the effect of driving the Timorese to identify with the church. Some figures indicated that by this time as many as 85 per cent of the population regarded themselves as members of the church. This suggested that the outcome in East Timor might yet be more hopeful than in some other parts of the archipelago or in the new states of the Southwest Pacific.

If East Timorese society had established a remarkable degree of coherence, East Timorese elites had demonstrated a surprising if still limited capacity to work together even despite the divisive events of the past. Even before the collapse of the 'New Order', the UN initiative of 1993–94 had brought together a range of political forces, including individuals affiliated with UDT and other groups who had cooperated, at one time or another, with the Indonesian occupation, along with elements of FRETILIN. After the fall of the Suharto regime, a series of meetings with wide representation convened in London, Melbourne and elsewhere sought to produce a blueprint for a new East Timor. However, talks in Jakarta between Xanana Gusmão and pro-integrationists were unsuccessful after details were publicized of the help the latter were continuing to receive from the Indonesian administration. If such strengths as East Timorese civil society and elites possessed were to be brought into play, therefore, armed conflict had to be minimized. With important elements of the Indonesian armed forces profoundly unhappy with the central government's handling of the issue, the argument for the necessity of intervention from a third force had many supporters in Australia (Daley 1999b; Kelly 1999).

A new departure in policy

Such was the context of the Australian decision to become engaged in the resolution of the East Timor issue. With the acceptance by Indonesia in late January 1999 that a test of East Timorese opinion was necessary before the territory's future status could be determined, it can be said in retrospect that the Rubicon was crossed. The logic of integration was dependent upon a complete identification of the interests of the population with those of Indonesians at large. Once the possibility of those interests being distinct was admitted, and given the sentiment that existed for independence, change was inevitable. And in light of the Australian government's encouragement of Indonesia to take that final step, further entanglement in the fate of East Timor also could not be avoided. In the future lay Australia's encouragement for the May agreement between the UN, Indonesia and Portugal for a plebiscite in the territory, the prominent support then given to the UNAMET mission, the INTERFET intervention amidst the chaos and blood letting in the aftermath of the popular ballot, which then issued in a major role in UNTAET as the new country of East Timor/Timor-Leste was constructed. The legacy has been a now continuing commitment to the development and security of East Timor and a complete redefinition of Australia's relations with Indonesia and with the Southeast Asian region.

While the case for Australian participation in that intervention was strong, even compelling, experience suggested nevertheless that it might be less than fully successful, irrespective of the cost expended. The comparison with Papua New Guinea (PNG) is instructive. Although Australian colonialism was far from ideal as a preparation for independence, Australia's record was better than that of Portugal in East Timor, and the decolonization that was realized in 1975 proceeded in an orderly fashion. Yet despite its resource riches and a generation of assistance for development, PNG is a fragile and in places a very disordered state. Violence is endemic in some parts. A subvention from the Australian government, of around A$300 million annually, is still required and in 2003 the decision was taken to dispatch Australian officials and police to work to address the issue of government failure. And to complete the picture, it should be recalled that in 1999, while attention was focused on East Timor, one of Australia's continuing commitments was to meet the additional cost (of about A$60 million annually) of maintaining a peace monitoring force in Bougainville. Timor is certainly smaller but also poorer; the divisions among its population are both greater and less – many share the same language and religion, though 24 years of Indonesian occupation led to some deep political divisions. In 1998–99, Australian aid to East Timor was budgeted at A$6 million, making Australia the largest donor of bilateral aid. To make a real impression on the political, social and economic problems confronting the territory, it was the consensus amongst aid specialists that many times this amount would need to be found for an extended period (Soesastro 1991: 207–29; Hill and Saldanha 2001). And this judgement was in relation to conditions prior to the catastrophe of September 1999. The commitment to Timor was therefore to become a major departure in Australia's regional policy not only in diplomatic and security terms, but also in relation to future aid budgets.

2   Australian relations with Indonesia and the East Timor issue

> Indonesia's incorporation of East Timor is the greatest difficulty in the relationship between that country and Australia.
> (Parliament of the Commonwealth of Australia, Joint Standing Committee on Foreign Affairs, Defence and Trade 1993, *Australia's Relations with Indonesia*: 95)

From a realist perspective, Indonesia is the key to Australia's defence. It commands the nation's Northern approaches from which or through which any military attack on Australia would be launched. A stable and friendly Indonesia is therefore crucial for Australia's security. From a common security perspective, there are added (or perhaps alternative) reasons for fostering good relations with Jakarta. Indonesia is the key to any wider multi-lateralist strategies for creating regional order. Indonesia is the dominant power in ASEAN, and this group is both the core of the ASEAN Regional Forum and the pioneer of the modalities for cooperation adopted by APEC. As has been indicated, since the 1980s Indonesia's forcible annexation of East Timor had support from the leaderships of both the major political parties. The decision by the Howard government to overturn this bi-partisan legacy was the most significant development in policy towards the Asia Pacific region and especially towards Indonesia since the Vietnam War. This chapter provides the context for that decision by considering the longer narrative of Australia–Indonesia relations, devoting particular attention to the crucial 1974–75 period.

The beginnings of the bilateral relationship

The Australia–Indonesia relationship has a long and complex history. At its beginning, despite the fact that each nation was the product of historical and cultural factors that could hardly have been more disparate, early Australian support for the new Indonesian Republic helped bring the final phase of decolonization to a successful conclusion. The initial Australian assessment of the independence movement was that it represented a force that could not be denied, and Australia maintained contacts with the nationalist leadership despite Dutch, British and US disapproval. When the Dutch launched the 'police action' of 20 July 1947 against the Indonesian Republic, Australia took the issue to the United Nations, referring the conflict to the Security Council as an 'act of aggression' under Article 39 of the Charter, the first time this provision had ever been invoked. From that point Australia was intimately involved in the diplomacy that finally led to the recognition of the Indonesian Republic as a sovereign state in December 1949 (Goldsworthy 2001: 134–70).

But if Australian support played a positive role in the initial formation of the Indonesian state, within a decade the conditions of the Cold War and movement of the Indonesian leadership to the left produced a very different policy. The Australian government was a participant in a US-led campaign to subvert the unity of the republic through covert assistance to separatist movements in Sumatra and Sulawesi (Kahin and Kahin 1995; Toohey and Pinwill 1990: 68–73). Though this campaign was an ignominious failure, its outcome provided for President Sukarno validation of his strategy of opposition to great power intervention in the region. Australian support for continued Dutch occupation of West Papua was similarly interpreted (Pemberton 1987: 70–106). The latter source of bilateral tension was skilfully defused by Foreign Minister Garfield Barwick in 1962 when he won the argument for abandoning this support in the interests of a long-term accommodation with Indonesia (Woodard 1998). The mediated agreement between the Dutch and the Indonesians adopted in September 1962 provided for the transfer of West Papua to an interim Dutch administration after which it would be governed by Indonesia pending a test of local opinion as to its future. At the time, Australian endorsement of this plan made much of the importance of the preparation of the territory for 'self-determination', though it soon became clear that there would be no free expression of Papuan opinion. This undoubtedly established a precedent, at least in Indonesian official thinking, that later had a bearing on policy towards East Timor.

This improvement in relations was short lived. The following year, Sukarno rejected the formation of Malaysia as a neo-colonialist creation designed to maintain British and US interests in Southeast Asia. In September 1963, his declaration of 'confrontation' with Malaysia evoked the response from the Australian government that it was prepared to provide military assistance to defend Malaysia, though Foreign Minister Barwick endeavoured to convince his own government as well as the British that the wisest course was to adopt a graduated response, with only such force exerted as would counter Indonesian actions (Woodard 1998). However, in February 1965 Australian troops were directly committed to serve on the Sarawak border with Borneo where Indonesian infiltrators were active and where the Indonesian military were training dissidents from East Malaysia (Edwards, with Pemberton 1992: 340–4). Until it terminated in 1966, 16 Australian service personnel were killed during this commitment.

The advent of the 'New Order' defused these tensions. Whether Australian agencies had any hand in the events of 30 September is not clear, but the rise to power of Suharto and his military associates was greeted with relief. On the one hand, the confrontation policy was abandoned, thus removing the possibility that border clashes would escalate into a wider conflict. On the other, the New Order was seen to be (with some qualifications) market friendly, a major positive consideration given Australia's alignment in the Cold War. For these reasons, the extensive blood letting that occasioned the rise of the Suharto regime passed almost without comment.

The reasoning applied by Australian policy makers should be understood. At this time Australia was involved in the conflict in Vietnam on the (quite clearly mistaken) assumption that this would involve the US irrevocably in the frustration of the expansionist designs of Chinese communism in Southeast Asia and beyond. The commitment to Malaysia derived from long-standing defence cooperation with Britain in the Malayan peninsula, but by 1965 it appeared that the Indonesia–Malaysia dispute was becoming part of the wider regional conflict. The fear in Canberra, given the fact that the PKI (Indonesian Communist Party) was by then the largest political movement in the archipelago and a participant in government, was that Sukarno would realize his avowed project of constructing a new Jakarta–Beijing axis. Then Australia would be prosecuting a war on two fronts, its commitment in Malaysia (despite the ANZUS Treaty) not necessarily being underwritten by the United States, its shipping and air routes all subject to interdiction, and given the (then) common land boundary in New Guinea possibly also having to contain guerrilla infiltration on that front. When the East Timor issue came to attention of policy makers it was seen through this lense.

Australia and the 'New Order'

By 1967 a profound reassessment of Indonesia had occurred in Australia (Mackie 1974). Canberra committed aid for the reconstruction of the country. It encouraged Japan and the United States to join the Inter-Governmental Group on Indonesia (IGGI) which coordinated the provision of international aid. In 1968, the prime minister, John Gorton, on a visit to Jakarta proposed that the two nations enter into a non-aggression pact.

Though this proposal was rejected, the two governments moved expeditiously to negotiate a seabed border, one motivation for which was undoubtedly that the region in question might hold exploitable oil and gas deposits (King 2002). By May 1971 the area to the east of Timor was delimited, roughly on the basis of equidistance between the land territories of the two countries. The western sector was considered in negotiations conducted in October 1972, with the boundary deviating somewhat from the line of equidistance in recognition of the existence of the 'Timor trough'. The Australian view was that this geological feature indicated that the continental shelf between the two countries was not continuous but divided at that point, and as this was located much closer to the Indonesian archipelago, Australia had a claim to a more extensive seabed zone than did Indonesia. Indonesia accepted this claim to some degree, a situation which later led Dr Mochtar Kusamaatmadja (who had been a negotiator in 1972 and later became foreign minister) that Australia had 'taken Indonesia to the cleaners' in securing this outcome (Richardson 1978). A provision of the agreement of 1972 allowed for the sharing of cross-border seabed resources, which later had an impact on the Australia–Indonesia 'Timor Gap' negotiations. Of course at this time the latter zone was subject to Portugal's jurisdiction, and the Portuguese view was to await the further evolution of relevant international law before proceeding towards any agreement with Australia.

But despite these developments, this is not to say that relations with the new regime in Jakarta were uniformly harmonious. During the Whitlam government (1972–75), a conscious attempt was made by the prime minister and members of the policy bureaucracy to repudiate any of the past associations with colonialism – the Vietnam commitment was terminated, independence for PNG was accomplished, and in the United Nations Australia supported a number of third world initiatives. In this spirit, Whitlam went out of his way to develop a close personal relationship with Suharto in order to underline this new international stance. However, as has been indicated in Chapter 1, he chose to encourage Indonesian designs on East Timor as a way of indicating that Australia was in earnest in seeking a new and equal partnership with the region's most important power.

The handling of the East Timor issue has been the largest influence on the subsequent course of Canberra–Jakarta relations. Neither is the nature of Australia's involvement in East Timor in 1999 and beyond intelligible without reference to the actions of the government in Canberra during the territory's abortive decolonization. This episode therefore deserves an extended treatment. While many of the participants and principals in policy-making circles at the time subsequently published their own view of events, and significant documentary evidence appeared in the public domain – notably in a collection assembled by Richard Walsh and George Munster in 1980 which was then banned as a result of a High Court injunction at the instigation of the Commonwealth (Walsh and Munster 1982) – the mechanics and logic of that policy making remained unclear. This situation changed as a result of the decision by Foreign Minister Downer in 1999 to make DFAT records on the issue available in advance of the usual 30-year exclusion on the publication of such materials. In doing so he adverted to the strong public interest in the issue, though the fact that the reputation of former Prime Minister Gough Whitlam would suffer from the disclosures they contained was perhaps also a consideration. Even at this juncture the Australia–Indonesia relationship had a bearing on the collection as its release was delayed for some months while Jakarta–Canberra relations were at a delicate stage during the tenure of office of Abdurrahman Wahid.

The Australian record on the Indonesian incorporation of Portuguese Timor

Whatever the precise reasons for its appearance, the history of Australia's policy towards East Timor, and especially the record of Australia's tangled exchanges with Indonesia on that issue, were placed on a much surer documentary foundation with the appearance of *Australia and the Indonesian Incorporation of Portuguese Timor 1974–1976* (Way 2000). This volume published 484 documents from the (then) Department of Foreign Affairs covering the crucial years 1974–76, plus a selection of materials from 1963 (when the Timor issue was the subject of an exchange of letters between the Portuguese and Australian prime ministers, Salazar and Menzies) and also to the end of 1978 (when the Australian government decided to acknowledge the *de jure* annexation of East Timor). For the most part these materials were made available ahead of their de-classification under the 30-year confidentiality rule. The full run of documents, of which these were a comprehensive selection, was simultaneously released for public perusal at the National Archives. Neither Cabinet records nor intelligence assessments were included, though many inferences could be drawn from materials in the 2000 collection regarding the wider activities of the policy community. The avowed purpose of their publication was to permit the public to develop an informed judgement of this diplomatic and national episode at a time when this was a matter of intensive public interest, and in a context where there was already an extensive but selective body of leaked material in the public domain.

Aside from the question of Timor policy, this collection conveys many messages. It is telling on the respective roles of ministers and the Department in the making of policy. It is informative on the (somewhat chaotic) structure of power in Indonesia's 'New Order' in the 1970s. For those so attuned, there are other semiotic readings. It is surely remarkable that, apart from Susan Boyd (a Second Secretary in Lisbon and then a member of the West Europe section of the Department), all the hundreds of policy makers that feature in its pages are men. But most readers were concerned with the dynamics of internal policy debate and implementation which are the focus of this chapter.

Here there are relatively few surprises. The text demonstrates that Prime Minister Gough Whitlam and Deputy Secretary of Foreign Affairs (later Ambassador) Dick Woolcott were the central figures in the making of Australian policy. Whitlam's meeting with Suharto in early September 1974 conveyed the impression to the Indonesian leadership that Australia would prefer the incorporation of East Timor into Indonesia, though the management of public opinion in Australia would require 'obeisance' to the principle of self-determination. Once in Jakarta as Ambassador (from March 1975), Woolcott, a figure extremely close to the prime minister from the time of his election, dexterously managed this policy. But while these documents show that Whitlam was a dominating presence throughout the period, they also reveal that important elements of the foreign policy bureaucracy were willing instruments in a design that helped deliver the East Timorese to Indonesian annexation.

It had not always been thus. In the very different circumstances of 1963, Cabinet had considered the Timor issue and had come to the conclusion that there was 'no practicable alternative to eventual Indonesian sovereignty over Portuguese Timor' (Cabinet Minute 5 February 1963, Way 2000: 26).[1] But Sir Arthur Tange (then Secretary, Department of External Affairs) is shown to have been aware that any incidence of Indonesian aggression 'will do the greatest harm to Australia's long-

---

1   Way 2000. The collection is referred to in the body of this chapter both by document and page number. Document numbers are only ascribed to materials from the period 1974–76.

term interests' (Memorandum of 25 February 1963, Way 2000: 28). Consequently, the working group he establishes on the question recommends that Australia go on the record at the United Nations, and also speak to the Indonesian side stressing the need for self-determination, otherwise Australia may become 'an accomplice of Indonesia in an exercise of "realpolitik"' (Way 2000: 33).

Though these sage recommendations were on the East Timor file, they were not heeded when the issue arose in the following decade. In a policy-planning document of 3 May 1974, East Timor is described as economically unviable and without an elite capable of leading it to independence (Way 2000: Doc. 3, 51). Consequently the 'logical long-term development' would be for it to become 'part of Indonesia'. How was this to come about? In early July 1974, the Embassy in Jakarta began receiving intelligence that key Indonesian figures were contemplating the acquisition by covert means of East Timor, this information being conveyed from Harry Tjan of the Centre for Strategic and International Studies (CSIS) to Jan Arriens, the First Secretary (Way 2000: Doc. 12, 62). Tjan claims that the idea arose partly as the result of an informal discussion with Peter Wilenski, principal secretary to the prime minister. This prompts an exchange later in the month between Graham Feakes, in charge of Southeast Asia and PNG in the Department in Canberra, and (then) Ambassador in Jakarta, Robert Furlonger. While Feakes (Way 2000: Doc. 16, 71) at this stage has doubts about a positive role for Australia in these plans, he neither accepts that integration is necessarily in Australia's interests, nor believes that Indonesian covert operations could so easily achieve their objective. Furlonger, however, has no such reservations. Anticipating the September Whitlam–Suharto meeting, the Ambassador remarks, 'Could the Prime Minister not say that he shares the assessment that it would be in the interests of the region that Portuguese Timor unite with Indonesia?'(Way 2000: Doc. 17, 73) Lest the president let slip mention of covert activities against East Timor, which would have to be repudiated for the record by the prime minister, Furlonger considers 'it is important that we forestall any such possibility' (Way 2000: Doc. 17, 73) by arranging for Arriens to brief Tjan accordingly. This briefing was subsequently held (Way 2000: Doc. 20, 79).

And the nature of the future Indonesian operation was apparent to the Embassy even in July 1974. After a field trip to West Timor, Third Secretary Denis Fisher reports on a conversation with an OPSUS (Special Operations) agent who served in Irian Jaya in the time of the 'Act of Free Choice' and whose task was clearly to produce the same result in East Timor (Way 2000: Doc. 18, 76). It should be recalled that 1025 'delegates' in West Papua under OPSUS tutelage voted unanimously in 1969 for incorporation into Indonesia, a process that was regarded even at the time as a travesty. As early as the end of July 1974 responsible members of the Department were well aware, therefore, of the manner in which East Timorese assent to integration would be engineered. This information was appropriately and as a matter of course conveyed to Whitlam. Tjan himself visited Australia prior to the prime minister's journey to meet with Suharto, and officials seek to persuade him, they believe successfully, to delay the covert operation in East Timor until after the leaders had conferred (Way 2000: Doc. 24, 91). In the briefing document prepared for Whitlam for that meeting, therefore, references to 'a genuine and internationally acceptable act of self-determination' (Way 2000: Doc. 24, 92) in East Timor are more gesture than substance. Both parties know clearly which course is being charted. And lest it be thought that these words were being placed on the record for the benefit of Indonesian officials, the Australian side is well aware that they are often not in the loop. In late September the ambassador recommends that the minister, when in New York, seek out Lim Bian Kie, private secretary to General Ali Murtopo, head of OPSUS (and an associate of Tjan) as the person 'best informed', since the Indonesian foreign minister himself is neither fully informed nor in sympathy with his leader's policy (Way 2000: Doc. 33, 107).

Denying the independence option

Such was the case at the outset of East Timor's decolonization. Given the extremely small Timorese elite and the very low level of development of the territory there may have been some justification, perhaps, in taking the view that the East Timorese were in no position to manage their own fate. In the space of 12 months it became apparent, first, that a political leadership had emerged with a coherent programme and widespread acceptance among the population, and second, that the Portuguese meanwhile had demonstrated that they had neither the capacity nor the intention to sustain the programme of decolonization they had affirmed in February 1975 and which had envisaged independence in October 1978 (Gorjão 2001a). At this point a reassessment of the Australian position might have occurred, either on the grounds that ignoring domestic political trends within the territory would be an altogether blatant denial of the right to self-determination, or because an unwelcome Indonesian intervention might be met by a sustained resistance perhaps even inviting that foreign entanglement that Jakarta's policy was supposedly designed to avoid.

However, despite members of the policy bureaucracy warning of these dangers, no change of policy occurred. Instead, Australian complicity with the Indonesian design deepened with knowledge of it. In August 1975, the UDT party attempted to seize power but were displaced after fighting with forces loyal to FRETILIN. Within days Australian policy makers know that the coup makers acted with the foreknowledge of BAKIN, the Indonesian State Intelligence Organization (Way 2000: Doc. 164, 303). In the confused situation the Portuguese authorities withdrew to the offshore island of Atauro, and there were suggestions that a multi-lateral intervention with regional participation be mobilized to end the fighting. In a submission to the prime minister, Secretary of the Department Alan Renouf notes the advantages of Indonesian participation in such an exercise, as against the unilateral action that Jakarta was contemplating. This 'regional cover' would 'help legitimise the Indonesian operation and neutralise opposition. It would enable Australia to support the Indonesian move and portray [it] in the context of preservation of regional peace' (Way 2000: Doc. 211, 382). Renouf is clear that this strategy will also deflect domestic criticism:

with the lull in the fighting in Portuguese Timor the moment for Indonesian intervention might well have passed: that is, with the fighting dying down apparently of its own accord, and with a Portuguese special envoy hoping to engage the parties in peace negotiations, it is difficult to see any pretext for Indonesian intervention which could be 'sold' to our domestic opinion. But the Department's feeling is that the breach between Fretilin and UDT is now irreparable so that any cease-fire might be short-lived. Timor, in short, is displaying all the characteristics of a South East Asian Angola. If so, the next lapse into political chaos may be the moment for Indonesians to move. So much better if Indonesia is seen to be acting not as a neo-colonialist but as the agent of a group of like-minded countries seeking regional peace.

(Way 2000: Doc. 211, 382)

In the meantime, Tjan and Lim confirm to the Embassy that key figures in the UDT are aligned with Indonesia and are being used as surrogates (Way 2000: Doc. 207, 371). In short, the Department was anticipating a clash between the Indonesian fifth column and FRETILIN that would be staged for Jakarta's purposes and which would then provide the pretext for a regional intervention, to be supported by Australia, which would serve to mask Indonesian annexation. Indonesian intellectuals who maintain, as a result of the events of 1999, that the Australian government was never wholehearted in its support of the integration strategy should attend to these passages of the documents now available very carefully.

Against this current, and especially in light of the fact that FRETILIN now appeared to be in firm control of East Timor, some officers within the Department, notably Geoff Miller, Ross Cottrill and Michael Curtin, endeavoured at various times to scrutinize critically the premises of Australian policy. In September 1975, Cottrill prepares a paper questioning the assumption that Indonesia could not live with an independent East Timor, and arguing that if problems later developed in such a state Indonesia would be quite capable of taking action to deal with them (Way 2000: Doc. 233, 417 n1). In a minute to John Rowland, Deputy Secretary of Foreign Affairs, Miller points out that there are two choices open to Australia, acquiescence in Indonesian annexation plans or attempting to persuade Jakarta that a *modus vivendi* with a FRETILIN ruled independent state could be reached. Referring to Cottrill's research, Miller argues that the cost of persisting with support for Indonesian subversion may be very high for both countries:

The disadvantages of this course are that in so far as it consciously encourages Indonesian intervention it is indefensible in terms of the Government's stated policies and principles, and that intervention may lead to a protracted struggle which will distract Indonesian attention from more important tasks and opportunities, distort its perceptions, and harm it internationally in both general (the United Nations) and particular (the United States) ways.

(Way 2000: Doc. 233, 419)

At the beginning of October, Miller tries again, adding that Australia–Indonesia relations may well also be a casualty of annexation, and the protracted conflict that is likely to result inside East Timor may actually attract the very involvement of the communist powers that intervention is ostensibly designed to prevent (Way 2000: Doc. 247, 440). After the event this reasoning provokes a querulous response from Woolcott, who maintains that nothing Australia could have done would have deflected the Indonesians from their intention to seize the territory. He reserves his sharpest barb for Cottrill, observing that 'I find Cottrill's point, that if an independent East Timor turned sour as far as Indonesia was concerned then Indonesia could do something about it, glib and untenable' (Way 2000: Doc. 423, 707). It should be recalled however that this remark was made in the context of the leaking of Woolcott's lengthiest defence of his 'pragmatic and realistic' advocacy (Way 2000: Doc. 393, 652–60), an event which may well have coloured his view of elements of the policy bureaucracy.

Despite these developments Woolcott remains convinced that the Indonesians are firm in their resolve to acquire East Timor and will not be swayed. He quotes the prime minister to the effect that 'Portuguese Timor is part of the Indonesian world' (Way 2000: Doc. 250, 445) against doubts on the part of Renouf, who by early October sees that FRETILIN is in charge and that the UDT has probably lost what influence it had formerly wielded. Renouf pleads that some account needs to be taken of principle: Whitlam's comment to Suharto in Townsville cannot be taken as '*carte blanche*' (Way 2000: Doc. 251, 446–7). This and other exchanges leave the impression that Renouf was a little unsure of his ground, perhaps as a result of his close association with Whitlam.

Portugal having so obviously lost its power to influence events, and with civil strife in the territory, it was logical for the issue to devolve to the United Nations. Former Permanent Representative Sir Laurence McIntyre advises that calls for the UN to be involved should be deflected. If Portugal requests a Security Council debate on Indonesian interference, this outcome might well be embarrassing for Australia and damaging for Indonesia (Way 2000: Doc. 228, 409). Thereafter Australian assistance to Indonesia at the UN was considerable. Australia opposes the circulation of FRETILIN documents to the Committee of 24 (Way 2000: Doc. 252, 448 n1), pressures the Indonesians to mount a campaign in the General Assembly (Way 2000: Doc. 333, 561), and two days after the invasion when many nations are looking to Australia to take the lead, Ralph Harry cables to Canberra to say that at the UN 'our immediate diplomatic problem and task has been to do what we can to reduce the pressure on the Indonesians' (Way 2000: Doc. 369, 617).

With the Embassy informed, almost on a daily basis, of Indonesia's invasion plans, the lack of coordination of national policy that is exposed by the killings at Balibo is strikingly in evidence, although it should be recalled that by this stage much attention in Australia was focused on the deepening constitutional crisis. On the question of the deaths of Greg Shackleton and his four media colleagues at Balibo on the morning of 16 October 1975, the documents make no mention of any intelligence intercepts that identified them as specific targets for the infiltrating

Indonesian forces. Of course such intercepts might well have been made, as Des Ball and Hamish McDonald have claimed (Ball and McDonald 2000), though the complete absence of any hint of their existence in this collection is noteworthy. However, the material shows that the Department had a close and correct knowledge of Indonesian military plans and was also aware of the danger posed to any Australians who were caught in the conflict. On the day before the killings, a cablegram from Woolcott states that 'Initially an Indonesian force of 800 will advance Batugade–Balibo–Maliana–Atsabe' (Way 2000: Doc. 262, 468), information confirmed in a 'very frank discussion' Woolcott has with General Benny Moerdani (Intelligence chief of HANKAM – the Department of Defence and Security) on the night of 15 October (Way 2000: Doc. 265, 472–6). At the very least it is extraordinary that those officials responsible for monitoring events who were working in the knowledge that a major Indonesian push was being launched did not, when seeing Shackleton's memorable reports on their television screens, put two and two together, even though they were not necessarily aware that by this stage the television crews were at the border. The mention in a brief for Willesee dated 16–17 October (Way 2000: Doc. 266, 478) for planning in the next week for the evacuation of Australian citizens, all of whom are in some danger, is tragically too late; though as the author is Renouf, who would have seen the putative intercepts, other interpretations of this material are possible.

The publication of this documentary collection clarifies the issue of the responsibility for the East Timor disaster. In December 1975, Renouf states in confidential remarks to the Ambassador of Japan that Whitlam had 'gone outside his brief' (Way 2000: Doc. 383, 638) in his discussions with Suharto in 1975, neglecting the Department's favoured position of self-determination for East Timor. He echoes this claim in his later memoir, where he states that at his talks with Suharto in September 1974 Whitlam 'changed the policy' by placing the emphasis upon integration (Renouf 1979: 443). This assertion (disputed by Whitlam, though on different grounds (Whitlam 1997: 72–3)) is hardly credible in the face of the material that has become available. At least part of the blame for encouraging the Indonesians must lie with the Department. With some exceptions and reservations, senior officials amongst whom Woolcott was only the most prominent, were pro-active advocates of a policy that positively assisted the Indonesian regime in its design. Support for this design was such that there was no concerted review of its acceptability even after the situation in East Timor changed profoundly with the virtual abdication of the Portuguese.

Whitlam and Woolcott

The fact that Whitlam was virtually unchecked, even by his own foreign minister, in the pursuit of his policy was a consequence of the nature of the Australian political process at the time, as well as of his lack of preparedness to debate such issues in Cabinet. On the latter point, former senator and minister John Wheeldon, commented in 1983 on the East Timor annexation that 'had there been any discussion of foreign affairs in Mr Whitlam's Cabinet, the then Prime Minister would have won anything but unanimous endorsement for his attitude' (Wheeldon 1984: 61). In the 1970s, lobby groups on foreign policy issues were less vocal and well-informed, but the Timor issue nevertheless stimulated a great deal of public comment much of which foretold the disastrous outcome of the drive to annexation.

As the only established democracy in this sorry episode, therefore, Australia's political processes did not contribute to a felicitous outcome. Visits by parliamentarians to East Timor to make up their own minds on the situation are regarded as an annoyance by the nation's leaders (Fry 2003). A Labor Party sub-branch taking an interest in the Timor issue has to be restrained. Stories in the Australian press – some by Bruce Juddery and Michael Richardson, remarkably prescient as it turned out – are noticed chiefly for their capacity to inflame Indonesian sensibilities. In a submission to the caretaker foreign minister, Andrew Peacock, Renouf observes that regarding the present turbulence in relations with Indonesia, 'many of the problems which have arisen have been caused by the well-publicized activities of private Australian groups' (Way 2000: Doc. 336, 565) rather than by Jakarta's policies.

But however supportive the Department of Foreign Affairs might have been for Whitlam's Timor policy, a significant counterpoint was provided by the Department of Defence. As early as August 1974, in a working paper forwarded to Foreign Affairs, W. B. Pritchett, First Assistant Secretary, Defence Planning Division, argues that Australian acquiescence in an Indonesian annexation would undermine the nation's credibility elsewhere in the region, and Australia's strategic interest would be best served if East Timor became through self-determination an independent state (Way 2000: Doc. 21, 83). In a brief prepared by Pritchett during preparations by Defence Minister Lance Barnard for a visit to Jakarta in December 1974, it is suggested that during exchanges with his Indonesian counterparts 'opportunity should be taken to remind the Indonesians of the unfavourable reactions to be expected to any immoderate action, and the importance Australia attaches to the free choice of the Portuguese Timorese being seen to be exercised' (Way 2000: Doc. 63, 140).

Despite the drift of events, Pritchett does not give up. He proposes in February 1975 that an independent East Timor enter a treaty relationship with Indonesia, giving the country a stake in Timorese security, a device that would remove concerns about security threats while offering Jakarta a way out of the looming impasse now it is becoming clearer that the territory will not be delivered easily into Indonesian hands (Way 2000: Doc. 90, 190). Thereafter Defence evidently provided a realistic view of the disposition of domestic political forces in the territory. Following the UDT attempted coup in August 1975, strategic assessments warn that FRETILIN has become an effective political and military force and would not be readily dislodged (Way 2000: Doc. 257, 460). In a document leaked in the late 1970s (and not yet in the public domain as it constitutes part of the Defence archive), Pritchett develops what is perhaps the most clear-sighted of all analyses of the issue. Writing at the beginning of October to the minister, Bill Morrison, he succinctly indicates the inconsistency of Australian policy:

Basically . . . we have pursued incompatible lines of policy – that Portuguese Timor should be integrated into Indonesia but that there should be an act of self-determination and that Indonesia should not effect integration by coercion. Since the weight of evidence from the outset has been that any act of self-determination would oppose integration, in effect what we have offered Indonesia with the one hand we have sought to deny them with the other.

(Walsh and Munster 1980: 221)

In its submissions over the past ten months, according to Pritchett, Defence has maintained that aggressive action by Indonesia to seize East Timor will have two likely consequences. First, the domestic reaction 'from both the left and right of the domestic political spectrum' to such action would threaten many of the fundamentals of the present Australia–Indonesia accord, including the defence cooperation programme. Irrespective of how this might be managed, the Indonesian response to this reaction might then undermine the friendly relationship that has long existed between the two countries.

Policy must be based on the assumption that FRETILIN is a plausible political movement that might be displaced by outright invasion but would surely then sustain a guerilla resistance. Taking issue specifically with Woolcott, Pritchett finds the current approach to the issue impractical. Urging the Indonesians not to use force and to negotiate with FRETILIN will not achieve either end. And an invasion will surely provoke international condemnation. The wisest course would be to seek to convince the Indonesians that they must accept East Timorese independence under the domination of FRETILIN. If they were skilful enough they could guarantee a role in the new state's security and this outcome might also create a potentially fruitful field for Australia–Indonesia cooperation, thus excluding any possible third parties.

Although the material that became available in 2000 does not offer a comprehensive picture beyond July 1976, it should be noted that there is clear evidence of a bi-partisan approach to the Timor issue. At one point Suharto wryly comments, after hearing of Whitlam's domestic difficulties, that the prime minister would seem to prefer Andrew Peacock as his successor, in preference to some in his own party, given that he had described Peacock as seeing foreign policy issues in much the same light (Way 2000: Doc. 109, 221). Even while in caretaker mode, following the November *coup* (after the Balibo killings, and within weeks of the final invasion), Prime Minister Malcolm Fraser sends a message to Suharto expressing his regret regarding domestic irritants to good mutual relations and stating his understanding for 'the need for Indonesia to have an appropriate solution' for the Timor problem (Way 2000: Doc. 343, 579). The latter enigmatic phrase was suitably glossed by Woolcott. Fraser has subsequently claimed that the Department took advantage of his caretaker status to initiate this communication: 'There was great pressure, I think deriving from the ambassador, for a message to be sent.' He also stated that he did not believe he had been briefed at this stage of Indonesia's invasion plans, though it is difficult to imagine what information he could be given regarding foreign policy issues at that time that was of greater moment (ABC 2000).

If Australian policy was clear enough, that of the other parties is depicted as highly confused. Suharto presided over a fluid and competing collection of factions. He failed to act in August 1975 when an intervention would have had some international credibility, because his spiritual advisor was sure that Timor would fall into his lap without effort. The chronic instability of the post-Salazar Portuguese political system prevented any coherent policy emerging in Lisbon. Decolonization on the African model – handing power to the most powerful group or coalition – was favoured by some policy makers, while others paid more attention to developments in East Timor or Indonesia. The Timorese of necessity took their cue from Portugal, with disastrous results. In the light of this record, it is ironic that Portugal should enjoy such a favourable reputation in its forsaken colony. The United Nations was immobilized by the Cold War.

However, there was one common element in the fact that foreign policy was not made by foreign ministers. In Portugal the military often took the lead. To his enduring credit, Senator Willesee resolutely disputed the prime minister's approach, which produced some awkward problems for the bureaucrats. Foreign Minister Adam Malik in Jakarta was initially kept in the dark and therefore his expressions of approval for Timorese independence were genuine. Later he learned of his nation's covert campaign of destabilization, and became a leading advocate of its consummation. When Professor Mochtar Kusumaatmadja assumed most of the responsibilities for handling the Timor issue he was deliberately kept uninformed so he would be a more credible international spokesman for Indonesia. Given his role in the events of 1999, the reader is left to ponder how much Alex (soon to be Ali) Alatas, then private secretary to the foreign minister and as is evident from this collection already an important member of the Indonesian policy community, learned of his craft at this time.

The prime minister's predominance in policy making on East Timor was apparent to his contemporaries. Woolcott's central role was also evident even in 1975, but the sheer volume and persistence of Woolcott's voice in the documents published in 2000 must lead to some re-evaluation of his importance. In September 1974 he was not averse to reminding Secretary Renouf, his superior at the time, that the prime minister's policy was one of incorporation of East Timor with 'obeisance' to be paid to self-determination in order to appease sentiment in Australia (Way 2000: Doc. 37, 111). He is a consistent advocate of an avowedly 'realist' assessment of the prospects for East Timor. Indonesia is intent on a policy of absorption. Australia is in no position to deny that intention, but any effort will only cause harm to a bilateral relationship so important to Australia's security. And at the same time, an independent East Timor would be an unstable micro-state in Australia's immediate locality, and thus a decided liability.

Woolcott's assessment was wrong. This is not to take issue with realist assumptions that are less fashionable now than in the 1970s, as the material in the 2000 documents collection shows that some members of the Department at the time were unhappy with a policy which denied values normally held as central to the Australian world view, including self-determination and an abhorrence of aggressive state action. Rather it is to say that those analysts who disputed

Woolcott's prescriptions while sharing his realist premises were much closer to the mark. In retrospect it can be seen that there were three serious flaws in Woolcott's analysis. First, without the sponsorship of a major power (indeed in the face of positive assistance given by the United States to the Indonesian military), FRETILIN managed to maintain a 25-year resistance against the occupiers of the territory. It was Woolcott's view immediately after the December invasion that 'without the intervention of a great power on its side . . . FRETILIN's cause has always been lost' (Way 2000: Doc. 393, 653). Second, Australia's support for this occupation did not deliver the positive relations that were the promised reward. Specifically, the Timor annexation had the exact opposite effect, poisoning relations with Jakarta for almost a generation, an outcome manifest in Suharto's inability to visit Australia from that time onwards. Third, the annexation severely damaged the reputations of Indonesia and its regime whose credibility as a regional player and as a leader in the non-aligned world was thereafter suspect. The reader of the key documents is likely to be struck by the absence of a vigorous and unconstrained debate as to the possibility of these outcomes. This seems to have been the result, in part, of Woolcott's style which led to some conflation of reporting, analysis and advocacy. Given the fact that many of the officials in the Department concerned with Indonesian policy had served during the Vietnam commitment during which similar problems were in evidence, this shortcoming is surprising.

In his memoirs, published in 2003, Woolcott complains that on East Timor he has been made a 'scapegoat' by 'partially informed academics' and others who have generated a 'mythology' about the issue by advancing the view that he was instrumental in persuading the Australian government to pursue 'an immoral policy of appeasing an Indonesian dictatorship and encouraging its military involvement in East Timor' (Woolcott 2003: 144). In his review of one of the major items in this mythology, Woolcott rejects any suggestion that Australian diplomats were compromised by their access to the thinking of the CSIS. However, though he refers to the existence of the documentary collection released in 2000, he ignores the evidence discussed above. To return to Furlonger's cable to Feakes of 30 July 1974 (Way 2000: Doc. 17, 72–4), the ambassador's preference for integration is plain and he is clearly suggesting methods by which Australia could become associated with the Indonesian plan, already well known to the embassy, to acquire the territory by any means including subversion. The context is the forthcoming visit by Whitlam when Furlonger is urging a discussion of the East Timor question:

> I think that the very least that Soeharto would expect from us would be to share his judgment that it would be in the interests of the region – not only Indonesia – if Portuguese Timor were to become part of Indonesia. I personally have no difficulty in accepting this as a proposition: the thought of poor, uneducated, probably unstable, independent East Timor on our doorstep, and susceptible to subversion and exploitation by other Powers, should be no more attractive to us than to Indonesia. Despite Indonesia's imperfections, the Timorese would probably be no worse off under Indonesia than if they were independent. And we would have one problem, which we

have developed some skill in understanding and dealing with, and not two, one of them completely unpredictable. Let us not be too swayed by possible criticism from radical academics.

(Way 2000: Doc. 17, 72–3)

Furlonger, of course, was successful in this regard. Woolcott is careful to observe that his two predecessors as well as his successors in Jakarta 'shared the same views' on East Timor (Woolcott 2003: 144). In these circumstances, any references by any of these officials to 'self-determination' can only have been for the purposes of public relations. As he writes of later events in August 1975, 'the potential contradiction between the two main aspects of Whitlam's policy – the logic of East Timor's incorporation into Indonesia on the one hand, and the need, on the other, for this to be an outcome of self-determination – was daily becoming more obvious' (Woolcott 2003: 159). If otherwise intelligent and well-informed individuals affirm two contradictory propositions it is bound to be the case that they actually believe only one of them.

On the death of the journalists, a further element in the 'mythology' is the allegation that the Australian Embassy knew of their presence at Balibo sufficiently early so as to have been able to warn them of the troop movements they knew were impending. Woolcott rejects this suggestion that he had advance knowledge of their whereabouts, though he does state that he learned of their deaths 'on the night of 17 October' as a result of 'an intercepted message' (Woolcott 2003: 154). But his account is clouded by the most extraordinary claim that 'the journalists had identified themselves with one side in the civil war, Fretilin' (Woolcott 2003: 154). This statement deserves close inspection. According to all observers there was no civil war by mid-October, though the Indonesian campaign of border incursions was getting underway (as Woolcott himself reported). Woolcott seems to have convinced himself, however, that there were still 'two sides' in the territory, clearly a situation that would help justify intervention. Now in order to do their job – to suggest that they 'should not have been where they were' is to demonstrate a profound misunderstanding of their professional responsibilities – the journalists certainly sought the cooperation of FRETILIN. By this time the leaders of the party were the de facto administrators, being in charge of the territory all the way to the western frontier, and the visit of the journalists could only be arranged with their approval. Indeed, they were pleased to help since they knew that their claims of foreign invasion would thereby be substantiated by a team of inter-national media. To hold the view that they were doing anything other than trying to obtain an important story is nothing less than an unwarranted slur on their characters.

There are other surprising elements in Woolcott's account. He appears to believe that 'all' of 'the people of West Timor' were Tetum speakers (146), whereas the use of Tetum was and is confined to the border areas. Most West Timorese being Atoni, Helong or Roti, thus speak distinct Austronesian languages which though related to Tetum are mutually incomprehensible. Clearly a common language might be used in favour of the argument for integration – did Woolcott believe this claim in 1975, and if he did, did it influence his judgement? He is also somewhat uninformed on Washington's policy on East Timor. As he maintains, 'the United States simply had not focused on the issue' and as the Ford–Kissinger meeting with Suharto occurred 'just hours before the invasion' (148) there was little that could have been done to influence the course of events. However it is now well known that Suharto discussed East Timor with President Ford during his visit to Washington in July 1975, when he described an independent East Timor as 'unviable' and supporters of this notion as 'almost communists' (National Security Archive 2002b). Given Indonesia's emerging role as the most important anti-communist power in Southeast Asia, it cannot be believed that this escaped the notice of Suharto's hosts. It has even been claimed that members of the US military helped train the paratroopers selected for the invasion of Dili (Conboy 2003: 237). Altogether, Woolcott's more contemporary view of East Timor seems no better founded than his view in 1975. And although recording his dismay at the brutality of Indonesian rule in East Timor, he is nevertheless candid enough to record his personal role while serving in 1982 as Australia's representative at the UN in having the East Timor issue withdrawn from the agenda of the UN General Assembly (Woolcott 2003: 195–6). Though this was done, he writes, as a result of a direct request from Prime Minister Bob Hawke, this manoeuvre closed off a vital forum for the East Timorese resistance to argue their case internationally and seemed to portend, at the time, the extinction of their hopes. It is perhaps little wonder that Woolcott's name has come to be so closely identified with East Timor.

It is perhaps an indication of the realist moral outlook that still characterizes the world of diplomacy and of which Woolcott is an exponent that Lim Bian Kie, now better known as Jusuf Wanandi, is a born-again champion of civil society and advocate of civilian control of the military in Indonesia. Yet if on the Australian side Woolcott is the dominant figure, for the Indonesians the key players are Moerdani, Tjan and Lim. When it is recalled that East Timorese mortality in the long night under Indonesian occupation was of around the same order (in proportion to population) as that of Pol Pot's Kampuchea, it is surely remarkable that Lim remains an influential figure with an apparently unsullied international reputation. If, however, a comparison is made with the standing of the comparable Australian actors a local analogue may be detected. Neither Whitlam nor Woolcott have indicated the slightest intention of modifying their view that the policy of 1974–75 was appropriate in the circumstances of the time. And their role still has its present day apologists as any perusal of the press occasioned by the release of the 1974–76 documents will show.

Reflections on the costs of 1975

What new insights can be derived from the 2000 documents collection? Woolcott's persistent and authoritative voice has already been noted. Given the later history of this relationship, it is noteworthy that early efforts are in evidence to quarantine defence cooperation from the fall-out from Indonesian action in East Timor.

However it is perhaps a measure of the doggedness of some journalists as well as the willingness of some of their sources to reveal the workings of the engine of policy that many of the themes that characterize this volume had already found their way into the literature. Whitlam's personal role, Woolcott's realism, the identity of the proponents in Indonesia of annexation, the means by which Australia came to learn of and become involved with this scheme, are all part of the existing record. However a solid documentary basis is now available for what have been up until the present unsubstantiated or contentious conjectures. But we are now in a much better position to assess the existing secondary literature. Here perhaps Nancy Viviani's account of policy during the Whitlam era (Viviani 1976), and Hamish McDonald's exposé of Indonesia's campaign of subversion (McDonald 1980: 189–211), both originally published more than 20 years ago, stand out as largely correct. Though the former author had the advantage of working in Willesee's office, it is noteworthy that she was able to validate most of her critical points from newspaper accounts. And the relevant section of the best summary view of East Timor's contemporary history, that by James Dunn, though published in 1983, remains substantially accurate (Dunn 1983: 122–64). Similarly, Jill Jolliffe's pioneering work on the events of 1975 is shown to be still the most comprehensive guide (Jolliffe 1978).

It is still not clear to what extent, at this time, Australian and US policy was coordinated, given the estrangement that existed between Washington and the Whitlam administration, though it can be assumed that the national intelligence agencies exchanged data. In a cable of 17 August 1975, Woolcott reports US Ambassador Newsom's comment to the effect that if the Indonesians should intervene militarily they should do so 'effectively, quickly and not use our equipment' (Way 2000: Docs. 169, 314). Washington was certainly aware of Indonesian designs as a result of a direct communication from Suharto himself. As has been noted, at his meeting with President Gerald Ford at Camp David in July 1975, Suharto indicated his interest in events in East Timor, characterizing those in the territory who desired independence as 'communist influenced', and expressing the view that given East Timor's poverty and lack of resources its only future (and one desired by a 'majority' of the population) was integration with Indonesia. The extent of US support for the policy of annexation is most clearly exhibited in the record of the meeting between Presidents Ford and Suharto and Henry Kissinger on the eve of the invasion, plans for which were already known to the American side. When Suharto adverts to the planned invasion, Ford remarks 'We will understand and will not press you on the issue' and Kissinger undertakes to 'influence the reaction in America' the chances for which would be maximized if the invasion could be delayed until the US party has left the country. Kissinger's later manoeuvres to avoid the consequences that should have followed, given Indonesia's violation of its end-user arms agreement with the United States, are well documented (National Security Archive 2002a).

Perhaps the greatest contribution to understanding the place of East Timor in the narrative of Australia–Indonesia relations is to be found in the silences of the document collection published in 2000. A significant silence in this collection is on the argument that East Timor would become a base for communist trouble-making in the region if placed in the hands of an independent régime. Later discussions of the events of 1975 make much of this rationale for both Indonesian and Australian actions, especially given that this was the year of communist victories in Indochina. But in this collection, while the phrase 'the Cuba of the South Seas' appears, neither Australian nor even Indonesian policy makers spend much time on the grounds for this claim. Nor is any hard evidence of communist influence within FRETILIN ever assessed. The consequences of annexation, moreover, are discussed only in the narrowest of terms, with advisers pointing out that an aggressive invasion would evoke condemnation in the UN which Australia, given its record, would have to support. But there is little evidence that on the Australian side much thought was given to what Indonesian rule might entail for the inhabitants of the territory. It is left to a Portuguese spokesman to point out that as the New Order had come to power on a sea of blood, it could not be assumed that the East Timorese would necessarily escape such treatment, especially given the allegedly leftist character of its government (Way 2000: Doc. 209, 374). This information was certainly available to Indonesia specialists at the time (Cribb 1990: 12), though estimates of the killings that followed the *Gestapu* incident ranged very widely from 200,000 to one million. In 1966, *The Economist* (1966: 727–8) reported deaths of one million; later Ben Anderson and Ruth McVey (1971) put the number at 200,000. The official estimate by KOPKAMTIB (the military command set up by Suharto to eradicate the PKI) of 500,000 did not become available until 1976 (Cribb 1990: 12). It can only be surmised that in the aftermath of 'Confrontation', the nation's policy makers were not inclined to scrutinize too closely the domestic performance of a régime that was perceived as more favourably disposed towards Australia than its predecessor.

Nor is there sign of a debate on what the impact of annexation might be on Indonesia, much beyond arguments regarding Woolcott's glib assertion that its government was 'not inexperienced' in dealing with 'residual' guerilla problems (Way 2000: Doc. 393, 653). Though Australia had had little experience with the consequences of giving authoritarian governments *carte blanche*, it is a little surprising that no comparisons were made with the experience of United States policy with some of its allies in Asia and Latin America. Though for long the focus was on the 'stability' that the New Order supposedly delivered, we can now see that the outcomes have been damaging to Australia's interests. The Timor commitment proved expensive to the Indonesian nation and became the top priority of the military. Resources flowed to the latter, guaranteeing the predominance of the military sector at a time when economic development and the introduction of market oriented reforms might otherwise have favoured the emerging middle class. Timor became a training ground and source of shared experience for the officer corps who developed the mentality and approach of an army of occupation, an approach that was extended to other localities including Aceh, Maluku and also West Papua. Though a poor territory, Timor even enriched such officers as Moerdani, whose wealth then assisted their further political ascent (Aditjondro 1999b). In this connection it was surely the case that Whitlam and Woolcott did not anticipate the venality of elements of the Indonesian military leadership. This policy thus helped to maintain a militarized and authoritarian (and ultimately unstable) Indonesia with which Australia could only pursue 'engagement' at a high cost to principles and values.

What is also noticeably lacking in the material released in 2000 is any sense that the Australian Embassy was being used in the perpetual struggle for influence that characterized Suharto's court. It is not that Australian policy makers were ill-informed on these matters. Document 374 contains a careful analysis by Furlonger of foreign policy making in Indonesia. The Foreign Ministry deals with 'minor and routine questions' (Way 2000: Doc. 374, 157), but as most regional issues possess a security dimension, the military and BAKIN exercise a powerful influence in the Ministerial Committee that has oversight in this area. This Committee, though, shares its role in a rather imprecise manner with the Political and Security Stabilisation Council, which also receives advice from such unofficial bodies as the Centre for Strategic and International Studies (CSIS). Suharto has the final and deciding voice in matters of policy, but he is very much dependent upon a circle of advisers, mostly military and in some senses representatives of rival organizational and factional groups. As in most such systems, information is not necessarily shared as often its possession imparts power.

The intention of Tjan and Lim in keeping the Australian Embassy so closely informed of matters not always even known to the foreign minister can only be hypothesized. Malcolm Dan, who often acted as Tjan's interlocutor, is adamant that he is an authoritative spokesman on the subject concerned, and is so communicative as a result of the relationship of trust that has been established with the Embassy (Way 2000: Doc. 157, 294). Geoff Miller is of the opinion that Tjan's revelations served to compromise Australia, though members of the Department sometimes regarded the latter's statements as 'deliberately outrageous'. Another purpose may well have been to influence Australian thinking, in the hope that approval for plans which were perhaps much less than firm policy would then be retailed to Suharto himself or other influential members of his entourage thus reinforcing prospects for their full adoption and subsequent success. In retrospect, it can be seen that if this was their objective they were enormously successful. By early September 1974, in a brief for Whitlam in advance of his trip to Indonesia, Tjan is described as 'Soeharto's principal adviser on Portuguese Timor' (Way 2000: Doc. 24, 90). There can be little doubt that Australian advocacy of his schemes aided immeasurably in their realization. As Feakes informs Willesee in December 1974, Murtopo was candid enough to remark to the ambassador in Lisbon that 'Australian support for the idea of incorporation had helped Indonesia crystallize its own thinking' (Way 2000: Doc. 61, 136).

Bilateral policy following the invasion

There can be little dispute that the strategy of encouraging Indonesian designs on East Timor, far from laying the foundations for a solid bilateral relationship, had the opposite effect. The independence movement in East Timor was widely and sympathetically reported in 1975 in the Australian press. The deaths of the five journalists in Balibo, an event for which it was widely believed even at the time Indonesian led forces were responsible, alienated many Australians and government inaction compounded the sense of outrage. If there had not also been a domestic constitutional crisis it can be assumed that Whitlam would have faced enormous public pressure over his handling of the Timor issue. By the time of the paratrooper landings on Dili, Australia was governed by a caretaker administration required under the prevailing political convention to take no new initiatives. Nevertheless, Australia voted in the UN General Assembly in favour of the resolution (which was adopted) condemning the invasion and calling for an act of self-determination in the territory to take place. This led to bitter criticism from Indonesia and a period of very cool official relations, notwithstanding the fact that behind the scenes Australia had been active to deflect criticism from Indonesia and, by inaction, had helped sabotage the UN mission led by Winspeare Guicciardi which had been dispatched to assess the situation in East Timor.

Influential voices in Australia soon argued that expressing criticism of Indonesia's handling of the East Timor issue served no constructive purpose. As the Defence Department's confidential 1976 *Strategic Assessments* maintained:

> Indonesia has been made aware of Australia's objection to its use of force beyond its borders to settle a dispute. The defence interest therefore favours acceptance of Indonesia's *fait accompli* in East Timor, and cessation of political criticism of Indonesia about self-determination.
>
> (Toohey and Wilkinson 1987: 238)

Nevertheless, the Timor issue dogged relations between the two governments (Parliament of the Commonwealth of Australia 1993). The reason why Suharto undertook no visit to Australia after 1975 was the sure knowledge that he would be greeted by public protest. In February 1979, Australia accepted the *de jure* incorporation of East Timor into Indonesia, but the opposition Labor Party continued to support 'the inalienable right of the East Timorese to self-determination and independence' until it came into government in 1983. As has been noted in an earlier chapter, under Prime Minister Bob Hawke the new Labor government decided to pursue a policy of rapprochement with Jakarta, reversing its previous support for self-determination. To underline this reversal of policy, former defence minister, Bill Morrison, who had led the parliamentary delegation to East Timor in 1983 which had reported favourably on conditions in the territory, was appointed ambassador to Indonesia.

Though the major political parties were by then in full accord on the Timor issue, lobbyists and pressure groups continued to insist that a country committed to human rights standards and accountable government could not in all conscience condone the forcible annexation of one country by another. The steady flow of reports of killings and human rights violations fed this insistence, the details of which were well known to the intelligence community. Accordingly, it could be claimed that events in Timor coloured the entire Australia–Indonesia relationship.

Perhaps for this reason, the New Order never enjoyed a positive image in the Australian media (aside from in the Murdoch press), and a full decade before the regional financial crisis some journalists were warning of the shaky economic foundations of Indonesia's growing apparent prosperity. At the same time, research in the academic world (much of it undertaken by the students of Heinz Arndt at the Australian National University) was much more positive on the sustainability of the New Order's development strategy. The exposure of the increasing cupidity of Suharto and his family owed therefore much more to investigative journalism than to mainstream academic analysis. A major controversy was stirred by David Jenkins, then a correspondent in Jakarta, who in April 1986 published an article in which he compared Suharto's record to that of the Marcos kleptocracy (Jenkins 1986). Jenkins was elaborating upon the work of Richard Robison, whose book *Indonesia: the Rise of Capital* (1986), revealed the extent to which the military elite of the 1960s had become the business elite of the 1980s. In retrospect, Jenkins' revelations hardly did justice to the size of the family fortune, but they had serious repercussions for bilateral relations. Entry visas for Australian journalists were suspended, and for a brief period even Australian tourists were denied entry into the country. The newspaper of the armed forces published articles in which Australian arrogance and racism were the chief themes, and it was also claimed (without, it should be said, much foundation) that Australia's new defence doctrine (associated with the 'Dibb Report') identified Indonesia as a possible future enemy. It was not until February 1988 that Australian journalists were permitted to reopen residential bureaux in Jakarta.

In handling the Jenkins issue the government in Canberra struggled with conflicting objectives. The defence of a free press and the freedom of commentary could not be impugned, even though the government was clearly discomforted by the affair. On the other hand, Australia was by this stage in the throes of a major economic realignment premised upon the need to liberalize and internationalize what had until then been a relatively protected economy and which, to succeed, required much greater integration with the booming markets of Australia's immediate region. In the event, Foreign Minister Hayden managed to engineer a reconciliation at the official level, though for several years Indonesian coolness was evident in the lack of visits from senior officials to Australia.

In 1979, the Fraser government had begun negotiations with Indonesia over the delimitation of the seabed boundary between Australia and East Timor. Indeed, these negotiations, as Foreign Minister Peacock stated, marked the practical recognition of Indonesia's *de jure* control of East Timor. The possibility of significant hydrocarbon deposits being found in the 'Timor Gap' was high, as Australian policy makers had known even in the Portuguese era.

These negotiations (interrupted in the aftermath of the Jenkins controversy) were inherited by Gareth Evans when he became foreign minister in 1988. Evans was a diplomatic activist of the 'big picture' school; his major project in this area was his avowed intention of putting more 'ballast' in the Indonesia–Australia relationship so that it would not be blown off course (to pursue this metaphor) by single events like the Jenkins article (Department of Foreign Affairs and Trade 1989;

Evans and Grant 1991: 190). Evans cultivated a close 'personal' relationship with his Indonesian counterpart, Ali Alatas, partly on the basis that such relations were in keeping with the indirect and consensual diplomacy of the ASEAN region. Regular ministerial and senior official meetings were initiated, again on the ASEAN model. The most important single outcome of Evans' tenure of this post was the final negotiation of the Timor Gap Treaty, concluded in 1989 and gazetted in 1991. As has frequently been pointed out, while a number of states (32 according to one survey) indicated by various diplomatic means that East Timor was a province of Indonesia, only Australia signed an international treaty specifically affirming this position. It is perhaps not entirely an accident that the conditions of the treaty were very favourable to Australia's interests. Nevertheless, in a less than edifying spectacle, Australia then found itself arraigned before the International Court of Justice by Portugal on the grounds that the Treaty denied the rights of the administrating power (Portugal) and by extension the rights of the inhabitants to self-determination. The best known image of Evans in Australia is the video clip of him toasting in champagne, in an aircraft overflying the Timor Sea, the signing of the treaty with Alatas, an image which has not assisted his pursuit of a high profile international diplomatic career following his tenure of the foreign ministership.

The Dili massacre of 1991 forced Evans to visit Jakarta to express Australia's concern. Initially Evans claimed that the episode was an 'aberration' and not to be compared, for example, to the Tiananmen killings in Beijing in 1989. But Prime Minister Hawke, responding in part to pressures from within his own party, but also from personal conviction – his emotional outburst after hearing of the events in Beijing in 1989 was by this time legendary – signaled a new and much less compromising line towards Indonesia. He even intimated that East Timor policy would be reassessed, though at this point domestic political dynamics intervened.

The Keating policy of engagement

Notwithstanding the 'ballast' for which Evans' labours were responsible, the new relationship with Indonesia was not sufficiently robust to deliver for the foreign minister during his visit meetings with any policy makers of consequence. But while Evans was in Jakarta, the Labor Party leadership passed from Hawke to Keating, and the tough stance of the former prime minister was quickly forgotten as Keating moved to make his personal mark on Australian external policy. Not known before this time as a leader with a great interest in Asia (or even in foreign policy as such), Keating had become convinced by close advisers that Australia's relationship with its immediate region was the key to national prosperity and security. It should be recalled that at this time growth in the new Asian tiger economies (and poor performance in the Australian economy) was such that many Australian policy makers were assuming that they would soon be dealing with a group of countries, individually and collectively, the national strength and capacity of which would outweigh Australia's (Garnaut 1989; Meredith and Dyster 1999: 287–9).

Keating determined that his first official visit abroad would be to Indonesia. In April 1992, he met Suharto in Jakarta, and in the bilateral meetings the Dili massacre was not discussed. It would not be too much of an exaggeration to say that Keating became an enthusiast for Indonesia, with all of the zeal of the neophyte. In 1994, he described the bilateral relationship thus:

> . . . no country is more important to Australia than Indonesia. If we fail to get this relationship right, and nurture and develop it, the whole web of our foreign relations is incomplete.
>
> (Keating 2000: 136)

During his tenure of office, Keating visited Indonesia on six occasions, as well as holding bilateral discussions with Suharto on the margins of APEC leaders' meetings in Seattle and Osaka. To be fair to his leadership record, it should be noted that Keating was instrumental in interesting Suharto in economic liberalization to a surprising degree. At the 1994 APEC meeting in Bogor, Indonesia committed itself to a complete opening of its markets by 2020. Though this was during the initial optimistic phase of APEC's growth, Suharto was originally sceptical that such a timetable would be in Indonesia's best interests, and Keating's powers of persuasion might have been the factor that made the difference.

But Keating's perception of Indonesia was selective. He was determined to believe that under Suharto the country was on the road to prosperity, and that this prosperity would eventually deliver political liberalization. Nor was the Australian view an isolated case – there are some parallels in the approach taken by Canada to Indonesia at the same time (Sharfe 1996). Of the Dili massacre, Keating said even in 2000 that it was the result of 'an appalling lapse of control by individual security forces on the ground in Dili rather than deliberate policy instructions from Jakarta' (Keating 2000: 129), despite the endorsement of these actions at the time by senior members of the military command. Keating undoubtedly regarded the December 1995 'Agreement on Maintaining Security' (AMS) as the crowning achievement of his pursuit of bilateral accord, though it only lasted (as will be shown) until September 1999. But even as this agreement was being secretly negotiated, a crisis emerged which again had its roots in the unhappy history of the East Timor issue. In early 1995, Indonesia nominated General Herman Mantiri as its ambassador to Canberra. Mantiri's senior military rank, his service in East Timor and especially his forthright statement defending the actions taken by the troops in Dili in 1991 caused outrage in Australia (Mackie and Ley 1998: 87).

There are several interpretations of this affair. It is surely extraordinary that neither Evans nor his key advisers acted sufficiently promptly to deter the Indonesian government from appointing a senior military official to this post so this outcome could have been accomplished without publicity. On the Indonesian side, either no thought was given to the possible reaction in Australia (a situation altogether likely given the lack of interest in foreign opinion in such circles), or this appointment was an uncompromising message that Australian criticism of Indonesia's 'internal affairs' was inappropriate and illegitimate. In the event, the nomination was finally withdrawn, though the post of ambassador thereafter remained vacant for some months. Even at this late stage there was a reluctance to admit the extent of the impact of East Timor on bilateral relations. On this issue, the co-author of one of the few book-length studies of the Australia–Indonesia relationship, an academic and former Labor MP, could ascribe the source of the controversy not to Indonesia's policy in East Timor and its failings but the activities of 'the "anti-Indonesian" element within the Australian community, led particularly by the pro-East Timorese groups and the left wing of the ALP' (Catley and Dugis 1998: 226).

In the following year the Indonesian government had the satisfaction of expressing displeasure with Australia's candidate for ambassador to Jakarta, on the grounds that an internal report he had prepared (which was subsequently leaked to the press) expressed criticisms of Suharto's failure to arrange an orderly political succession. In response the candidate nominated withdrew.

The AMS was a major departure in both Australian and Indonesian policy (Hartcher 1996). It appeared to contravene Indonesia's affirmation of ZOPFAN (Zone of Peace, Freedom and Neutrality) and was not discussed in advance with other members of ASEAN; for Australia, this was the first formal entry into the imprecise and consensual diplomacy for which ASEAN had become by this time very well known. However it was emblematic of the fact that, in addition to economic engagement, the Australian government was by this time also building a much deeper and more consequential military and security relationship. When Keating came into office as prime minister, the foundations had already been laid for closer forms of defence and military cooperation (Ball and Kerr 1996: 85–98).

Cooperation of this kind was being considered by policy makers as early as the 1960s. Even in 1964, with the policy of confrontation unfolding, Indonesian officers were attending the Australian Army Staff College. After a hiatus at the end of the Sukarno period, Australia and Indonesia recommenced security cooperation in 1968–69, in 1973 under the Defence Co-operation Program (DCP) the first joint military exercises were held, and by 1975 Australia was providing A\$6.1 million in defence aid, including training over 100 military personnel at Australian facilities (Boyle 2003). To a great extent the fortunes of security cooperation fluctuated in line with the larger relationship, the DCP being abrogated altogether in 1988 in the aftermath of the Jenkins controversy.

Personal military diplomacy revived the security connection, with the Chief of the Australian Defence Force, General Peter Gration, visiting Indonesia in late 1988; this visit reciprocated in July 1989 when the Commander-in-Chief of ABRI, General Try Soetrisno, led a high level delegation to Australia. After a suitable interval as a result of the Dili massacre, there were further visits from senior military figures including that of General Edi Soedrajat, Minister for Defence and Security, in 1993. In this atmosphere joint training and exercises, information sharing and other cooperative activities proliferated, and the mutual security relationship transcended the point reached in the 1980s. On the eve of the regional financial crisis, Australian and Indonesian special forces were undertaking extensive joint training.

What reasoning lay behind these developments? With the development of the post-Cold War notion of 'cooperative security', that is (according to its proponents, who included Gareth Evans) security by mutual confidence building and acculturation so that neighbouring nations could enjoy 'security with' and not 'security against' each other, it was argued that closer relations between the two militaries would dispel any residue of belief that they were antagonists (Ball and Wilson 1991: 145–60). It would also develop the foundation for cooperation in dealing with common problems including smuggling, illegal fishing and cross-border drug trafficking. Such cooperation would provide the 'building blocks' for a consensual regional order. In retrospect, of course, it is unsurprising that the record of the Australian government has been criticized on the grounds that taxpayers' funds should not be used to cultivate linkages with the military of a personal dictatorship.

The Liberal–National Party government and the impact of globalization

The Labor administration led by Paul Keating was replaced by a Liberal–National coalition government led by John Howard in March 1996. At the outset, the new administration adopted quite a different tone in its approach to regional issues. It described its philosophical position as 'realist' and defined its principal objective in this area as a pursuit of 'the national interest' specified in terms of the physical security of Australia and its citizens and their economic prosperity (Department of Foreign Affairs and Trade 1997: iii).

Whereas in the Keating era republicanism was on the political agenda and aspects of the British inheritance and historical record were derided, Howard rejected such re-evaluations as the 'black arm band' school of history and, in a phrase that often occurred in public pronouncements, declared: 'we do not have to choose between our history and our geography'. Accordingly, though the government did not reject the idea of 'engagement' with Asia, it was more inclined to view this strategy as desirable only if it served 'the national interest' and if it did not require or encourage the abandonment of essential values and traditions including transparency and the rule of law.

The Coalition government's stewardship of foreign and defence policy might, in other circumstances, have resulted in little substantive variation from that of its predecessor, and consequently relations with Indonesia would have continued at least for some time on the established track. The Howard government, however, soon had to grapple with developments in the region that overturned many of the established assumptions of the foreign policy community. The regional financial crisis that began in mid-1997 negated the widely shared expectation that an increasingly prosperous Asia would inexorably bring Australia into its economic orbit, while compelling a more judicious and nuanced approach by Canberra to more self-confident and perhaps even more assertive and capable neighbouring powers.

As a consequence, the relatively benign and predictable regional environment became turbulent and uncertain. The political repercussions of the crisis, especially the attempted democratization of Indonesia, inevitably subjected past attempts to build bridges with regimes and leaderships in the region to new and critical scrutiny. But it was not just previous relations with individual regimes that came under question. The backlash of Asian governments against perceived Western indifference to their financial plight, and the stimulus this gave to the creation of an East Asian identity, threatened to undermine Canberra's attempts at fostering regional organizations (in which Indonesia invariably had the role of central player) across the Pacific Rim.

The financial crisis highlighted the ambivalence in the Coalition's approach to the region. On the one hand, the government responded quickly and generously to the international relief programme for Indonesia (and also for Thailand and Korea). On the other, the crisis provided an opportunity for the government to point to the distinctiveness of Australia's economic and even social systems as an explanation for why the nation was immune from the regional contagion (Wesley 2002). As the foreign minister remarked of Australia's record, 'what other country in the region has managed, in the face of the toughest economic conditions for fifty years, to maintain both strong economic growth and successfully renew democratic institutions through the holding of a free and fair general election?' (Downer 1999: 4). From being a pupil of the Asian dragons in the previous decade, Australia now volunteered itself as an instructor in the ways of reform, though this new role was not well received in many parts of the region. It is also worth recording that the Australian government foresaw the social disruption that would be caused by the inflexible application of the IMF's rescue formula to the Indonesian economy, and Foreign Minister Downer himself lobbied in New York for modifications to the package.

ASEAN and APEC proved ineffectual in dealing with the crisis, and Canberra's somewhat sceptical approach to regionalism manifest after 1998 was in part a response to this poor performance. But the Howard government's manifest preference for closer cooperation with traditional allies and a more discriminating attitude towards regional and global institutions was challenged by developments not just in the region but throughout the world system. The growing interdependence of states threatened more restrictive conceptions of the national interest with obsolescence. The financial crisis itself demonstrated the vulnerability of important economies to a world financial regime constructed on the foundation of new technologies in the 1990s. A major casualty of this trend was the Indonesian economy.

Domestic political developments – linked though in different ways to the impact of globalization – also challenged the Howard government's policies towards the region and on important global issues. Even in the less turbulent times of Prime Ministers Hawke and Keating, Australian elites were in some danger of outpacing popular opinion on many of the aspects of Asian engagement, from security to immigration (Cotton and Ravenhill 1997b: 12–13; McAllister and Ravenhill 1998). In a domestic development with significant and still continuing impact on Australia's external policies, the Howard government was forced to deal with a new political force seeking to mobilize voters in the name of what was alleged to be a growing gap between elite preferences and popular aspirations.

Pauline Hanson appeared in the political arena, first as an outspoken independent, then as the leader of a party that won 8.4 per cent of the vote in the federal election that returned the Coalition to office in 1998. Hanson was never clear on the policies to be used to achieve her goals, but she was outspoken on what she disliked. In her parliamentary maiden speech she complained of the actions of many malevolent agencies in Australia: 'financial markets, international organisations, world bankers, investment companies and big business people'. She also warned of the dangers of 'being swamped by Asians', and specifically criticized the government for giving aid to Indonesia when that country was controlled by a 'dictator'. All of these phenomena could be traced to the impact of globalization on Australia, and to the government's partial dismantling of policies of social protection.

The movement Hanson created, for all its temporary popularity, lacked coherence. 'Pauline Hanson's One Nation Party' disintegrated and she lost her federal parliamentary seat in 1998. However the revival of her movement for a time suggested that it might not be a transient phenomenon – and certainly that the fears that sustained such a populist upsurge were far from ephemeral. Moreover, it was a political force that posed the greatest threat to the Coalition, since those who voted for the party were largely individuals who had previously voted for the National or Liberal Parties and thus the Howard government (Jackman 1998).

This phenomenon presented the government with a powerful electoral motive to underscore its scepticism of regional engagement, the most prominent example of which was the close Keating–Suharto relationship. In what can be seen in retrospect as an extraordinarily active period in foreign policy making, the Australian government's performance and utterances from 1997, especially regarding the Asia Pacific region, cannot be properly understood without a consideration of this domestic dimension. The most important policy innovation over these years was undoubtedly the decision to abandon support for Indonesian sovereignty in East Timor, a decision that led first to extensive and prominent support for the UNAMET ballot in the territory and then to the September 1999 military intervention. This phase of Australian policy is the subject of Chapter 5. The East Timor issue thus can be seen to cast a 25-year shadow.

3   The failure of Indonesian policy

The East Timor problem was no ordinary case of Southeast Asian separatism. In Indonesia, at different times there have been separatist movements in parts of Sumatra and Maluku, and the OPM (*Organisasi Papua Merdeka*) remains a shadowy movement in West Papua/Irian Jaya. During *konfrontasi* armed guerillas backed by Indonesia endeavoured to detach the Borneo territories from Malaysia. In Myanmar the Shan and Karen have maintained armies and fought campaigns for years in opposition to the central government, and in Mindanao the various Moro groups have never been reconciled to government from Manila and indeed enjoyed a resurgence of support in 2002. None of these quite represent what might be termed 'alternative states'. The GAM (*Gerakan Aceh Merdeka*) in Aceh, having fought the Indonesian military to a standstill, won a form of recognition as a result of international mediation in 2002. However, further military intervention in the context of the post-September 11 security environment demonstrated that independence for Aceh is still a decidedly remote prospect.

In East Timor, by contrast, there was a situation where for a time, albeit brief (to be precise, formally from 28 November, in practice from mid-August, up to 7 December 1975), a political movement constituted an independent and more-or-less effective administration prior to the incorporation of this territory into Indonesia. Though at this point a loose coalition, FRETILIN seems to have been successful in governing the territory. And while its title to power derived partly from its defeat of rival political forces after the UDT coup attempt in August, in local elections prior to that time held under Portuguese auspices, FRETILIN won a majority of the contests. Moreover, this incorporation did not occur formally until 31 March 1976, nor was it accomplished as a result of the post-colonial adjustments that led to the original formation of most of the states of Southeast Asia. Indeed, the FRETILIN administration seems to have survived in many parts of East Timor until the second half of 1978.

East Timor was formally incorporated into Indonesia as the nation's twenty-seventh province on 17 July 1976, even while ABRI were still engaged in battles in the mountains within sight of the capital. On 27 September 1999, the Indonesian commander in Dili, Major General Kiki Syahnakri, formally transferred authority for security in the territory to the INTERFET command, and the final elements of his force embarked on 27 October, Indonesia having formally rescinded its territorial claims on 25 October. Between these dates Jakarta expended, given East Timor's insignificant size and population, prodigious amounts of blood and treasure in pursuit of a policy of integration. Yet this policy was evidently a failure, as became apparent with the irrevocable internationalization of the issue by early 1999.

The resistance to integration

Indonesian claims to title always rested on dubious foundations. It was difficult to disguise the fact that East Timor was seized by an act of military force. Nor was the Indonesian case assisted by the fact that some East Timorese who initially were prepared to testify in international fora that the integration was popularly conducted were later to recant their stories. At the United Nations in 1975, though Indonesian spokesmen raised the issue of dealing with the problem of the influx of refugees from over the border, and also dwelt on East Timor's alleged kinship with the rest of the island and the archipelago, the burden of the Indonesian case rested on the plea for 'integration' contained in the 'Balibo Declaration' (Krieger 1997: 60–3). The latter was released in the name of four of East Timor's political parties – UDT, Apodeti (*Associação Popular Democrática Timorense*), KOTA (*Klibur Oan Timur Aswain*) and Trabalhista – on 30 November 1975 and was intended to counter FRETILIN's independence declaration of two days previously. Thereafter the fact that *four* parties had sought integration was adduced as an indicator that the majority of the East Timorese were of like mind. This claim is repeated in Jakarta's official account of East Timor's 'decolonisation' (Department of Foreign Affairs, Republic of Indonesia 1977) and also in the version of events given by former Ambassador Sabana Kartasasmita. He argues that the programme of the Declaration was endorsed by the 'People's Representative Council' established in Dili in 1976 and thus international standards for self-determination were met (Kartasasmita 1998: 23–6). The official Indonesian government narrative (still available on the Foreign Affairs website in February 2003) restates this contention, claiming that 'Apodeti, UDT and other political groups . . . with Indonesian military assistance . . . retook Dili from Fretilin forces and 10 days later proclaimed a Provisional Government'. This narrative continues:

> Both the Provisional Government of East Timor and the Indonesian Government sought UN participation in oversight of the decolonization process but the UN did not choose to act. So the Provisional Government proceeded to constitute an elected People's Assembly. On 31 May, in open session witnessed by members of the diplomatic Corps accredited to Jakarta and the international press, the People's Assembly voted to request formally that Indonesia accept the decision of the people of the territory for integration with the Republic of Indonesia as its 27th province.
>
> (Department of Foreign Affairs, Republic of Indonesia 2003)

This account incorporates a grotesque distortion of the UN position, given the Security Council's unequivocal condemnation of the invasion and its insistence that Indonesian forces withdraw in order to allow a proper act of self-determination to occur. This act, of course, was never conducted and the unanimous vote of the 'People's Assembly' was clearly a charade. But this interpretation is directly contravened by other Indonesian sources. The popular recollections by Hendro Subroto, a journalist who accompanied the invasion force from its very first operations in September 1975, though they seek to interpret Indonesian policy in a favourable light, are quite frank in describing ABRI's military strategy in which any East Timorese role was almost incidental (Subroto 1997). Similarly, a book based in part on interviews with General Moerdani and others, while it describes the initial border campaign as being conducted by 'UDT-Apodeti forces, backed by Indonesia "volunteers"', nevertheless characterizes the occupation of Dili as proceeding from a fully fledged military invasion by Indonesian forces which was 'a savage battle, with much plunder, looting and violence' (Singh 1996: 47). The most detailed documentation of the Indonesian military role, that contained in the account (based largely on interviews with key personnel) by Ken Conboy, demonstrates that as soon as OPSUS became involved in a consideration of the East Timor issue, it was assumed that military means would necessarily be employed (Conboy 2003: 196–9).

Whatever the constitutional manoeuvres, by the mid 1980s the Indonesian military were in charge of most of the territory of East Timor. Having lost their geographical base, the FALINTIL resistance army were reduced to waging mobile warfare in small bands. Indonesia achieved this result by the exertion of a pre-ponderance of force, facilitated by specialist arms supplies from the US and Britain. The early battles were not well conducted, and there are numerous eyewitness accounts of widespread civilian killings. Terror and famine as much as military action were used to destroy opposition to military rule (Taylor 1991; Budiardjo and Liem 1984).

FALINTIL by this time had effectively supplanted FRETILIN as the main vehicle of the independence struggle. Its leaders changed tactics in the 1980s, abandoning the doctrinaire implementation of a strategy of 'people's war', forging a common front with other political groups and shifting the focus of the struggle to the urban areas (Carey 1995). The umbrella political resistance, the CNRM (*Conselho Nacional da Resistência Maubere*) became the common political expression of the anti-integrationist movement upon its formation in 1988. While maintaining a relationship with FALINTIL, it was successful also in forging links with the emerging student-led urban resistance which emerged in the later 1980s (Pinto and Jardine 1997).

The reasons for the failure of Indonesia's policy of annexation are a matter of considerable debate. They may be sought in the assumptions fundamental to Indonesia's conduct. They may also be attributed to particular dynamics within East Timor during the 1990s, a time in which external pressures played an increasing role.

As to the former, it is clear that in the first few years Indonesian military policy was incoherent, producing widespread alienation of the population and many fatalities while being incapable of finally extinguishing the guerrilla resistance. An early attempt to use East Timorese troops was abandoned after Indonesian officers proved reluctant to trust them. Only much later and with some measure of success, were local recruits employed to track the guerrillas of FALINTIL (Conboy 2003: 266–72, 310–13). Throughout, the Indonesian military exhibited a remarkable capacity for self-deception regarding the nature of the resistance. The latter were regularly referred to as 'GPK' (*Gerakan Pengacauan Keamanan* – security disruptor gangs) rather than as FALINTIL, and even Indonesian strategists seemed to have believed that they were isolated groups of gangsters and thieves rather than the most visible element of an extensive resistance network. An early text of 1982 on theatre military strategy by Major Williem da Costa, a West Timorese officer later to become in 2002 TNI commander in Timor, exhibited the assumption that the 'GPK' could only win supporters in particularly disrupted communities (Budiardjo and Liem 1984: 176–82). A careful study of a surprisingly comprehensive collection of ABRI/TNI documents that survived the destruction of 1999 has shown that similar assumptions remained central to military thinking even after the Santa Cruz incident (Moore 2001). And it was a standard claim of Indonesian government publications on East Timor that as extensive 'development' funds had been expended in the territory, the support of the bulk of the inhabitants had thereby been secured. To support this proposition, the New Order concept of the 'floating mass' (Elson 2001: 190–1) was applied to the population, the argument being that as most of them were illiterate and preoccupied with subsistence issues, they could be easily controlled by the use of material rewards.

Economic policy, the main characteristics of which were the assumption by military-linked companies of the monopolies and properties controlled by the former Portuguese colonialists, did nothing to convince the population that development was for their benefit (Aditjondro 1999a, 1999b; Saldanha 1994). In the sphere of culture, the compulsory predominance in education and in the governmental administration of *Bahasa Indonesia* was imperfect as a vehicle for building a pro-integration consciousness when most positions in the state apparatus were reserved for personnel from outside the territory. That the latter was a feature of Indonesian rule was one of the findings of a survey of the territory conducted by a team of (rather courageous) Indonesian anthropologists (Mubyarto *et al.* 1991). During this time, in addition to civil servants posted to the territory, East Timor received around 85,000 trans-migrants from Indonesia (Durand 2002: 87).

However important the role of extra-regional forces became at a later stage, in the years up to the 'opening' of East Timor to visitors and trans-migrants in 1989, it should be emphasized that Jakarta had a free hand to adopt almost any policy it pleased. As has been demonstrated, successive Australian governments deliberately avoided the issue, and the continuing military effort against FALINTIL was only prosecuted with the assistance of counter-insurgency technologies knowingly supplied by the United States, and later France and the United Kingdom. Along with these failures, the continuing elements of the East Timorese cultural and political resistance also played a role. The local Catholic Church (led by a mostly indigenous priesthood) acted to a great extent as a protector of the identity and claims of the population, and there is good evidence that adherence to Catholicism increased markedly since 1975, perhaps accounting by 1999 for the religious affiliation of more than 80 per cent of the East Timorese (Archer 1995). Given the territory's uncertain status during the Indonesian period, the church was not part of the Indonesian diocese but was administered direct from the Vatican.

The resolution of these longer-term antinomies required a catalyst, and this was provided by the 1991 Santa Cruz cemetery massacre in Dili. It may be conjectured that this set in train a new trajectory for events, and may be considered thus as the starting point for the particular story that ended in 1999. The context for Santa Cruz included the appeal in 1989 by Bishop Belo, the primate in Dili, to the UN for a plebiscite to determine the wishes of the population on their future, and the visit by the Pope later in that year, which was the occasion for popular demonstrations and acts of government repression (Kohen 1999: 161–93).

Though there had been many killings of East Timorese before that time – the total number of fatalities during the period of Indonesian rule numbered at least 120,000 and could have been as high as 200,000 – the Santa Cruz events (during which between 200 and 500 people were shot or disappeared) were distinctive (Robinson 1994; Parliament of Australia 2000: 80–1, 86; Durand 2002: 87). A number of members of the foreign media (in Dili to cover a Portuguese official visit that did not eventuate) witnessed the killings, and Max Stahl's graphic film taken at the time and smuggled out of the territory provided the defining images for an issue that prompted renewed international attention. As a response, international aid agencies as well as foreign governments, including those of Canada, Denmark and notably the Netherlands, reduced or suspended aid programmes to Indonesia. Jakarta subsequently refused all further aid from the Netherlands, which in 1992 had become the chair of the donor consortium the Inter-Governmental Group on Indonesia (Baehr 1997).

Amid the growing disquiet, the Indonesian authorities themselves convened an inquiry into the conduct of the military. Although the Djaelani Commission recommended trivial punishments and sanctions for a small number of soldiers and junior officers (the most severe being imprisonment for 18 months), its findings amounted to a rare admission that the government and its local agents were at fault (*Inside Indonesia* 1992). The transfer at the same time of senior commanders responsible in 1991 for operations in East Timor also seems to have been part of Suharto's strategy of undermining Moerdani's power base (Crouch 1992; Kahin *et al.* 1992). In addition, the incident itself may have been a manifestation of differences at the highest military levels (possibly between Moerdani and Suharto's son-in-law Prabowo) regarding the best means to control East Timor and suppress the independence movement (Feith 1992).

After critical US Congressional hearings in 1992 on human rights violations in East Timor, at which Allan Nairn, whose skull was fractured as the result of a beating by Indonesian soldiers at the time of Santa Cruz, gave crucial testimony (Nairn 1995; United States Senate 1992), the Congress voted to withdraw funding for military training and cooperation (under IMET – The International Military Education and Training Program). As the result of a civil action brought in US courts by the family of Kamal Bamadhaj, a New Zealand citizen killed during Santa Cruz, punitive and other damages of $14 million were awarded in 1994 against General Sintong Panjaitan, who had been the responsible ABRI (*Angkatan Bersenjata Republik Indonesia*) Udayana Regional Military Commander at the time (Goldson 1999). Following the Djaelani Commission, Panjaitan was sent on sabbatical for study at Harvard University, but quickly decamped for home upon receipt of a subpoena to attend the court. As Secretary of Development Operations he later became a confidant of the president during the Habibie administration, and was responsible for defusing a possible coup attempt by another East Timor veteran, Lieutenant General Prabowo Subianto (O'Rourke 2002: 143). Bamadhaj held dual Malaysian nationality but his death was hardly noticed in the remainder of Southeast Asia.

In summary, most independent observers long believed that the bulk of popular opinion in the territory favoured independence. Despite the territory's contiguity with Indonesia, and the fact that Indonesia spent considerable 'development' funds there since 1976, Indonesian rule was never accepted. There are a number of reasons for this, including the historical record already mentioned. Briefly, they include the influence upon the society and culture of several centuries of distinctive Portuguese colonial rule. The 'decolonization' experience of 1974–75, when for a time it seemed that the people of East Timor would determine their own destiny, raised expectations that were then frustrated. In addition to the disasters of the early years of Indonesian occupation, considerable hostility was generated by ABRI's seizure of much of the property and commerce of the territory, and the extensive use of military personnel as an arm of the state administration did not endear the population to their Indonesian masters. If East Timorese were ever to be allowed to express their own opinions on their political future, there seemed little doubt that they would choose separation from Indonesia.

It was in the context of these factors that the UN was stimulated to resume a role essentially neglected since the mid-1980s. Successive resolutions had been passed by the UN General Assembly censuring Indonesia for failing to allow the East Timorese to exercise their right of self-determination, but from 1983 the issue was bequeathed to the Secretary General and the exercise of his good offices. In the aftermath of the massacre, the UN Human Rights Commission Special Rapporteur on Extrajudicial, Summary or Arbitrary Executions, Bacre Waly Ndiaye, produced a report on the incident which was a damning indictment of Jakarta's failure to change its policy or punish those responsible. Under UN auspices and with Indonesian and Portuguese participation, a series of conferences were convened between various representatives of East Timorese opinion, including the CNRM, who were thus accorded enhanced legitimacy (Gunn 1997). For the first time, an official meeting was held in 1995 between Indonesian Foreign Minister Ali Alatas and José Ramos-Horta, the CNRM's vice chair and foreign affairs spokesman.

With increased international attention and the first indubitable signs of Indonesian self doubt, continuing unrest was encouraged, manifest in major demonstrations in Dili in 1994 and again in 1996. The award of the Nobel Peace

Prize for 1996 jointly to Bishop Belo and José Ramos-Horta further enhanced the standing of the resistance. Policy intellectuals in Indonesia began to consider major changes to the approach taken to the territory, though any new departure was vetoed by the president. Alatas claims to have sought to persuade Suharto, though without success, of the advantages of a policy of autonomy as early as 1994 (Greenlees and Garran 2002: 28–9). Even some military figures began to discern advantages in reform of the system of control in the territory (McBeth 1994). The emerging discourse of human rights within Indonesia also identified East Timor as an area of concern. After an investigation in 1995 by Komnas HAM, the human rights monitoring body established in 1993 largely as an outcome of the Dili massacre, into the killing of six civilians by soldiers in Liquiça, the officer deemed responsible was sentenced in a court to a four-and-a-half -year gaol term, a hitherto unprecedented measure. This event helped focus democratic groups in the country on the issue (Naipospos 1996). When, within three weeks of Suharto's resignation, President Habibie remarked in June 1998 that a new status for East Timor should be contemplated, this was thus the culmination of a process begun in 1991.

The groundwork for the internationalization of the issue

From the time of President Habibie's dramatic announcement of a new approach to the East Timor issue, Indonesian policy was in disarray (O'Rourke 2002: 256–80). Policy makers and power-holders were in dispute both on the nature of any new arrangements for the territory, and on the extent to which the consideration of these would entail consulting the opinion of the population. As has been argued, renewed international interest in the East Timor question, and especially Australia's repudiation of its previously accommodating approach to the issue, exerted some influence on Jakarta's policy. By the end of January 1999, the Indonesian government took the position that a vote on autonomy could, after all, be arranged. By 10 May, Indonesia became party to an agreement with Portugal and under UN auspices which would establish mechanisms to determine whether the people of East Timor would accept a new autonomous status within Indonesia or whether they would prefer independence. If the East Timorese chose autonomy, on Portugal's initiative East Timor would be expunged from the list of Non-Self-Governing Territories of concern to the General Assembly. If autonomy was rejected, Indonesia (following constitutional steps) would withdraw and Portugal would oversee a transitional order to construct an independent government. On the basis of the May agreement, UNAMET (United Nations Mission to East Timor) was established and charged with the responsibility of gauging the views of the East Timorese on their political future. East Timor became, irreversibly, an international concern.

UNAMET's role was to explain to the East Timorese the nature of their choice, register all eligible voters and then conduct a 'popular consultation'. In all, around 1000 staff, observers and officials were sent to East Timor to organize the vote.

It was not a peace-keeping operation, though it did contain a civilian police contingent and a small military liaison group. Throughout its mission, Indonesia was responsible for maintaining appropriate security in the territory and for the protection of UN personnel, with the role of the international police contingent strictly advisory.

The May agreement provided for a significant UN presence (UNAMET 1999b; Martin 2001). The ballot was superintended by some 241 international staff, 141 of whom were stationed in the field. Some 420 volunteers observed the conditions of the ballot. An international police force (mandated at 280 members) was deployed with the task of advising their Indonesian counterparts. The police force included a significant Australian contingent, and was commanded by Australian Federal Police (AFP) officer Alan Mills, who was appointed UNAMET Civilian Police Commissioner in June. Earlier in 1999 militia leaders threatened to kill any Australians who became involved in a political transition in the territory, so their safety was surely at risk.

The UN role ahead of the ballot was crucial. The UN was required to enrol prospective voters, educate them as to the nature of their choice, and report the outcome. Throughout, the Secretary General was in control of the process, being empowered to delay or even abort the ballot if the security environment was not conducive.

Some discussion of the legal foundation of the UN mission is necessary, especially given the fact that Indonesia had not relinquished claims to sovereignty of what was still regarded as the nation's twenty-seventh province. Intervention in the affairs of a member state of the UN is always a doubtful undertaking, given that the organization's fundamental legislation contains the statement (in chapter 1, article 2/7) that 'nothing contained in the present Charter shall authorize the UN to intervene in matters which are essentially within the domestic jurisdiction of any state'. However, in the post-Cold War era such interventions have become more common (Damrosch 1993), and under the terms of the UN Charter there are three possible routes. One, described in chapter 8, gives a role to regional organizations in preserving peace and order. A second, described in chapter 6, gives the UN and its organs a possible role in the peaceful settlement of disputes. A third, the subject of chapter 7, delegates wide powers to the UN Security Council to take whatever action it regards as appropriate to deal with 'any threat to the peace, breach of the peace, or act of aggression' (article 39). Only actions under these last provisions are specifically excluded from the general prohibition on interference in the domestic affairs of a state and are therefore unambiguously legitimate.

With ASEAN positively disengaged from the issue and there thus being no regional equivalent of NATO, chapter 8 was not relevant to the Timor case. This left the provisions of chapters 6 and 7. The establishment of UNAMET and the mission it had been given clearly had no connection with 'chapter 7' operations. Indonesia remained exclusively responsible for order in the territory. The UN was assuming a presence by mutual agreement, and its personnel only had such authority as was specifically endorsed by the mandate. In particular, police personnel were only acting as advisers. In the light of the disorder and violence endemic in 1999, there had been an intense debate in Australia and elsewhere on the need for a 'peace-keeping' force in the territory, to be imposed as a curative for that disorder and thus deployed with or without Jakarta's consent. But in the circumstances of mid-1999, and especially with much global attention focused on the Kosovo crisis, the UN Security Council would not have approved such a force. The UN might have been expected, therefore, to have applied the provisions of 'chapter 6' to the ballot arrangements. But though all parties concerned had consented to the arrangement, even this mode of 'intervention' was evidently considered too sensitive. Accordingly, the UNAMET mission was assembled on the specific request of the Secretary General and became the responsibility, not of the UN Department of Peace Keeping Operations (DPKO) but the UN Department of Political Affairs. The DPKO did, however, play a role in the organizing of the police and military components of UNTAET.

This type of mission was not, therefore, even 'peace-keeping', at least in the classical usage of that term. Now it is true that in the post-Cold War era, international interventions which began with the assent of the parties concerned sometimes took on dimensions that exceeded peaceful settlement or relief delivery by a considerable margin. Action to protect the Kurds of Northern Iraq and to impose order in Somalia are good examples. Indeed, according to the UN DPKO, the single most important lesson from the Somalia debacle was that 'chapter 6' and 'chapter 7' ('peacekeeping' and 'peace enforcement') operations overlapped, confusing the purpose of the mandate and rendering the role of forces and personnel on the ground uncertain (United Nations DPKO 1995; Clarke and Herbst 1997). But in these and other cases what was required was either a disrupted or a pariah state within which there was perceived to be a human security problem, as well as a coalition of powers prepared to supply the military means to deal with the problem. Further, none of the five permanent members of the UN Security Council could be opposed to the action, and the coalition of powers had to possess the political will and the international influence to have the proposed action sanctioned.

In the East Timor case, on the view of the key actors in mid-1999, Indonesia was neither sufficiently disrupted nor enough of a pariah to justify the mobilizing of an action that was, formally speaking, any kind of interventionist peace-keeping operation. In short, the United States and other major powers were not likely to call Indonesia to account. Even the military initiated and orchestrated killings and violence prior to September 1999 did not prompt any more than verbal warnings. Moreover, intervention in Timor, even if its possibility had reached the stage of being discussed in the UN Security Council ahead of the August ballot, might well have been vetoed by China (perhaps regarding the question as analogous to Chinese action in Tibet). Neither is any parallel with the UN mandate in Cambodia very helpful. UNTAC only assumed a virtual trusteeship over those parts of Cambodia not controlled by the Khmer Rouge after the powers concerned were delegated by the Supreme National Council of Cambodia, a body constructed for just this task. The various faction leaders in Timor were never going to negotiate a comparable accord, and in any case some of these groups resolutely opposed the creation of a separate national entity, an alternative that was also rejected by Indonesia.

Nevertheless, once a significant UN presence became involved, the issue was discussed repeatedly by the Security Council, and was also a matter for the General Assembly. Problems in the run up to the ballot stimulated further UN action. The situation remained that a delayed ballot or a distorted result would generate other demands for a resolution to the problem. Indonesia's options were constricted. In short, despite the rhetoric of 'integration', the issue inexorably became an international question as Jakarta lost control of events. Ultimately the full powers of a 'chapter 7' mandate were exercised.

As a result of the Secretary-General's initial report to the Security Council on conditions in East Timor, the UN requested that in addition to police advisers, a team of military liaison officers serve as part of UNAMET. The Indonesian command agreed to the presence of 45 officers (with Brigadier Rezaqul Haider of Bangladesh serving as Chief Military Liaison Officer of UNAMET), whose task was to monitor the behaviour of the security forces stationed in the territory.

UNAMET and Indonesian policy

Even before the May agreement, security in the territory was an issue of serious concern. In 1995, 'ninja' gangs, operating with apparent impunity, had abducted and murdered independence supporters. In late 1998, Indonesian policy took a new tack, with the formation of various 'militia' groups, organized and supplied by elements of the Indonesian military, including the Kopassus special forces (East Timor International Support Centre 1999a). While the legality of these armed formations was extremely doubtful, they nevertheless drilled and paraded with Indonesian military in attendance, and their activities seemed to conform to a general plan to intimidate the population and destabilize the independence camp (East Timor International Support Center 1999b; McDonald *et al.* 2002).

This unsatisfactory security environment underlined the shortcomings of the political processes that had generated the May agreement and thus of the mandate that UNAMET was required to discharge. First, its political foundation was slender. The initiative seems to have been largely the result of decisions taken by President Habibie and his close advisers. Habibie's motivation appears to have been a desire to demonstrate his own democratic credentials, partly to secure the confidence of international creditors and partly to distinguish his own polices from those of the discredited New Order with which he was otherwise closely associated (O'Rourke 2002). But his candidacy for the presidency was always a doubtful venture, and ironically his handling of the Timor issue did much to damage his standing in the People's Consultative Assembly (MPR). Second, for the East Timorese to exercise an informed choice the independence movement needed to be able to put their case openly by campaigning in the cities. Few informed observers ever believed that this would be permitted, which indeed proved to be the case. Further, even to have their opinions registered, FALINTIL and their immediate supporters needed to travel into areas under Indonesian control at least twice, once to register and once to vote, thus clearly being required to put their lives at risk

The third shortcoming of the process related to the maintenance of security. Under the May agreements, Indonesia was solely responsible for 'peace and security' in the territory. From the Indonesian point of view, this had been the case since the 'integration' of 1976. At the time of the 1991 massacre at the Santa Cruz cemetery, military commanders said openly that the outcome was consistent with maintaining security. But it was a different kind of security that was now required. The 'absolute neutrality' of the armed forces and police, and of all state functionaries, was mandated by the agreements. In seeking to minimize the role of ABRI, it was the police who were to be 'solely responsible for the maintenance of law and order'. Here it should be recalled that until the beginning of 1999 the police and the armed forces were under a combined command. The police dispatched to East Timor inevitably contained members with combat experience in the territory. The UN police advisers were expected to play some restraining and mediating role, but they had no direct responsibility for peace and order.

It is important to grasp that the May agreements, including the document on security arrangements, did *not* actually provide for the disarmament of the various forces in the territory. They suggested a code of conduct should be established, and that intimidation cease. The agreements gave an important role to the Commission on Peace and Stability, which was tasked with disarming the factions, but this Commission (though established at a public ceremony in Dili on 21 April 1999 and the subject of a meeting of the major faction leaders in Jakarta on 18 June) was slow to function effectively, and in any case was dominated by pro-integration members. Significantly, ABRI was not given this role. The UN Secretary-General in his memorandum on the security modalities said that he would be looking for indications that there had been a general 'laying down of arms' as a condition for the ballot to proceed, but all the UN could do was delay or abort the ballot if this condition was not observed.

Fourth, there were significant ambiguities in the autonomy proposal that the East Timorese would choose if they rejected independence. Under this proposal, the armed forces remained responsible for defence. Neither the areas they might legitimately occupy nor the actions they might reasonably take were specified. There was nothing in the autonomy law relating to the return of all the properties seized and monopolies created since 1975. In many ways, this was the biggest burden assumed by East Timor, and without reform in this area political autonomy would be largely an empty gesture. There was nothing on the employment of East Timorese, as opposed to Indonesians from elsewhere, in the future administration of the territory. In the end, under this option East Timor remained a part of Indonesian territory, and the autonomy law might be lawfully (and thus without legitimate international complaint or sanction) repealed or amended. There was no comparison, for example, with the guarantees (such as they were) that provided the foundation for the separate Hong Kong polity in post-1997 China.

In retrospect, the most serious shortcoming lay in the post-ballot arrangements.

Under the May agreement, if the ballot favoured autonomy, then the UN was only to have a limited formal role. Without mechanisms to scrutinize Indonesian conduct, in relation to adhering to the autonomy package and regarding its treatment of those who had been identified with the independence cause, Indonesia would have enjoyed a free hand. If the ballot had had this result, few countries would have been likely to take a further interest, and without such an interest the UN would have had no authority to act. It should be recalled that in not dissimilar circumstances, Indonesia acquired control over the administration of Irian Jaya in 1963 after the brief UNTEA (UN Temporary Executive Authority) interregnum, quickly turning it into a creature of Jakarta's policy.

Similarly, if the ballot favoured independence, concrete arrangements would be required for an international presence to monitor the transition. While an adequate and timely UN presence was clearly needed to effect whatever transfer of authority was to occur, planning for a post-ballot presence proceeded slowly and on the assumption that if the East Timorese chose independence there would be a more-or-less orderly Indonesian disengagement from the territory. Indications to the contrary were not taken seriously (Dodd 1999).

There is considerable evidence that many in the military hierarchy had convinced themselves that the autonomy proposal would receive extensive and probably majority support. For this reason, as much as by virtue of the fact that conditions in the territory very much favoured the Indonesian option, the military permitted the consultation to proceed.

The fortunes of UNAMET

On 6 April around 62 civilians were killed in and around the church at Liquiça, where eye-witnesses maintained that Indonesian personnel were in attendance during the incident. This outrage was followed on 17 April by a rally of militia members in Dili at which, in the presence of the leading military and civil authorities, Aitarak militia leader, Eurico Guterres, exhorted the crowd to hunt down resistance leaders. In the ensuing melee around 30 individuals, mostly refugees, were killed. The fact that Aitarak was officially sponsored was well known, with the organization actually receiving recognition as a civil defence entity only two weeks after this incident (McDonald *et al.* 2002; Moore 2001: 32–3). These were the worst of many such acts of terror, which continued despite the presence from 3 June of members of UNAMET. Militia members displaced thousands of people from their homes, and were responsible for attacks on UN offices in Maliana and elsewhere (Bartu 2000). The CNRT (*Conselho Nacional Da Resistência Timorense*), a coalition of all major political parties which replaced the CNRM in April 1998, could not campaign openly, civil servants were instructed to vote for autonomy or face dismissal, and Indonesian flags were required to be flown on every building. The ballot process was twice delayed because of this disorder, and as UNAMET amassed evidence of Indonesian military complicity in incidents of violence, the UN requested the central authorities to withdraw named officers who they considered were responsible.

In the event, this campaign of intimidation was not successful, despite the mobilization of thousands of armed militia in a situation where Indonesia remained in complete control of security (Martin 2001). The reasons for this failure must remain a matter of conjecture, but it may be supposed that the internationalization of the issue and the consequent intense foreign scrutiny restrained the full potential for intimidation. Despite being sorely tested, FALINTIL (apart from several isolated incidents) remained in cantonments and did not engage in retaliation against the militias, which would have provided a pretext for more concerted action against independence supporters or for the aborting of the consultation process. In this period, divisions may have occurred within the military chain of command the members of which were undoubtedly distracted by Indonesia's internal political crisis, serious instability in the regions, and the need to manoeuvre to maintain an influential role in the post-Habibie order.

An important element in deterring the complete sabotage of the ballot was the leakage of secret Australian intelligence assessments that illustrated the direction by elements within the Indonesian military of the militias. The Australian government made repeated representations to Jakarta on the need for Indonesia to observe all the elements of the May agreement and especially the preservation of a security environment that would allow the population to exercise a genuine choice. The deterioration of public order and the apparent connection between the TNI (*Tentara Nasional Indonesia* – as ABRI was by that time known) and the militias were also the subject of pointed resolutions of the UN Security Council. On 21 June the Vice Chief of the Australian Defence Force while meeting with TNI commanders in Jakarta made available to them intelligence reports incorporating specific details of military involvement with militia operations.

The consultation indicated a resounding preference for independence, with 98 per cent of the enrolled voters casting their ballots, and 78.5 per cent of these in favour of bringing to an end the 24 years of association with Indonesia. Even before the result was officially announced on 3 September, violence had broken out, with two local employees of UNAMET early fatalities. UNAMET was forced to withdraw all its personnel from centres outside Dili where, despite the presence of thousands of troops and uniformed police, the UN compound (which by that time also housed 2,000 refugees) was placed under siege (Cristalis 2002). A delegation of five members of the UN Security Council visited Jakarta and East Timor and upon their return to New York reported 'that the violence could not have occurred without the involvement of large elements of the Indonesian military and police' and concluded therefore that 'the Indonesian authorities were either unwilling or unable to provide the proper environment for the peaceful implementation of the 5 May agreement' (United Nations 1999b). Acting on this assessment, the Security Council urged Indonesia to accept the intervention of an international security force to restore order. Meanwhile East Timor's housing and infrastructure were being systematically trashed, and hundreds of thousands of people were being moved by sea and land to West Timor and other parts of Indonesia. It was clear to all observers that this forced migration could not have occurred without extensive planning, including the mobilization of ships and aircraft.

These events brought to a head international demands for more credible means to provide a secure environment. Right through the ballot period and as a reaction to the endemic disorder it had been suggested that an international force was needed to perform the security role so inadequately discharged by Indonesia and which should have been available to facilitate the free elicitation of East Timorese opinion. But this demand had been rejected by Jakarta as inappropriate and indeed a threat to the very consummation of the popular consultation. Despite ordering two delays in the process and repeatedly criticizing the partiality and ineffectiveness of Indonesian security efforts, the UN Secretary-General in his reports to the Security Council never found the situation to have deteriorated so badly as to warrant the withdrawal of UNAMET. Consequently, quite apart from the fact that there was insufficient time – in the light of the normal pace of UN proceedings – to bring the Council to the point of debating the issue, it is very unlikely that a majority could have been mustered for sterner UN intervention, even setting aside its likely veto by China.

But the concerted infrastructure trashing and population displacement in East Timor, which became the focus of intense international media attention, provoked new efforts. Even so, it took some time to engineer a UN-sanctioned solution. On 14 September, UNAMET members and the refugees they were sheltering were airlifted to Darwin by the ADF. The UN compound was subsequently looted and burned, though apart from TNI troops and police most of the inhabitants of the capital had fled or been deported.

On 15 September, the United Nations Security Council (in Resolution 1296/1999) unanimously authorized the establishment of a multinational force in Timor. The resolution, under the terms of chapter 7 of the Charter, gave the force three tasks to perform: to restore peace and security to East Timor, to protect and support UNAMET, and to facilitate within force capabilities humanitarian assistance. This was therefore a fully fledged peace making or peace enforcement mission with a 'robust' mandate. The background to and the discharging of this mandate is the subject of the following chapter. But with this development the Indonesian phase of the East Timor narrative was virtually at an end though not without, in the manner of its expiry, severely damaging the nation's reputation.

ABRI/TNI policy – origins and responses

In retrospect, the systematic despoliation of East Timor seems to have served little purpose, neither advancing the political careers of key military leaders nor enhancing Indonesia's reputation in the world. Nevertheless, the comprehensiveness of the destruction and the logistics involved in the movement of hundreds of thousands of people seemed evidence enough of a deliberate plan. The ABRI/TNI perspective on East Timor therefore deserves some consideration, especially in the light of the evidence that has since emerged on the role of the military.

It hardly needs stating that the military never regarded the political aspirations of the East Timorese as legitimate. This attitude undoubtedly survived the fall of Suharto. As soon as Habibie announced that Indonesia would be accepting a referendum to determine East Timor's future, the TNI launched *Operasi Sapu Jagad* (Clean Sweep), intended to destroy the remnants of the CNRT (TAPOL 1999b). The commander of the operation, Major General Zacky Anwar Makarim, was later appointed liaison officer to UNAMET, underlining the military's lack of concern with the opinions of the population. Given the events of September 1999, it is clear that in the formulation of the UNAMET mandate, the chief source of miscalculation lay in a profound underestimation of the importance of East Timor to the ABRI/TNI.

ABRI's honour and record were at stake. The military took approximately 20,000 casualties, with between 5,000 and 10,000 killed, the actual number never officially being released. General Wiranto had his first combat experience in East Timor (serving as a captain), and returned for a second tour of duty, ultimately to rise to the position of armed forces commander in February 1998. It was said that one of the conditions that was laid down for ABRI to consent to the August ballot was that there be no revision of the historical judgement that the army's conduct of the intervention was beyond reproach, and that its casualties were not in vain. There was clearly some awareness that important officers might eventually be prosecuted for human rights violations: the Bosnia and Kosovo precedents might then become applicable.

Military interests (along with Suharto family companies – in practice the two overlapped) held much of the property and commerce in East Timor in 1999. PT Batara Indra – linked to former Timor commander and Defence Minister Moerdani – was the largest commercial operation. From the early 1990s, Suharto family companies (including some connected with the president's son-in-law, Lieutenant General Prabowo) also assumed an important presence. Immediately upon the invasion, the extensive properties of the Portuguese development companies were seized and assigned to military interests, and the currency was demonetized, destroying the fortunes of the local business class (many of them ethnic Chinese). Although comprehensive data is not available, in the coffee, sandalwood, timber and pearling industries, Indonesian interests predominated (Saldanha 1994; Aditjondro 1999b; Wain 1982).

ABRI's record in East Timor also had a bearing on its 'dual function', the continuance of which was hotly debated at that stage of Indonesian democratization. This, arrangement, of course, had been part of the fabric of the Indonesian political system since the advent of the 'New Order'. In particular, ABRI had been the most important element in the administration of the territory. In 1979, a Sub-regional Military Command (Korem) was established to assume 'territorial' responsibility for East Timor. Korem 164, consisting of 61 military sub-districts, posted personnel in every village and became the sole military command in 1993 (Kammen 1999). At the same time, as is now clear, the Indonesian Special Forces, Kopassus, assumed responsibility for the command of non-territorial units, a change that rendered them less visible while also legitimizing the widest use of 'counter-insurgency' tactics (Moore 2001). If history was to judge the territorial-administrative role of the military in East Timor, whatever its precise structure, to have been a failure, then this was likely to become an additional reason to seek its general abandonment in other parts of the republic.

Failure to frustrate Timor separation might also have been regarded as a signal to dissident forces in regions – Aceh, Irian Jaya, Maluku – that they might attempt the same strategy. Finally, the desire to take revenge and to spite the East Timorese cannot be entirely discounted. If they were to have independence, they would start with less than nothing. The military therefore had many motives to take such action, the most weighty being destroying evidence of past abuses and giving a stern warning to separatists elsewhere.

In the event, fears of being called to account for the East Timor debacle proved justified. In September, President Habibie, under considerable international pressure, instructed the National Commission on Human Rights (Komnas HAM) to establish a nine-member Commission of Inquiry into Human Rights Violations in East Timor (KPP HAM) to determine whether sufficient evidence existed to bring particular officers to court for crimes committed in East Timor during the transition. After some resistance General Wiranto, Major General Zacky Anwar Makarim and other key members of the TNI appeared before the Commission. In testimony to the Commission, Joni Marques, a militia commander from Los Palos, described his training by Kopassus and admitted responsibility for the killing on 25 September of eight civilians, including two nuns and four priests. The Commission also established the authenticity of the 'Garnadi Paper', a memorandum prepared by P4-OKTT, which was a military group established under the authority of Coordinating Minister for Political and Security Affairs, Feisal Tanjung. This document, which became available to UNAMET prior to the ballot but which was rejected as a hoax by the TNI command, urged the military to make every effort to support the integration cause, but if the ballot was lost to make contingency plans to evacuate their supporters 'possibly destroying facilities and other vital objects' (*The Jakarta Post* 2000a; *Indonesian Observer* 2000b). In an interim report the inquiry found that there had been collusion between the TNI, the militias and the police, and thus the military were directly or indirectly involved in extra-judicial executions after the 30 August self-determination ballot. In a final report released on 31 January 2000, a total of 32 individuals, most of them senior military and police figures, were named as being responsible for the most serious violations of human rights amounting to crimes against humanity.

These issues were also a matter of concern for the UN. On 15 November 1999, the UN Economic and Social Council, acting at the urging of the UN Commission on Human Rights and the UN Secretary-General, established a Commission of Inquiry to investigate possible violations of human rights and breaches of international humanitarian law in East Timor during 1999. After visiting East Timor and hearing the testimony of witnesses, the Commission reported that evidence existed of military complicity in the violence and disorder that ensued following the August ballot. During this time, INTERFET and UN investigators were discovering burial sites of Timorese murdered by militia. UN visits to refugee concentrations in West Timor also raised concerns regarding the role given to former militias in the control and coercion of these refugees. At the end of December the Commission, having conferred in Jakarta with the members of KPP HAM, recommended to the UN Security Council that an international tribunal be established to try individuals suspected of war crimes and human rights violations if Indonesia failed properly to investigate these questions. However, President Abdurrahman Wahid stated that he would not allow Indonesian officers to be tried by an international tribunal as this would constitute a breach of the nation's sovereignty (*Jakarta Post* 1999). Of concern also to the United Nations was the presence in West Timor of around 200,000 refugees, most of whom had been unwilling deportees. Though former militias seemed to be in control of many of the camps into which they had been settled, Jakarta did little to address this problem until shamed by the murder in Atambua in September 2000 of three UNHCR refugee workers, one a US citizen.

At the time, this unprecedented review of the past conduct of the military posed significant problems both for Indonesia and for its new democracy. With six generals (including General Wiranto) in his original 35-person cabinet, President Wahid was clearly aiming to maintain military support, and such support remained vital given the unrest in Aceh and Maluku threatening the integrity of the state. Yet once the KPP HAM report of January 2000 recommended that Wiranto and other senior military officers be further investigated for complicity in or failure to prevent the violence and destruction in East Timor, President Wahid had little choice but to suspend Wiranto, who had been serving as Coordinating Minister of Political and Security Affairs. This undoubtedly alienated some elements of the military, and there were claims of military complicity in various bombing incidents in the capital. Yet with the UN apparently insistent that the issue of human rights abuses during the transition period be investigated in such a way as to satisfy international opinion, Jakarta had no choice but to launch judicial proceedings.

The dimensions of the military responsibility for Indonesia's policy failure became clearer as a result of these proceedings, even as the flaws in the process revealed the inability of key actors and institutions still to come to grips with the errors of the past. The responsibility for pursuing these matters was passed to the Attorney General, Marzuki Darusman, who delayed the proceedings pending the establishment of a proper legal basis (given the absence at that stage of an appropriate law rendering serious human rights violations an offence). Darusman also made the decision to restrict prosecutions to five particular cases, a decision that survived the transition to the government of Megawati Sukarnoputri. Most observers of these cases have commented unfavourably upon many aspects of their conduct, from the lack of protection offered to witnesses, to deficiencies in documentation, major inconsistencies and shortcomings in the indictments, and even the absence in some instances of a proper court recorder. Perhaps the major fault in the process was the fact that as the focus was exclusively and solely on these five cases, a pattern of systematic military support for the East Timorese militias could not be established (Judicial System Monitoring Program 2003; International Crisis Group 2002).

One of the most prominent defendants was Brigadier General Timbul Silaen, the former East Timor police chief. He was accused of neglect and inaction in the face of major crimes, notably the attack on the Liquiça church on 6 April 1999, the attack on the home of Manuel Carrascalão on 17 April (when militia members murdered 12 refugees sheltering there), and in connection with various incidents in the days after the ballot. However, during the first two incidents Silaen was absent in Jakarta, thus diminishing his immediate responsibility, a point undoubtedly known to the prosecution when the charges and defendants were being nominated. Silaen was acquitted, as were the five military and police officers (one of the former *bupati* of the district) who were charged with responsibility for the attack on the Ave Maria church in Suai, when some 27 people, including three priests, were massacred. However there were some guilty verdicts, including former governor of East Timor, Abilio Soares, and Aitarak militia commander, Eurico Gutteres. Whereas these individuals are both East Timorese, the guilty verdict on Brigadier General Noer Muis, the commander (then holding the rank of colonel) who took charge of military forces in the territory just two weeks before the ballot, was unexpected. He was given a five-year sentence for failing to prevent the deaths of around 42 civilians, including individuals who died during an attack on Bishop Belo's residence. However he was released on appeal, and the final outcome in his case is uncertain. The most surprising verdict was in the case of Major General Adam Damiri, the Udayana Regional Military Commander in 1999. The charges he faced included murder as a crime against humanity in connection with deaths in Liquiça and Suai, as well as in Dili immediately after the ballot. In August 2003 he was sentenced to a three-year gaol term, though he also lodged an appeal. However there were some puzzling anomalies in the conduct of the trial, including the fact that at one point the prosecutor suggested that all charges be dropped for lack of evidence and also the fact that the length of the sentence would appear to be shorter than the minimum prescribed in Indonesian law.

What is probably the most important question in relation to the issues discussed here is the fact that the defendants often cited the still official account of Indonesia's past role in the territory as justification for their actions, a stance which apparently many in the Indonesian public as well as in the court system found credible. And the troubles of 1999 were attributed to conflict between two sides or forces which it was the duty of the security authorities to mitigate, rather than being the product of Indonesian military orchestration of the militias and consequent intimidation of the population.

In relation to East Timor a flawed accounting by Indonesia for the outrages of 1999 will have several unfortunate consequences. The Indonesian public will continue to regard East Timor's separation as somehow the result of the machinations of malevolent external forces and interests. And if independent East Timor proceeds with its own accounting, possibly of the kind advocated by the East Timor Serious Crimes Unit in February 2003, bilateral and thus to an extent regional relations will be impaired. The Unit, funded by the UN but answerable to the Dili government, recommended the indictment not only of Silaen and Guterres but other senior military and militia figures including General Wiranto himself. Though there was no prospect of Indonesian citizens being surrendered into custody in East Timor, this development issued in a major diplomatic incident, even despite President Gusmão's plea that harmonious bilateral relations were in the interests of all parties. The context for his intervention was undoubtedly the fact that the security forces were dealing at precisely the same time with several bands of former militia who had infiltrated across the border from West Timor. The failure of Indonesian policy in East Timor continues to condition the TNI response to disorder across the archipelago.

Conclusions

The measure of the failure of Indonesian policy in East Timor is indicated by the fact that its outcome was a major and continuing UN intervention in the region. The emergence of East Timorese independence raised acute questions within Indonesia on the political role of the military, while it also subjected the country's record to unprecedented international scrutiny. Rather than serve as the unifying force of a nation still under construction, the military came to be seen by its critics as self-interested and destabilizing. On this view, far from establishing conditions for unity, the military and its policies could only breed dissent. From this perspective, the 2003 campaign against the 'separatist' GAM movement in Aceh will have the same disastrous consequences as the various campaigns over 25 years against FALINTIL and its supporters.

Indonesian policy must be seen in its regional context. Within ASEAN, the East Timor crisis seemed to indicate the need for critical reflection on the practice of non-interference in the domestic affairs of member states, as well as on the question of the group's response to a situation where regional and global norms may not coincide. But just as there has not so far been a thorough assessment within Indonesia of the meaning of the East Timor adventure for the republic and its institutions, so in the organizations that embody regional order the issue has yet to receive the attention that it warrants. The chance to avoid further crises of this kind, notably in West Papua, has been reduced accordingly. Quite how far the events of 1999 tested regional norms of order is the subject of the next chapter.

4 The East Timor intervention, humanitarian norms and regional order

Despite evident conceptual and political difficulties, the doctrine of humanitarian intervention has become influential in the post-Cold War era (Murphy 1996; Ramsbotham and Woodhouse 1996; Wheeler 2000). Countries in Asia, however, have doggedly resisted this trend, promoting the principle of non-interference as an integral part of the modalities of what has been termed 'the Pacific way' (Mahbubani 1995). The prominent participation of regional countries in the 1999 intervention in East Timor, an intervention sanctioned by the United Nations with a specifically humanitarian rationale and under Australian leadership, was therefore uncharacteristic. The regional response to the Timor issue does not reflect a re-evaluation of the doctrine and thus a major change in the rules constituting regional order, but rather was a consequence of specific historical and political factors. Most important of these was the fact that the UN had never accepted as legitimate the Indonesian incorporation of the territory. Once the United States adopted a more critical attitude, in the context of an Australian choice (against a long-term trend of 'engagement' with Jakarta) to pressure Indonesia to accept demands for a test of local opinion on East Timor's future, the internationalization of the issue became inevitable. In the aftermath of the post-ballot militia violence, Indonesia's uncertain transitional leadership could not resist calls for an intervention by peace-keepers, amongst whom regional nations were to be preferred. The latter, however, did not abandon their general preference for a regional order based upon the non-intervention principle. Nevertheless, the events of 1999 pose important lessons, including for coalition operations and for other potential interventions in the region.

Asian security and intervention

The prevailing regional order in Asia is largely a product of intervention. The United Nations sponsored intervention in East Timor in 1999 no less than Indonesia's initial invasion of the territory should be seen in this light. In Asia since 1945 there have been a series of interventions that have had a lasting impact on the societies directly affected as well as on regional relations. Asian and Pacific countries were significant participants in the Korean and Vietnam Wars (in the former, the Philippines and Thailand, as well as Australia and New Zealand; in the latter, the

Philippines, Thailand, South Korea, Australia and New Zealand). The territory of Irian Jaya/West Papua was acquired by Indonesia after brief stewardship by the UN, but after Indonesian guerrilla operations had undermined the resolve of the Netherlands to hold the territory. The longer-term consequences of Soviet Russian intervention in Afghanistan are still a major source of regional instability. The intervention by India in East Pakistan in 1971 facilitated the birth of Asia's fourth most populous nation, Bangladesh. In addition to its annexation of Portuguese Goa, India has also intervened in the Maldives and with somewhat less success in Sri Lanka. Vietnam's displacement of the Khmer Rouge regime in Kampuchea/ Cambodia in 1978 exhibits some parallels with Indian action in Bangladesh. Later, under UN auspices, the political system of Cambodia was fundamentally re-engineered in 1992–93. Throughout the intervention in Cambodia, moreover, the ASEAN countries were prominent players. The first Jakarta Informal Meeting (of July 1988) was the initial step in ASEAN attempts to secure cooperation between the Cambodian factions. With the establishment of the UN Transitional Authority in Cambodia (UNTAC), ASEAN countries, including Indonesia, Malaysia and the Philippines, were prominent in contributing to the military component of the mission. Finally, the role of the Russian Federation in policing the internal borders of Tajikistan satisfies some of the descriptors of intervention.

But if Asia is the continent of intervention, none of these incidents may be described as having been initiated in defence of humanitarian norms. Whether it quite merits the label of 'intervention', the Korean case was sanctioned by resolutions of the UN Security Council that referred to the obligation of the international community 'to repel armed attack'. The Indonesian action in West Papua was defended as the final realization of the decolonization of the Netherlands East Indies. Neither the Vietnam nor the Bangladesh cases were sanctioned by international agreement, and the Afghanistan war was fought in the teeth of international opposition. Though grave humanitarian issues (including the cost of supporting as many as ten million refugees on Indian soil) were prominent in the rationale initially offered by India of its conduct in Bangladesh, ultimately the Indian justification rested on claims of self-defence. India's action was not performed in concert with others, and censure in the UN Security Council was only avoided due to the exercise of a Soviet veto. The fact that this crisis also represented an opportunity to dismember long time rival Pakistan of course cannot be ignored. Vietnam's actions in Cambodia were largely applauded for their humanitarian consequences, and this issue became an item in Vietnam's subsequent justification for its actions, but again (and not without good reason) at the time self-defence was advanced as the rationale. The UN intervention in Cambodia was ultimately legitimized by the fact (or fiction) that UNTAC was acting as legatee for the Cambodian Supreme National Council whose objective was national political reconciliation. A subordinate aspect of the exercise was to resettle around 360,000 Cambodian refugees present in Thailand. Russian actions in Tajikistan are in pursuit of a security end. In short, the addressing of humanitarian issues were at best ancillary objectives in all these interventions where they did not, indeed, serve as the actual cause of additional human suffering.

If the practice of intervention in Asia has not been in pursuit of humanitarian ends, neither has the theory had any influential supporters in the region. Any suggestion that international standards or obligations might lead to censure or sanction, let alone interference in domestic affairs, is stoutly resisted. Thus the Bangkok Declaration of April 1993 was framed by Asian nations specifically to limit the applicability of the Universal Declaration on Human Rights and its Covenants to the political and social systems of its signatories. Humanitarian problems were not to be considered grounds for infringing the political sovereignty of national actors. In matters of security, this resistance is overt. Since its inception, ASEAN has been committed to the principles of non-interference and consensus (Snitwongse 1998: 184–94). In 1997, on the thirtieth anniversary of its inception, ASEAN admitted Myanmar despite the very poor humanitarian and human rights record of its government, and in the face of international condemnation of that government's refusal to accept the results of the democratic elections of May 1990 (Funston 1998: 22–37). Attempts to modify these modalities, following the organization's poor performance during the regional financial crisis and in response to new transnational issues (including environmental threats, piracy and drug trafficking) have not been successful, even though some ASEAN leaders and policy intellectuals have been candid enough to concede that the organization courted 'irrelevance' if it did not respond to its perceived shortcomings (Wanandi 2000). China is even more opposed to the expedient of intervention. Humanitarian relief should have UN Security Council sanction as well as the approval of the countries concerned, and, in the words of an influential Chinese analyst, 'the principle of non-intervention must be further strengthened not weakened' (Jin 2000: 56). Consequently, provisions for intervention are neither prominent in the equipment and training nor in the doctrine of most Asian military forces. The exceptions are South Korea, and also to some extent (having been significant providers of various forces to UN operations) Bangladesh, Pakistan and India. Japan also has a commitment to humanitarian intervention, though under special (though evolving) constraints.

The original intervention in East Timor by Indonesia in 1975 matches the regional pattern. The ostensible grounds for Indonesia's invasion were provided initially by an appeal by opponents of FRETILIN for integration with Indonesia. FRETILIN, after victory in a brief civil conflict, had declared independence on 28 November 1975, Indonesian led forces having by that stage occupied a number of border regions (Carey 1995: 9–55; Dunn 1983; Gunn 1999; Jolliffe 1978). The Indonesian case for acquisition of the territory was never clearly stated, but rested on putative historical ties, shared cross-border cultural affinities, and suggestions that any other course would produce an impoverished and unsustainable state (Krieger 1997: 60–3). Here there is some evidence that India's annexation of Goa had provided a precedent. Indonesian spokesmen did also claim that the influx of refugees into West Timor from late August 1975 generated a burden for Indonesia, but danger to the Indonesian state was the main theme of Jakarta's justification both at the time and later.

On first acquaintance the East Timor intervention of 1999 appears to mark a significant departure for the region and a new stage in regional order. Firstly, the humanitarian issue was a most prominent item in the rationale offered for the insertion of INTERFET (International Force East Timor). Indeed, it could be argued that without the systematic and wanton abuses visited on the population of East Timor immediately following the UN-conducted ballot of 30 August 1999, international opinion would not have been sufficiently mobilized to make the intervention possible (Sebastian and Smith 2000: 64–86). Secondly, regional countries were prominent in the 'coalition of the willing' mobilised to provide personnel for the intervention. The commander of the military component of the successor to INTERFET, UNTAET (United Nations Transitional Administration in East Timor), was an officer from the Philippines, who was replaced after a short tour by a colleague from Thailand. Perhaps most remarkable was China's contribution to UNTAET of civilian police. But upon examination the Timor case is profoundly ambiguous, with humanitarian questions at best serving as a trigger for addressing international and regional issues of longer standing. It would not be excessively cynical to observe that if humanitarian abuses had been of primary importance at that time, intervention would surely have occurred in 1975 or 1976, or at least the original invasion would have been roundly condemned in the neighbourhood. In retrospect it is clear that the terror and dislocation experienced by the population in 1999 though horrible were much less than their sufferings in the later 1970s.

The East Timor intervention

The background to, grounds for and regional response to the East Timor intervention will now be reviewed in order to illustrate its exceptional character. UN Security Council Resolution 1264 of 15 September 1999 authorized the commitment of a multinational force to East Timor. The resolution notes the 'worsening humanitarian situation in East Timor' and expresses concern at 'reports indicating that systematic, widespread and flagrant violations of international humanitarian and human rights law have been committed'. It also adverts to the need to punish those responsible for such violations as may subsequently be verified (United Nations 1999c).

The intervention was grounded on the assessment that the present situation was a threat to peace and security, and that while the provision of humanitarian assistance was an urgent task, this was to be performed in the context of the transfer of sovereignty required by the result of the August ballot and in light of the invitation by Indonesia for the insertion of such a force. In turn the ballot organized by the UNAMET mission was framed by the agreement between the UN, Portugal and Indonesia signed on 5 May which explicitly set aside the positions taken by the parties on the status of East Timor. Throughout the events of 1999, the uncertain political status of East Timor was thus an irreducible element in the UN position. It is the argument here that without this uncertain status international intervention on the putative territory of the world's fourth largest nation would not have been contemplated.

All of the UN operations in East Timor have been coalition operations with a significant regional component. UNAMET contained many personnel from the neighbourhood and was conceived to fulfil major confidence-building tasks. While Australian logistics and personnel were crucial, the 321 police and military component also included members from Bangladesh, Japan, Malaysia, Nepal, New Zealand, Pakistan, the Philippines, South Korea, the Russian Federation and Thailand, as well as others from beyond the Asia-Pacific.

Australian personnel comprised the core of INTERFET, but regional states were also contributors to that force, with Thai Major General Songkitti Jaggabatara serving as the deputy commander, 1,580 Thai military comprising the second largest element, and support being provided also by forces from the Philippines, South Korea and Singapore with a small staff component also from Malaysia (Dupont 2000: 163–70). With the advent of UNTAET, the first commander of the military component was Lieutenant General Jaime de los Santos of the Philippines, his position being taken by Lieutenant General Boonsran Niumpradit of Thailand in July 2000. The UNTAET military and civilian police component included personnel from Bangladesh, China, Malaysia, Nepal, New Zealand, Singapore, South Korea, Sri Lanka and Thailand. A substantial body of the force was Australian, and a significant number of Australian troops remained to serve on the security force component of the post-independence UNMISET mission.

From this roll call it might be supposed that countries in the region are committed to peace-keeping operations as a matter both of doctrine and of force characteristics. It is certainly the case that some Southeast Asian countries have been prominent in peace-keeping missions. Malaysia, for example, had taken part in 18 such exercises prior to the Timor crisis (including UNTAC, UNOSOM II and UNPROFOR). However, the strategic reality is that as most of these countries have been preoccupied with internal threats, their forces, though numerous, have been trained and configured to operate close to home and thus with supplies and support to hand (Mak 1999: 102, 108). These priorities are reflected in the White Papers of the various nations (Department of National Defense, the Philippines 1998; Ministry of Defence Thailand 1996: 31). Malaysia devotes more attention to this issue than any of its neighbours, though it should be noted that its published guidelines on commitments to peace-keeping operations require acceptance by all disputing parties and impartiality from intervening forces (Ministry of Defence, Malaysia 1997: 71).

An exception to this generalization is South Korea. The Republic of Korea presently regards participation in UN peace-keeping operations as both a duty and a source of useful experience (Ministry of National Defense, Republic of Korea 1999: 149). Prior to the East Timor commitment, the most numerous Korean contingents served in Somalia (UNOSOM II) and in Angola (UNAVEM III). From 1995, South Korea has kept one infantry battalion and an engineering company, as well as other support forces, earmarked for service under the UN. Korea's participation in the East Timor intervention, although unexpected in military circles, was consistent with the nation's force structure and doctrine. The decision was taken to commit forces on 13 September, and by 24 September 1999 two liaison officers were attached to the theatre command in Sydney. On 30 September advance elements of the Korean force were transferred to Australia by Korean C-130 for training in Townsville, with commitment to the theatre beginning from 16 October.

South Korea's decision to contribute to INTERFET, announced by President Kim Dae-jung at the Auckland APEC meeting on 13 September, was a major step forward in assembling the 'coalition of the willing'. Asian participation was crucial if the operation was not to resemble an instance of 'Western' interference, yet ASEAN reservations on transgressing the rule of non-interference, and differences between Thailand and Malaysia on their respective roles, if the necessity of such a force was agreed, stood in the way. Korea helped tip the balance, with President Habibie and General Wiranto responding to an approach the next day by the Thai foreign minister, Surin Pitsuwan, by assenting to an ASEAN presence in INTERFET (Cheeseman 1999: 34). Even so, many regional commentators, and even the Malaysian prime minister himself (Mahathir 1999), detected in the unfolding of events a sinister Western purpose.

In the light of South Korea's readiness for this role, and the subsequent success of its contingent, it might be supposed that this indicates a new acceptance of intervention amongst Asian nations. Yet Korea is an exception to many of the region's rules, as this episode demonstrates. President Kim Dae-jung, while in opposition, was vocal in his support of democratic causes in the region, specifically aligning himself with dissidents in Hong Kong, Taiwan and Myanmar, and seeking to refute the arguments of 'the Singapore school' on the appropriateness of author-itarianism for Asian political systems. Relations between South Korea and Australia have always been close, reflecting not only the events of the Korean War but subsequent economic complementarities, including Australia's early contribution of US$1 billion to the IMF-managed relief fund for Korea assembled in 1997. President Kim had many reasons to support this UN initiative. He was also mind-ful that he was due to visit Australia immediately after the APEC meeting, and was therefore under some personal pressure from Prime Minister Howard. But the commitment was controversial in Seoul. The major opposition party, the *Hannaradang*, moved a motion in the National Assembly critical of the commitment, an initiative that was supported by Korean business groups with commercial links with Indonesia (*The Chosun Ilbo* 1999: 100–3). With support from prominent NGOs, President Kim prevailed, but the impression left from this episode was that a different political leadership might not have taken this course.

Finally, Japan's contribution should be noted. Japan's support for the inter-national effort in East Timor was crucial. Japan was an early and generous contributor to the UN East Timor Trust Fund, and Japan also coordinated the donor's conference that raised more than $600 million for the reconstruction of the country. The contribution of actual military forces was not for Japan an option. The 'Five Principles' for Japan's participation in peace-keeping operations prescribed at that time that Japanese contingents may only carry arms minimally sufficient for their own protection (Japan Defense Agency 1999: 98). Not only was INTERFET's mandate to restore security, but it was unclear at the outset whether that mandate would be resisted by members of the militias who remained in the territory. Subsequently, with the Japanese legal framework revised, Japanese forces served with the UN peace-keeping force in the territory.

It can be maintained, therefore, that without Australia's role as the lead nation in the coalition, INTERFET would not have proceeded. As early as March 1999 the Australian Defence Force moved an additional brigade of troops to Darwin, and readied further elements for a possible regional deployment at short notice. Staff officers in the ADF (Australian Defence Force) formed a planning team to work on possible East Timor scenarios. Exercises were held in June simulating a possible landing in the territory. According to press reports, Australian special forces were inserted covertly in mid-1999 to scout possible landing sites (Hunter 1999). At this time, interception of TNI communications by Australian signals intelligence clearly demonstrated high level military support for the East Timorese militias (Bartu 2000: 35–42). The ADF had therefore to assume that if an intervention became necessary it would likely be into a hostile environment. While on a visit to Dili on 30 July 1999, the Australian foreign minister, Alexander Downer, indicated that Australia would consider committing troops to an international peace-keeping force in the post-ballot period (Murdoch and Riley 1999), should this expedient be adopted by the UN. In the aftermath of the August ballot the need for an international force became abundantly apparent (Fox 2000: 109–18). Australia offered on 7 September to lead such a force if this was consistent with UN intentions, and ADF units in Northern Australia were placed on 24-hour readiness (Cole-Adams and Alcorn 1999). At first it was expected that Australia's contribution would be around 1,500 troops plus logistics, but this number was increased, by stages, to 4,500 as the urgency of the commitment increased and as the misgivings of potential regional partners became more evident.

Initially there was great reluctance to support a coalition-based intervention. The United States cited other commitments, and the ASEAN countries had no wish to offend Indonesia, irrespective of the humanitarian crisis on their doorstep. President Habibie hinted that an invitation might be extended to such a force if the disorder could not be contained, but was adamant that a unilateral action by Australia would be considered a warlike act. A full UN peace-keeping operation would take months to arrange, and even the UN legitimation required for an international force was delayed by the slow processes of the organization. As the potential leaders of a 'coalition of the willing', Australia's delegates contemplated setting out for the APEC conference in Auckland scheduled for 12–13 September with no assurance that there would be any resolution to the problem. There was talk in Australia of a crisis in the alliance relationship with the US, and of the country's isolation in the region. Finally, in a speech of 9 September, President Clinton threatened dire economic and other consequences should Indonesia fail to comply with the international demand for intervention that he had now come to support:

> If Indonesia does not end the violence, it must invite – it must invite – the international community to assist in restoring security. It must allow international

relief agencies to help people on the ground. It must move forward with the transition to independence. Having allowed the vote and gotten such a clear, unambiguous answer, we cannot have a reversal of course here. The overwhelming weight of international opinion, from Asia to Africa to Europe to North America, strongly agrees with this position. Right now, the international financial institutions are not moving forward with substantial new lending to Indonesia. My own willingness to support future assistance will depend very strongly on the way Indonesia handles this situation. Today, I have also ordered the suspension of all programs of military cooperation with Indonesia effective immediately. Our military leaders have made crystal-clear to senior military officials in Indonesia what they must do to restore our confidence. . . . It would be a pity if the Indonesian recovery were crashed by this, but one way or the other, it will be crashed by this if they don't fix it, because there will be overwhelming public sentiment to stop the international economic cooperation, but quite to the side of that, nobody is going to want to continue to invest there if they are allowing this sort of travesty to go on. So I think one way or the other, the economic consequences to them are going to be very dire, but I think – my statement clearly signals where I'm prepared to go on the economic issue.

(Clinton 1999)

The International Monetary Fund followed this lead by suspending further aid to Jakarta, pending progress on this and other problems (*Financial Times* 13 September 1999). This pressure was sufficient. Weakened by the effects of the financial crisis and thus crucially dependent upon international aid donors, and in the hands of an uncertain transitional political leadership, Indonesia authorized an intervention. The United States agreed to make available vital logistics support, and some ASEAN countries then joined the coalition. However, there are grounds for the argument that if the key players had not, fortuitously, been committed to a regional gathering at that very time, the operation may have been delayed further or may even not have occurred. And it is almost certainly the case that if the territory concerned had not been East Timor, Australia would not have assumed the leadership role.

In summary, the extent of the UN's commitment to East Timor is undoubtedly a function of its long association with the territory. This association includes the fact (to be considered below) that demands for self-determination were for so long denied, and also the indubitable truth that East Timor's parlous condition in September 1999 was a consequence of the revenge taken after a UN sponsored and conducted ballot demonstrated the extent of popular opinion in favour of independence.

The denial of self-determination and its consequences

The central theme in the history of the East Timor conflict is, as has been argued, Indonesia's consistent denial of international norms and opinion. In this policy

Jakarta was abetted by the determination of regional and other states to ignore what was by all accounts a human rights disaster. The belated recognition of these aspects of the conflict lies behind the action of many states in 1999.

As has been illustrated, Indonesia acquired East Timor as a result of military conquest, begun in October 1975 and largely accomplished by late 1978. Indonesia's conduct was in violation of important principles and conventions in international law, a fact the UN could never thereafter completely ignore. Specifically, Indonesia's purposes were accomplished by aggressive action, and in the process the right of self-determination of the population was denied (Clark 1995: 65–102). The aggressive use of armed forces against the population of another state or territory is specifically proscribed by the UN Charter (as well as by other international instruments prohibiting the use of force). The right of self-determination is both a recognized feature of international law, and also a major operating principle of the various organs of the United Nations. It is an objective that for the UN has been qualified in the sense that while decolonization has been pursued single-mindedly as a major global preoccupation of the organization, secessionist movements within already decolonized states have not generally received recognition. It should be noted that Indonesia itself was a beneficiary of this principle of the non-recognition of secessionist movements, in that Jakarta could claim West Papua as an integral part of its territory on the grounds that it had been part of the Netherlands East Indies. East Timor, however, had never been part of the Netherlands empire, had been recognized as a colonial territory by the UN (despite non-acknowledgement by Portugal) and had never been previously claimed by Indonesia. Indeed, in a letter of 17 June 1974 to José Ramos-Horta, the Indonesian foreign minister, Adam Malik, explicitly acknowledged that 'the independence of every country is the right of every nation, with no exception for the people in Timor' (Jolliffe 1978: 66).

In addition, there are also grounds for holding Indonesia guilty of breaches of international law in so far as its actions led to serious humanitarian and human rights abuses (Nettheim 1995: 181–204). Census and other data, as well as the statements of some of the principals concerned, indicate that between 120,000 and 200,000 of the inhabitants of East Timor died during the period from 1975.

While the Indonesian invasion was still under way, the issue was considered by the UN Security Council. Resolution 384/1975 of 22 December called for an immediate Indonesian withdrawal and for 'all States to respect the territorial integrity of East Timor as well as the inalienable right of its people to self-determination' (Krieger 1997: 53). These sentiments had already been expressed in Resolution 3485(XXX) of the General Assembly of 12 December (Krieger 1997: 123). The Security Council considered the issue again on 22 April 1976 (Resolution 389/1976) and restated its position in almost identical terms. While this was the last occasion for some time on which the Security Council considered the East Timor issue, it was a matter on which the General Assembly debated annually until 1982. While majorities for the resolutions passed successively diminished over that period, on each occasion the resulting resolution affirmed the freedom of the East Timorese to exercise the right of self-determination (Ramos-Horta 1987).

The issue was then devolved to the Secretary-General under his 'Good Offices' powers. Though these were exercised only intermittently, East Timor never disappeared from the UN agenda, and the frustration of self-determination and human rights abuses were regularly discussed in various UN fora. The latter became increasingly important as humanitarian concerns moved to the centre of international diplomacy with the waning of the Cold War. UN attentions were rekindled by the Santa Cruz incident of 12 November 1991. Indonesia's actions at the time and subsequently were the subject of UN censure. Aid donors, including the Netherlands and Canada, withdrew their support, and the international media turned its attention to other forms of malfeasance by the Suharto regime. In concert with the Catholic Church and others, the UN arranged meetings abroad of various East Timorese in an effort to encourage reconciliation.

Throughout this period, therefore, the UN continued to hold the view that Indonesia's annexation of the territory was illegitimate. Though a number of states signified in one form or another that they accepted that Indonesia possessed sovereignty over the territory, the majority did not. As long as Indonesia remained the key state of the region, and was in the hands of a leadership resolute in its determination to retain the territory, little movement could be expected on this issue. The regional financial crisis exposed the weakness of the regime, and the need for it to turn to the International Monetary Fund for emergency finance opened the way for external leverage to be applied. Under international pressure, and now in the hands of a transitional political leadership of doubtful credibility, Jakarta turned to the UN for the negotiation of new arrangements for the increasingly restive territory. Once its future political disposition passed to the forefront of the UN agenda, its past history could no longer be ignored.

Regional nations ignored the plight of the East Timorese, an issue considered later in this chapter. It is regrettable that the stand taken by those states generally predisposed to defend humanitarian standards was no more positive. Both the United States and Australia were complicit (as has been shown in the previous chapter) in the original invasion, and took steps subsequently to deflect criticism from Jakarta for its policies. Only much later were there any second thoughts, prompted by the Santa Cruz killings of November 1991 and their aftermath. US withdrawal of IMET (International Military Education and Training) funding for cooperation with Indonesia in 1993 was a major blow for the Suharto regime, and, especially in the 1990s, US NGOs and writers were instrumental in keeping the issue before the attention of the global public. Nevertheless, without US support the annexation would not have taken place, and without US materiel the war against FALINTIL would not have been successful. As has been noted, on his visit to Jakarta with President Ford on 5–6 December, Henry Kissinger gave approval to Indonesia's invasion plans, and deliveries of more than US$1 billion of arms, including counter-insurgency aircraft and other specialist items, gave Indonesian forces the upper hand from 1978. In the UN, the United States deliberately obstructed censure of Indonesia (Moynihan 1978: 247; Budiardjo and Liem 1984: 8–10; Taylor 1991: 84, 134; Nairn 2000: 43–8). It is not without some irony that it was Richard Holbrooke (US ambassador to the UN) who was entrusted with the task of reading the riot act to Indonesia's generals in 1999 regarding human rights abuses in the refugee camps in West Timor. As Assistant Secretary of State for East Asian and Pacific Affairs, Holbrooke was a major policy actor under the Carter administration during which time arms deliveries to Indonesia (despite an ostensible ban) made possible the prosecution of the war against the resistance.

As has been argued in Chapter 1, Australian policy paralleled that of the United States (Ball and McDonald 2000; Way 2000). From December 1978 Australia acknowledged East Timor as a province of Indonesia. Australia was the only nation to enter an international instrument positively affirming Indonesian sovereignty, when in February 1991 the Timor Gap 'Zone of Cooperation' Agreement with Indonesia was gazetted. Meanwhile, as has been discussed in Chapter 2, Australia had embarked on a major programme of defence cooperation with Indonesia, including training with the very forces in whose care East Timor was placed. This cooperation was codified in the Australia–Indonesia Agreement on Maintaining Security of December 1995.

The reassessment of the East Timor issue by the governments of the United States and Australia was undoubtedly fuelled by the impact of the regional financial crisis on Jakarta's policy capacity, and its fallout in the form of the collapse of the Suharto regime. Even so, as late as December 1998 the Australian prime minister could still express the view that he would prefer to see East Timor remain part of Indonesia, albeit within a framework of local autonomy.

The closest analogy for the UN intervention in East Timor is the role of UNTAC in Cambodia, which might suggest that this experience constitutes something of a regional precedent (Downie 2000: 117–34). However it should be recalled that UNTAC's role was to reconstitute political authority in the country through the convening of national elections, albeit acting as legatees for the Cambodian Supreme National Council. UNTAC's military forces were given the mission to ensure security during the preparations for the ballot. In practice, however, the Khmer Rouge remained hostile to the peace process, and the officials of the State of Cambodia did not always comply with the directives they received from UNTAC. In addition, all the factions retained their separate political status throughout the exercise (Peou 2000: 247–86).

By contrast, the United Nations in East Timor became both state and state builder. Though East Timor indigenous political factions remained active, prior to independence in May 2002 there were no political or administrative structures beyond or outside those engineered by UNTAET. Moreover, the CNRT, which in the initial stages of UN trusteeship incorporated most of the political factions, agreed initially to set aside the rudimentary local administration that it had instituted when the population moved back to their home areas once the militia violence had subsided. The movement then become an active participant in the advisory processes established by UNTAET. From 14 July 2,000 these processes incorporated a 33-person National Consultative Council and also a quasi-cabinet in which the CNRT was by far the largest group (UNTAET 2000: 23–4). By the time national elections were held in August 2001, the movement however had broken into its component parties. The full implications of these developments are discussed in Chapter 8.

In short, Australia's role as leader of the INTERFET coalition, its support by the US, the participation therein by key ASEAN countries, and its endorsement by the UN all represented, to some extent, a reversal of previous positions. In the case of Australia in particular, a growing awareness of the bad faith of the past touched the national conscience and was perhaps the key to what is otherwise a surprising and radical policy innovation.

INTERFET to UNTAET

The INTERFET operation quickly restored a measure of security to East Timor, but was not intended or equipped to resolve the many problems of administration or reconstruction. As an interim measure, UNAMET re-established a presence in Dili on 28 September, but there being no administrative personnel or structures remaining in the territory and faced with a major humanitarian crisis, a much more comprehensive effort was required. Reporting to the UN Security Council on 4 October, the Secretary-General recommended that a new authority be constituted with augmented powers (United Nations 1999d). On 25 October the Security Council (1272/1999) resolved to establish a UN Transitional Administration in East Timor (UNTAET) with executive, legal and administrative responsibility for the territory (United Nations 1999e). UNTAET was planned to incorporate three components: an administrative component (including an international police contingent numbering 1,640 officers), personnel responsible for humanitarian assistance and relief work, and a military component (of around 8,950 troops). UNTAET's mandate was extremely wide, being empowered to provide security, establish new administrative and legal structures, while simultaneously fostering the capacity of the East Timorese to govern themselves and establishing the conditions for sustainable development. Not since the formation of the UN administration in Cambodia had the world body assumed so many responsibilities for a given population. Unlike UNTAC, however, the legitimacy for the operation stemmed not from the consent of the East Timorese people but from the provisions of the UN Charter. Sergio Vieira de Mello, a Brazilian who had served as the Secretary-General's representative in Kosovo, was designated as the leader of UNTAET.

Two problems immediately confronted the implementation of this plan. Military forces had to be found for the security component, and funds had to be provided for reconstruction. While Australian troops were the largest group in INTERFET, their presence had generated both resentment from commentators in Indonesia as well as some expressions of apprehension elsewhere in the region. Consequently, while the Australian government offered to maintain forces in East Timor under UNTAET auspices, Canberra endeavoured to ensure that the majority of the UNTAET force would be provided by other nations and that its commanding officer would not be an Australian. In the event, Lieutenant General Jaime de los Santos of the Philippines was designated as force commander, with Major General

Michael Smith of Australia serving as his deputy. In addition to forces from the Philippines and Australia, significant contingents for UNTAET were provided by other regional countries. The international community also addressed the need for aid to East Timor. A meeting of donor countries convened in Tokyo on 17 December pledged US$522 million for the reconstruction of the territory, with Japan providing $100 million. This exceeded the $300 million estimated by the World Bank to be needed for adequate reconstruction of infrastructure, health care services and education. Aspects of the post-INTERFET phase of the East Timor intervention will be further elaborated in Chapters 7 and 8.

East Timor as a regional challenge

If the past conduct of the UN itself had been less than satisfactory in handling the East Timor problem, was there any alternative to UN stewardship? The UN Charter recognizes the potential contribution to security of regional organizations, and to some extent NATO has already assumed a security maintenance function in the European theatre and especially in Kosovo. In Asia, ASEAN and the ASEAN Regional Forum are the organizations whose chief focus is security. It might be expected therefore that ASEAN (or its constituent countries as members of the Regional Forum) would have taken an interest in the East Timor issue, especially given the long association of the UN with its humanitarian and sovereignty dimensions.

In fact the East Timor case illustrates the major deficiency of regional organizations acting in the role of custodians of regional order, namely, that as they generally include interested parties they can act in the global interest only rarely. It also underlines the lack of interest in this issue by nations in the region. As has been noted in the last chapter, aside from Singapore's abstention at the UN General Assembly votes on Timor in 1975 and 1976, the (then) ASEAN member countries always voted with Indonesia on this issue. China and the other Asian socialist countries were among Indonesia's sternest critics whereas Japan and India, on the other hand, accepted the Indonesian position. A consideration of this topic requires not only a review of the role regional countries played during the period of Indonesian annexation, but also some analysis of the response of the regional order to the events of 1999.

The New Order's commitment to the 'integration' of East Timor and the military's role therein have been adequately demonstrated. Given Indonesia's position as the key country in ASEAN and ABRI's major role in the Indonesian polity, the East Timor issue posed many challenges for the region. The general response of the member states was to ignore the violations of international law that occurred in 1975 and the human rights abuses that followed thereafter. As a consequence, the emergence of an independent East Timor posed unusually difficult problems for ASEAN. For a generation the strategy of Southeast Asia's elites had been to assemble a resilient and geographically inclusive regional organization conforming to broad norms of collective and inter-state conduct. For reasons unrelated to the issue at hand, though also themselves challenges to the non-intervention principle, since 1997 this organization had been under considerable strain (Funston 1998). East Timor was a further challenge to the organization's rationale and modalities.

As is widely acknowledged in the literature on regional order, the most important supra-national security actor in the region is ASEAN, though its precise status (whether security community or elite project) is disputed (Acharya 2001; Narine 2002; Tow 2001). The ASEAN 'norms' of mutual respect for sovereignty, the right of states to be free of external coercion, a prohibition on intervention in the internal affairs of other states, the settlement of disputes by peaceful means and the renunciation of the threat of force have come to be enormously influential in institution building in the Asia-Pacific. Since the 1970s Australian foreign policy makers especially have accorded ASEAN major status as a security (and also as an economic) interlocutor.

The record of ASEAN's response to the East Timor issue, however, is indicative of the limitations of this source of regional security order. On any reading, Indonesia's annexation of East Timor involved the sustained use of aggressive force and the systematic violation of the human rights of the population of the territory. In addition, Indonesia's actions violated the intent of the one common instrument developed by ASEAN to build a distinctive regional order, ZOPFAN (the Zone of Peace, Freedom and Neutrality). The East Timor venture led to Indonesia's military dependence upon the United States, the very further entanglement with foreign powers that the group ostensibly sought to reject. Yet ASEAN solidarity in support of Jakarta's policy was never breached. As Michael Leifer observed, 'Indonesia's neighbours who formed part of the same general political alignment were obliged, at first privately and then publicly, to come to terms with Indonesia's way of securing its own and their priorities' (Leifer 1983: 159). Vietnam was a strong supporter of the independence movement in the period 1975–82, but this of course was at a time long before Hanoi's ASEAN membership.

In the early 1990s, with Indonesian policy in the territory clearly a failure as was demonstrated by the Santa Cruz killings, many nations formerly supportive of or quiescent in Indonesia's role took a more critical approach. As has been noted, the training of Indonesian officers in the US was suspended, the panel of major aid donor governments raised objections, and the UN tried anew to convene negotiations between Lisbon and Jakarta on the status of the territory. Not all nations followed this trend, with Australia and Japan helping to deflect criticism of Indonesia in UN human rights fora.

ASEAN's posture of complete support for Indonesia's intervention in East Timor was however maintained. It is indicative that the Philippines, Thailand and Malaysia all, with varying degrees of willingness, took steps to obstruct East Timorese pro-independence meetings and gatherings on their territory (Ramos-Horta 1987: 125–58; Inbaraj 1995: 128–49). The 'Asia-Pacific Conference on East Timor' of May–June 1994 saw the Philippines, in response to pressure from Jakarta, impose entry bans on a number of participants and endeavour to have the meeting excluded from the grounds of the University of the Philippines. A meeting in July of the same year, in Bangkok, of the Southeast Asian Human Rights

Network devoted to the East Timor issue was similarly discouraged. At the November 1994 APEC meeting Singapore's prime minister, Goh Chok Tong, invoked ASEAN 'solidarity' as a reason for de-emphasizing the issue of human rights in the deliberations of the organization, at a time when the United States was seeking to induce President Suharto to introduce greater autonomy in East Timor. The second 'Asia-Pacific Conference on East Timor' convened in Kuala Lumpur in November 1996 was broken up by the youth wing of the ruling UMNO (United Malays National Organisation) party, with police taking the opportunity to arrest some 66 local activists and journalists. It was left to then Deputy Prime Minister Anwar Ibrahim to justify the use of the Internal Security Act in this instance (Singh 1996: 214–20).

Now the reasons for the group's avoidance of this conflict, and indeed their steadfast support at the United Nations and elsewhere for the Indonesian position were clear enough, as indeed was the rationale for Australia's similar behaviour in this period. But if, as some critics maintain, ASEAN's concern from 1979 with the Cambodia issue represented a partial undermining of the ASEAN norms, its complete lack of concern with East Timor until 12 September 1999 must be interpreted as an even greater denial. Thus, in the Joint Communiqué of the 32nd ASEAN Foreign Ministers' meeting, at the time when UNAMET had almost completed preparations for the fateful August ballot, and disorder was threatening the most important UN operation in Southeast Asia since UNTAC, East Timor did not rate a mention.

There can be little doubt that the East Timor crisis of 1999 was Southeast Asia's greatest security challenge since Vietnam's invasion of Cambodia, and in crafting means to deal with the crisis prominent figures in ASEAN called for a 'regional' solution that avoided intervention by external powers. Despite this history of solidarity, the 1999 crisis identified some tensions between the member countries. At the time, Australian Foreign Minister Alexander Downer was making strenuous diplomatic efforts to assemble a 'coalition of the willing' to provide the troops for the INTERFET operation, when indeed he was able to call upon the diplomatic capital amassed as a result of Australia's regional engagement strategy, there was some hesitation in Southeast Asian capitals ahead of Indonesian assent to the necessity for such a force (Lee Kim Chew 1999; Pura 1999).

The climate was also influenced by some outspoken commentary from Malaysian Prime Minister Dr Mahathir. In a newspaper column, Dr Mahathir expressed the view that 'the West would like to see Indonesia broken up into smaller countries' and 'to frustrate Indonesia at any cost'. The East Timor intervention apparently conformed to that alleged pattern, with Australia 'the main beneficiary' (Mahathir 1999). The tone of this commentary was in keeping with widespread media condemnation of Australia within Indonesia.

When confronted by the post-ballot bloodshed and the Indonesian government's clear inability or disinclination to discharge its obligations to the United Nations and to the East Timorese to maintain order, ASEAN as an organization could find no mechanism through which to influence developments. Further, as the APEC summit in Auckland convened, ASEAN foreign ministers initially refused to participate in a meeting on the East Timor crisis convened by the host, Prime Minister Jenny Shipley. After intensive lobbying by Australia, New Zealand and Canada, delegates from all the member countries (except Hong Kong and Taiwan) attended a gathering on 8 September, though on the basis that the meeting was unofficial and not formally part of the APEC proceedings. By this stage, however, privately some representatives from ASEAN countries were conceding that the issue had to be confronted (Reyes 1999). Once the UN had insisted on an international intervention and this intervention proved acceptable to the Habibie government, Thai Foreign Minister Surin Pitsuwan was then active, however, in encouraging contributions from the ASEAN nations to the intervention force. In the event, it is significant that Thailand, its government in recent years an advocate of a somewhat more interventionist approach regarding the common affairs of ASEAN, made a sizeable contribution to the force and provided the deputy commander (Major General Songkitti Jaggabatara). Malaysian policy at this time fluctuated, with a bid first to lead the force which was later withdrawn to be replaced by an offer to field only a small group of staff officers. This change was perhaps influenced by the claim of José Ramos-Horta that as Malaysia had always sided with Indonesia on the Timor issue, Malaysian personnel would not be welcome in the territory.

The failure of regional security structures was a major consideration in crafting the response to the crisis. INTERFET became, through necessity, an exercise dominated by Australia. And it should not be forgotten that so many of East Timor's present problems are the legacy of decisions taken in Indonesia – if not directly by the government in Jakarta – that proceeded on the assumption that there would be no effective accounting in the region or beyond for a post-ballot policy of devastation and revenge.

East Timor raised the issue once again of the appropriateness of other ASEAN members becoming involved in the internal affairs of a member state. The difficulty was compounded in that this 'internal' matter was the cause both of a UN presence in the member state, and also close scrutiny of the issue from the point of view of international human rights standards. These problems are reflected in the first statement on East Timor ever made in an ASEAN ministerial communiqué which, on 24–25 July 2000, 'commended Indonesia for all its efforts [sic] in resolving the East Timor issue' (ASEAN 2000).

And the INTERFET exercise and the abandonment of Indonesian claims to the territory did not resolve the East Timor problem for ASEAN. While East Timorese membership of ASEAN would realize a long supported principle of geographical completeness, ASEAN governments were divided on the possible reception of the new state into the organization. The original CNRT position had been that East Timor, once independent, would first seek entry into the South Pacific Forum. The wisdom of joining a group dominated by Australia was, however, questionable, and after extensive tours of the established ASEAN capitals by Xanana Gusmão and José Ramos-Horta in 2000, the latter was prepared to describe ASEAN as a possible 'security umbrella' for the nation when it finally achieved independence (Ramos-Horta 2001: 8). But a bid for closer relations with

ASEAN was confounded by Myanmar/Burma, as the regime in Yangon regarded the East Timorese leadership as being identified with support for Aung San Suu Kyi. A compromise was reached in 2002, when East Timor was represented at the thirty-fifth ASEAN Ministerial Meeting in Brunei by invitation from the chair, a practice that is likely to continue. If East Timor is to obtain full ASEAN membership, at some point some critical reflection upon the past record of the organization as well perhaps as on its modalities may be in order.

As has been noted, ASEAN set the pattern for Asian regionalism, and the group continues to function as the core of the region-wide security conference inaugurated in 1994, the ASEAN Regional Forum (ARF). Even though the ARF is a much wider organization neither beholden to Indonesia nor required to attend especially to the sensibilities of state elites generally, its reticence and inaction on the East Timor issue mirrored that of ASEAN. Given its character as a consensus based organization, the ARF does not articulate a policy on any given issue, though its general position can be inferred from the Chairman's Statement released after each annual meeting. The sixth meeting, convened just a month before the August ballot in circumstances that had led many commentators to predict disaster, did not elicit any comment whatsoever on the East Timor issue. A year later, on East Timor the chair merely 'welcomed the positive trends which had taken place there as well as [the] cooperation between Indonesia and . . . UNTAET' (ASEAN Regional Forum 1999, 2000). There was no suggestion of lessons learned or mistakes to be avoided. Even in 'Track 2' regional meetings in 1999 and 2000, East Timor was the missing agenda item. This indifference was despite their ostensible obligation to extend discourse into non-official and thus inevitably controversial territory. To the extent that ASEAN and the ARF are constitutive of Southeast Asian regional order, their contribution to the outcome of the East Timor crisis has been minimal.

But it is for this reason that the East Timor issue has had a major impact on regional order. Regional order is understood here to refer to the pattern or arrangements manifest in the regional security milieu and aimed at the maintenance of peaceful relations between the states in question. The precise nature of the impact depends upon a judgement made as to the essential character of ASEAN, given its role as the organization that is the principal bearer of regional order. On one view it is an association that embodies the 'sense of community' proposed by Karl Deutsch (Deutsch *et al.* 1968) and aimed at the 'peace in parts' project advanced by Joseph Nye (Nye 1971) as a possible role for regional organizations. This interpretation centres upon such shared norms as the pacific settlement of disputes and non-intervention in internal affairs that are 'constitutive' of the community (Acharya 2001: 24–6). Yet as has been shown, these norms were first systematically ignored during Indonesia's invasion and long occupation of East Timor, and then comprehensively set aside in the resolution of the problem, which depended upon a major international intervention backed by the sanction of force. On this interpretation of ASEAN, both the consistency of the alleged norms and their capacity to deal with regional security issues have been found wanting. The future behaviour of states in and towards the region must now be conditioned by a scepticism as to the real power and status of these norms and of the organization that espouses them. It is for this reason that the East Timor issue constitutes something in the nature of a 'critical experiment' for the security community view of ASEAN, and consequently it is somewhat puzzling that the best known contemporary exponent of this interpretation of the organization avoids an analysis of it (Acharya 2001).

There is an alternative view of ASEAN which posits the group as a regional system, or sub-system, of states, as opposed to a geographically delimited 'society of states' (Bull 1977: 8–16). On this interpretation, the logic of ASEAN exhibits 'the possibilities of collective maneuver and protection' (Hoffmann 1987: 110) thus offered to its members, or, to be more precise, to their political elites. Within that pattern of manoeuvre, while the sovereignty of the member states was affirmed, a hierarchy was acknowledged in which Indonesia assumed the status of *primus inter pares*. These arrangements provided the foundation of a regional order, the principal achievements of which have been to 'diminish the likelihood of resort to violent methods of resolving inter-member conflicts', and 'to prevent any one great power from achieving a position of hegemony in the region' (Jorgensen-Dahl 1982: 234, 239). On this more limited view of the organization, the East Timor crisis has had a less corrosive, but still deleterious, impact. ASEAN's members have not 'enhanced their standing in the international community' (Jorgensen-Dahl 1982: 234), they have failed to prevent the intervention of external powers in resolving a local security issue, and most particularly Indonesia's reputation and capacity have both been impaired, thereby undermining Jakarta's former leadership position. The future activities of the member states will now be constrained, in part, by the fact that Australia has been further drawn into regional security questions by virtue of its role as, in effect if not formally, security guarantor for the newly independent East Timor, now an aspirant for ASEAN membership. At the same time, suspicions of Australia in Indonesia consequent on the East Timor intervention are likely to complicate that role. ASEAN's capacity to 'maneuver' has clearly been compromised by the East Timor experience.

Lessons of 1999

If the East Timor crisis prompted an uncharacteristic involvement on the part of nations in the Asian region in an interventionist strategy, nevertheless there are protracted conflicts in the neighbourhood that may yet result in some form of international action. These include religious and ethnic separatism in Myanmar and the Philippines, where a failure in relevant state capacity may force external actors to assume a role. Elsewhere in Indonesia, notably in Maluku, Aceh and West Papua, it is even doubtful whether Jakarta has adequate means or the will to resolve conflicts that threaten the very integrity of the state. In one or other of these regions similar intervention may yet eventuate. Further, the collapse of the regime in North Korea may generate order and human security difficulties beyond the capabilities of South Korea alone. State failure is a possibility in Laos, Nepal, Pakistan and Sri Lanka, and even after the international intervention of 2002 may yet befall Afghanistan.

There are lessons therefore in the East Timor case for the states of the Asia Pacific and for regional order as well as for the entire international community. Perhaps the clearest lesson derives from the fact that Indonesia was entrusted with the maintenance of security during and after the UNAMET ballot. Throughout the ballot period, as is now clear, the militias were armed and directed by military personnel who indeed planned the post-ballot mayhem. Quite apart from the fact that Indonesia and the Indonesian security forces were interested parties in every sense, the actual security instrument was flawed and ambiguous. The police alone were tasked to keep order, which allowed the numerous army personnel present the excuse of non-intervention when this course was preferred. UNAMET contained both a military and a police component, but they served in an advisory capacity only (though sometimes at the risk of their lives) (Savage 2002).

This is not to say that alternative security arrangements would have been easy to organize, but were simply overlooked. From the outset and as a reaction to the endemic disorder it had been suggested by some critics that an international force with direct responsibility for security was needed (Taudevin 1999; Maley 2000b). But this demand was rejected by Jakarta as inappropriate and indeed as a threat to the very consummation of the popular consultation. Despite ordering two delays in the process and repeatedly criticizing the partiality and ineffectiveness of Indonesian security efforts, the UN Secretary-General in his reports to the Security Council never found the situation to have deteriorated so badly for him to recommend the withdrawal of UNAMET. Consequently, it is very unlikely that a majority of the Security Council could have been mustered for any modification to the UN role. It should be recalled that the Kosovo crisis was the subject of three strongly-worded Security Council resolutions in March and again in September and October 1998, yet these had no real effect on the worsening situation prior to the NATO decision of March 1999 to intervene.

This question then leads to a consideration of the timing of the ballot. Australia, Portugal and other parties encouraged President Habibie in his initiative to resolve East Timor's status in the knowledge that he was an interim leader with an uncertain mandate. Was this an inappropriate strategy, especially in light of the fact that the outcome of the ballot was zero-sum, with the alternatives thus identifying unreconcilable elements of a single political entity? Waiting until the outcome of the elections of 1999 might have been a better policy. However, the apparent front runner in the contest, Megawati Sukarnoputri, was on record as opposed to relinquishing control of the territory, and in the event when she did finally take office her administration was not prepared to countenance separatist movements in Aceh and West Papua. And once Habibie announced his intention to address the Timor issue, a delay might well have prompted the very violence that was the result in September.

The lesson here has become a commonplace in issues of this kind, namely that a swift response to humanitarian crises is required, and that global institutions are not yet adequate to this requirement. The potential for discord during and immediately after a ballot process is heightened if the results can be interpreted as zero-sum. Further, neither interested parties nor their surrogates should have a role in the maintenance of security during a popular ballot in a disputed political entity. Whether such a ballot should be aborted altogether in the absence of a neutral security force must, perforce, remain a matter of judgement.

'Operation Stabilise', the initial task of INTERFET, constituted a major test of the Australian military, its equipment and its systems. These performed surprisingly well, given the urgency of the operation. What is most noteworthy about the exercise was the fact, as the commander, Major General Cosgrove, candidly observed, that 'the Australian logistics contingents supported the whole [INTERFET] force – well above design capacity' (Bostock 2000: 27; Smith 2001). First, this meant that the coalition leader had to be prepared to provide whatever support was necessary for the force components. This included not only food and shelter, but also on occasion munitions, communications facilities and transport. This is consistent with what is known of other coalition operations where indeed successful logistics are essential if the coalition is to function successfully, politically as well as militarily (Walsh 1999). What was different in the East Timor case is the fact that, unlike the US in the NATO context, Australia did not have extensive experience of working with some of the particular military partners involved. Further, neither did the supply of materials and equipment even remotely resemble the munificence associated with the world's only superpower (Wright 2000). It should be noted that it took the INTERFET force from 20 September, when the initial landings were made at Dili, to 16 November, when they appeared in the Oecussi enclave, to complete the occupation of the territory. They faced little organized opposition, took no fatalities, and killed only a handful of militia members. In retrospect, the deployment may appear to have been excessively cautious. Yet the reality was that the logistics systems were fully stretched to deliver this result. If, as may well have happened, elements of the Indonesian military had been committed, even surreptitiously, the operation would have run into severe difficulties. The straining of the logistics would have had military and might even have had political consequences.

This last point leads to a further, major consideration. Despite the UN mandate and Indonesia's formal assent, it was never absolutely clear whether the TNI would observe its responsibility to cooperate with the international force. It was even a possibility that outright conflict might occur, perhaps after the displacement of the political leadership responsible for the agreement. When inserting the force, the INTERFET command had to have the demonstrated capability to protect it from any possible attack. Once inserted, the commander needed to have on hand whatever systems might be needed to deal with antagonists. Consequently, the INTERFET force, though charged with peace-keeping duties, had to be protected by advanced air and sea units, and its commander had to have available heavy armour and artillery for rapid deployment. This is a lesson both for coalition operations, where such protection may well be needed again, but also for states that consider training and equipment for peace-keeping operations appropriate and sufficient for the conditions of the twenty-first century. Further, if coalition operations are to become a regular adjunct to or even replacement for conventional peace-keeping forces, coalition leaders (who will not always be the US) must be prepared to move, provision and protect many of their partners. Once again the East Timor case is exceptional by virtue of the fact that Australia was prepared to act as coalition leader, and possessed the necessary capability. These issues are discussed in more detail in Chapter 7 of this book.

As a result especially of the Kosovo and East Timor experiences, the latest generation of peace-keeping activities have broadened far beyond those envisaged by the originators of the practice (Chopra 1999; Langford 1999: 59–79; Shawcross 2000: 362–75). UN peace builders now bring not only police, but also laws and courts, not only administrators but also administrative structures and tribunals, indeed almost all the requisites of a modern state except modern citizens. The military element, central in the original conception of peace-keeping, now must share the stage with other and perhaps more prominent and prestigious components. But if the inhabitants and their elites, or a significant number of either, fail to behave as modern citizens, not only is the entire intervention placed at risk, but those military forces that are an integral part of the exercise may be called to discipline or control recalcitrant members of the body politic. This outcome was narrowly avoided by UNTAC in Cambodia and also by UNTAET in East Timor, but given the appearance of civil disorder in late 2002 the latter's successor mission may have to grapple directly with this problem. From the point of view of political theory, the notion of engineering political form is somewhat problematic. From the point of view of perhaps a majority of the member states of the United Nations, it is a course to be rejected, except in highly unusual circumstances. Such political support as it has enjoyed might in retrospect be seen as a phenomenon of the 1990s.

Conclusions

Asia's uncharacteristic response to the East Timor crisis has done little to increase the probability of similar interventions in the region. No nation in the Asia Pacific yet appears as a willing and viable candidate for the role of coalition leader, and without adequate resources in diplomacy and logistics alike, humanitarian interventions in the territories of the region's failing states are unlikely to be attempted. In retrospect, the fact that Indonesian sovereignty over East Timor was never accepted by the United Nations, and that Australia for complex domestic and historical reasons (to be further discussed in the next chapter) was prepared to break with a policy of engagement with Jakarta pursued for almost a generation, is a concurrence of circumstances with few parallels elsewhere in the region. Regional order still rests upon modalities that reflect the pre-eminence of the principle of state sovereignty, as ASEAN's record on the issue conclusively demonstrates.

5 Australia's East Timor commitment

Causes and consequences

Before the events of the later 1990s, if there was one issue in Australia's external relations on which there existed unalloyed bi-partisan agreement it was East Timor. Governments of both persuasions had regarded the question of positive relations with Indonesia to be of far greater moment than the right to self-determination of the East Timorese, irrespective of the extent to which their Indonesian governors observed or denied their human rights. A Liberal–National Coalition government initiated the negotiation of the Timor Gap 'Zone of Co-operation' Agreement, and a Labor government signed and ratified it. But by 2000, this constant in Australia's regional posture had changed completely. This chapter examines this major shift in Australian policy, and then considers its many consequences. Not only had Australian intervention led to the birth of a new Southeast Asian nation, to which both government and opposition had committed themselves to provide security and economic assistance for some years to come, but the East Timor experience had also compelled a thorough revision of the policy and approach of 'regional engagement' that had been so prominent up until that time. As the alternative security strategy was closer cooperation with Australia's traditional treaty partner, the United States, regional order underwent significant change even prior to the events of September 11.

The Australian commitment to East Timor

As has been discussed in Chapter 1 of this book, the first overt sign of a re-evaluation of the Timor issue occurred in late 1997. Mindful of the political turmoil and the consequent prospects for political change that the Asian economic crisis had unleashed in Indonesia, the Labor Opposition debated the Timor question, adopting support for the right of the East Timorese to 'self-determination' as party policy in May 1998. This step stirred controversy and, as events unfolded, resulted in recriminations from former Labor prime ministers, Paul Keating and Gough Whitlam. It was also a factor in the decision taken by the Senate in November 1998 to undertake a thorough review of the Timor issue by the Foreign Affairs, Defence and Trade References Committee (Parliament of the Commonwealth of Australia, SFADTRC 2000).

Following the forced resignation of President Suharto in May 1998, the fundamental changes in the Indonesian political dynamic became a major preoccupation in Australia. The pace of democratization accelerated in a context in which the serious effects of the Asian economic crisis made many of Indonesia's leaders acutely aware of the importance of maintaining a positive national image in order to guarantee an uninterrupted flow of financial support. Suharto's vice president, B. J. Habibie, assumed the presidency, and on 9 June announced that a special form of autonomy was being contemplated for the nation's twenty-seventh province. The president seems to have taken both the military and the foreign policy establishments by surprise with this intervention. According to his foreign policy advisor, he recognized that, given East Timorese dissatisfaction with Indonesian rule, the territory was both a continuing financial liability that the nation could not now afford and a major threat to Indonesia's reputation abroad. In addition, a breakthrough on the issue would establish Habibie as a credible democratic figure (Alatas 1999; Anwar 2000: 19–20).

After the October 1998 Australian federal election, Foreign Minister Alexander Downer initiated a re-examination of Australia's approach to Timor, an issue that had been something of a personal concern from the beginning of the year (Greenlees 1999). With disorder and uncertainty developing in the territory, Downer went so far as to assert publicly that a resolution of the issue could not be achieved without the participation of the leaders of the East Timorese. In Canberra, DFAT officers embarked on a review of possible outcomes in East Timor. The opinions of refugee and political leaders were sought on the future shape of an autonomous or independent East Timor, and on what support would be needed if the territory was ever to become self-sufficient. When it was determined that even a nominal connection with Indonesia would be unacceptable to the East Timorese without a test of public opinion in East Timor, the decision was taken to seek to influence policy in Jakarta more directly.

In the light of later charges that Australian action was the major determinant of Indonesian policy, and thus the nation's policy makers should assume the greater part of the responsibility for the violence and mayhem of September 1999, it should be recalled that Habibie's announcement regarding possible East Timorese autonomy initiated a diplomatic revolution of international dimensions. Indonesia and Portugal, having pursued barren discussions through a series of ministerial conferences between 1992 and 1996, agreed at a ministerial meeting in August 1998 to begin negotiations on models of autonomy for East Timor (Gorjão 2001a). UN interest in the territory was also reaffirmed by the Secretary-General, and the UN proposed to both Portugal and Indonesia a model for a transitional regime. The EU, on the basis of a common policy formulated in 1996, also indicated a renewed concern with developments in East Timor, with a visit by the EU 'troika' of ambassadors to Dili, the first such visit in the history of the Indonesian occupation (Ward and Carey 2001). And in the US the independence movement's strong support in Congress was manifest in the Senate's unanimous adoption of a resolution on 10 July calling on President Clinton to work actively to carry out the UN resolutions on East Timor and to support an internationally supervised referendum on self-determination (East Timor Action Network 2000). Finally, Habibie's announcement touched off a strong popular upsurge in East Timor itself, which threatened a major internal upheaval unless there was progress towards a resolution of the issue (Soares 2000: 67).

All of these developments were closely watched in Canberra. In December 1998, the prime minister was persuaded to write to President Habibie to suggest that a new formula be found to permit eventual Indonesian disengagement from the territory if that outcome was in accordance with popular sentiment. Although he offered a positive evaluation of Habibie's commitment to reform, Howard recommended that a possible model for a resolution of the problem was to be found in the Matignon accords. President Habibie rejected the colonial parallel with New Caledonia, but the letter was an important influence in Indonesian policy making, as it led Habibie to the conclusion that if the East Timorese could not be reconciled after 25 years to incorporation, it was better that they separate from Indonesia completely (Alatas 1999; Anwar 2000). Indonesia's public position, at this stage, was to reject the option of a ballot. Downer pursued this initiative, suggesting in an official release on 12 January 1999 that the East Timorese should be permitted an act of self-determination after a lengthy period of preparation. Bowing to what by then had become the inevitable, on 27 January Foreign Minister Ali Alatas made the first public reference to the possibility of complete independence for the territory if other outcomes proved impractical.

The momentum of events increased. UN-brokered talks involving Indonesia and Portugal produced a draft plan for popular consultations, though differences on provisions for a referendum, a future constitution, and an interim UN presence prevented the principals from signing the document. In keeping with his mercurial reputation, Habibie declared that, whatever the outcome, Indonesia wished to be free of the Timor problem by the following year. The Timor issue then became drawn into the chaotic lead-up to the June parliamentary elections, with front-runner Megawati Sukarnoputri explicitly rejecting any form of separatism as a blow to national unity. Public awareness of the East Timor issue was stimulated by the publication of a new instalment of the Sherman Report on the deaths in 1975 of five Australian-based journalists in Balibo, near the Indonesian border. Sherman had revisited the issue in 1996, finding that the evidence still pointed to the deaths of the journalists in cross-fire between FRETILIN troops and an invading Indonesian–East Timorese force. Largely as a result of new revelations from an East Timorese, who claimed to have participated in the incident as an irregular with an Indonesian detachment, Sherman found that the troops who had occupied Balibo and killed the journalists were 'under the control of Indonesian officers' (Sherman 1999: 149; Ball and McDonald 2000).

Following talks in Jakarta in February with President Habibie, and a meeting with Xanana Gusmão, Downer traveled to Portugal for consultations with Foreign Minister Jaime Gama. In Lisbon there was a good deal of accord on the need to encourage institution-building in the territory. Prior to the meeting, the Portuguese government announced that it was prepared to assume the responsibility for funding the administration of Timor during a possible transition period. In a complementary measure, Australia announced a commitment to contribute 'within its capacity' to an international programme of relief. Portugal also agreed to the stationing of an Australian diplomat in Lisbon to maintain liaison.

At this time and later, differences emerged on the desirability of a UN intervention involving the dispatch of a peace-keeping force. The government of Portugal was insistent that a neutral force was needed while the political settlement was still under negotiation, whereas Australia took the view that the final status of the territory had first to be defined, otherwise peace-keepers would inevitably become parties to a civil conflict. However, contingency planning was already underway in the Department of Defence for the commitment – in a manner yet to be determined – of Australian personnel (Daley 1999a). In addition, DFAT established an East Timor Task Force to maintain constant scrutiny of the situation in the territory and to formulate policy options. Later a similar group was established in the Department of Defence.

The activities of pro-integration armed 'militias' in East Timor bred a climate of fear and led to whole populations leaving their villages to seek refuge. These developments underlined the need for additional security arrangements. Though some disputed it at the time, the evidence even at that stage pointed to the militias being the creatures of senior commanders in the Indonesian military, if not of the TNI itself (van Klinken 1999). While the government in Jakarta was talking as though East Timor was a problem to be discarded, not all in the armed forces were evidently in agreement with this judgement. Australia became inextricably involved when the leaders of two militias threatened the lives of Australians, and in response most Australian aid workers and residents left Dili in February 1999.

The next step was taken at negotiations conducted between Portugal and Indonesia under the auspices of the UN in New York. Indonesia finally abandoned its refusal to permit the East Timorese to express their wishes directly on their future. Consequently, UN Secretary-General Kofi Annan was able to announce on 12 March that all parties had agreed that 'a method of direct ballot will be used to ask the people of East Timor whether they accept or reject' a proposal for autonomy (United Nations 1999a). A UN presence would be required to administer a popular ballot, and it was proposed that an assistance mission charged with that task would be dispatched to the territory within several months.

The possibility of Australian participation was raised, and policy regarding Timor became a major element in domestic political debate. The chief difference between government and Opposition related to the precise role that Australian personnel would play. The government's position was that in the absence of any political settlement, the employment of Australian personnel as part of a peace-keeping force was most likely to lead to embroilment in an internal dispute. The Opposition's view was that without a third force to avert the descent into violence and fear, no fair consultation could be arranged. The agreements necessary to authorize such force were therefore required as a matter of urgency. Implicit in the government's position was the belief that relations with Indonesia still weighed heavily in the balance when the fate of East Timor was considered. But in order to be able to respond to any emergency, the defence minister announced that a brigade of Darwin-based troops would be upgraded to a state of 28-day readiness, thus doubling the forces available for rapid deployment (*The Australian*, 12 March 1999).

Meanwhile, at the UN, Indonesia and Portugal inched towards an agreement that would allow a test of popular opinion. Australian ministers and representatives made an unremitting effort to bring the parties to a common position. In addition to the concerted lobbying effort in New York, Australian diplomacy was active elsewhere. Following violent incidents and killings in East Timor that bore all the hallmarks of military complicity, the prime minister sought a summit with the Indonesian leadership. At a meeting in Bali on 27 April, the Australian side expressed its disquiet over the deteriorating security situation, and raised the possibility of an international force taking responsibility for security in the territory. While the Indonesian side would give no ground on the latter issue, the president did accept an offer of A$20 million towards the expense of conducting the expected ballot and also a role for personnel from Australia, including civilian police.

On 5 May, Indonesia, Portugal and the UN announced that agreement had been reached to set aside the issue of the status of East Timor, in order to test opinion in the territory on a choice between autonomous status and complete independence. As a consequence, the UN Security Council approved on 11 June the establishment of UNAMET, the purpose of which was to enrol the East Timorese, inform them of their rights and conduct a ballot to determine their opinion.

Although Australia was never a party principal, it would be fair to say that UNAMET was an Australian step-child. Australia was the largest donor to the trust fund established to support UNAMET (A$20 million from a total of US$46 million); Australian staff and resources made a significant contribution to the mission's programme; and Darwin was used as a logistics base and training ground. The Australian Electoral Commission conducted the ballot at the centres outside the territory and organized the processing of the electoral data. Australians were prominent among the volunteer contingent whose role was to serve as district electoral officers charged with the task of witnessing the ballot. And of the total contingent of 275 civil police – a greater number than originally envisaged, largely because of Australian lobbying in New York – 38 were Australians (including the Commissioner, Alan Mills). The Australian media, reporting in great and sometimes vivid immediacy and detail, ensured that not since the Korean War were the attentions of the nation so absorbed by the unfolding of a UN operation. Finally, leaks from the Australian intelligence community fuelled an intense debate on the security predicament faced by the East Timorese (Ball 2001).

The May agreement required adherence to a very tight schedule, in order to fit the timetable of the Indonesian political process. Given the sometimes ponderous nature of UN operations, initially there were doubts that the ballot could be held by the end of August, and Australian resources and support were material in allowing that deadline to be met. A timely delivery of vehicles from Australia speeded the UNAMET deployment, but concerns about the inadequate security arrangements dwarfed the logistics and material problems. Indonesia had insisted that, as a condition for assenting to the ballot, sole responsibility for security would remain in the hands of Indonesian police. Violent incidents in which 'militia' members not only displaced thousands of people from their homes but directly attacked the UN offices in the western town of Maliana were graphically reported in Australia and convinced many of the public that the Indonesian forces were intent upon fostering a climate of terror and thus preventing a free expression of opinion (Bartu 2000). This view was encouraged by the visible limitations on the CNRT campaign for an independence vote. In the event, this campaign of terror was not successful, and here the internationalization of the issue and the consequent intense foreign scrutiny undoubtedly restrained the full potential for intimidation.

An important element in deterring the complete sabotage of the ballot was the leakage of secret Australian intelligence assessments, which showed how senior elements within the Indonesian military were directing the militias. It is clear that intelligence analysts were receiving detailed information not only of the links between particular officers and militia leaders but also regarding plans for revenge upon the population if the ballot result favoured independence (McDonald *et al.* 2002). The media also reported that Australian special forces were active inside the territory, landing and extracting personnel clandestinely in order to prepare intelligence on possible landing sites in the event that Australian contingents were required for an intervention. More accessible sources told the same story. An experienced aid worker in the territory, Lansell Taudevin, provided reports to the Australian embassy in Jakarta that documented military connections with the militias, evidence that Taudevin later claimed was discounted by the embassy in Jakarta in the interests of 'the big picture' (Taudevin 1999: 197). The foreign minister and other government spokespeople were compelled to deny that the looming crisis was the deliberate result of Jakarta's policy, and the proposition that 'rogue elements' of the military were responsible was advanced. By June, however, it became clear that only concerted pressure at the very top of the political and military hierarchies in Indonesia would have any hope of averting a disaster.

According to the official count, the Australian embassy in Jakarta made 120 direct representations to the Indonesian government regarding the obvious deficiencies in the security regime (Wensley 2000: 5). On 21 June, the vice chief of the ADF, Air Vice Marshal Doug Riding, was sent to Jakarta to dissuade the military leadership from pursuing a disastrous course in the territory. While meeting with TNI commanders in Jakarta, he made available to them intelligence reports incorporating specific details of military involvement with militia operations (Lyons 1999b: 25). The deterioration of public order and the apparent connection between the TNI and the militias were also the subject of concerned discussions within the UN Security Council.

As was widely anticipated, the consultation, though twice delayed, indicated an overwhelming preference for independence. The ballot was witnessed by many international observers, including a delegation from Australia led by former deputy prime minister, Tim Fischer (Fischer 2000). Even before the result was officially announced violence had broken out, with the murder of two local employees of

UNAMET. UNAMET was forced to withdraw all its personnel from centres outside Dili, where, despite the presence of thousands of troops and police, the UN compound was under siege by armed militias.

In the words of Australia's representative at the UN, 'Australian diplomacy . . . went into over-drive' following the announcement of the result of the ballot (Wensley 2000: 7). At the UN, Australia convened a 'Group of Friends', including New Zealand and Japan, closely consulting with the US and the United Kingdom, in an attempt to build a coalition to intervene in the chaos. At first the proposal was to accelerate existing UN plans for a security force that would assume control once Indonesia had formally relinquished its connection with the territory. However, even on the fastest of tracks this would have taken some weeks. Over that weekend, members of the Timor group in the Department of Defence worked to adapt existing contingency plans for the employment of Australian troops to evacuate UNAMET and civilians from East Timor to a full peace-keeping role. At a meeting of the National Security Committee on Monday 6 September, these plans and Australia's other options were reviewed (Cole-Adams and Alcorn 1999). The decision was taken to commit a significant Australian force to a UN-legitimized intervention. The diplomatic task that then had to be accomplished was complex. Australia worked to secure sufficient support from other nations, especially from the region, so that the intervening force would have a genuinely international character, to gain US approval and participation, and to secure Indonesian assent. And an appropriate mandate had to be formulated and approved by the UN Security Council.

US support was crucial, but mixed signals were emanating from Washington. The Pentagon and Defense Secretary adopted the view that the US had too many other commitments, and National Security Adviser Sandy Berger was positively opposed to any involvement (Becker and Shenon 1999). On the other hand, key members of the State Department, the most prominent being Assistant Secretary Stanley Roth, took a more sympathetic view (Metherell and Skehan 1999; Alcorn 1999). This apparent indecision caused alarm in Canberra, and while every effort was being made to sway opinion in Washington, some commentators detected an emerging crisis in the ANZUS alliance.

In addition to unremitting efforts at the UN, the fortuitous timing of the APEC leaders' summit in Auckland on 11–12 September provided an additional venue for Australian diplomacy. As economic and foreign ministers gathered for the ministerial meeting on 9 September, the East Timor issue inevitably dominated many of the exchanges, even despite an explicit refusal of ASEAN members to make it part of official business. With New Zealand in the chair, and the Australian prime minister exerting his influence, regional countries including South Korea, the Philippines and Thailand were persuaded to support the intervention.

Acting on the report of a delegation of five of its members who had been dispatched to Jakarta and Dili, the Security Council urged Indonesia to accept the intervention of an international security force to restore order. All through this time, the militias were systematically trashing East Timor's housing and infra-structure, and hundreds of thousands of people were being forcibly compelled to leave the territory. In Australia's efforts to keep the international community focused on the issue, the close consultations held between New Zealand and Canada, and the United Kingdom's very prominent role were evidence that Commonwealth ties still had some substance.

The IMF warned Indonesia that future support would be prejudiced by a failure in East Timor. Finally, as has been noted in the previous chapter, the international effort was completed, with President Clinton stating, immediately before his departure for New Zealand, that if the violence could not be restrained, then Indonesia must accept intervention, a position finally acknowledged by Habibie in a telephone call to the UN Secretary-General. In adopting this position, it is noteworthy that Clinton cited the alliance relationship with Australia as a factor in his decision to support intervention.

The Security Council mandated the intervention force, INTERFET, on 15 September under the chapter 7 – 'peace enforcement' – provisions of the UN Charter, the Secretary-General having formally invited Australia to assume the leadership. In this fashion, Australia emerged as the leader of a 'coalition of the willing'.

In East Timor the militias remained in control, although many of the population had fled to the hills. The siege of the UN compound was lifted on 14 September when the Australian Air Force flew UNAMET's remaining members and the refugees whom they had sought to protect to Darwin, an exercise that also saw the deployment of Australian special forces to protect the operation. The air force was in action again on 17 September, when, with Indonesian assent, it made the first in a series of airdrops of relief supplies.

Following successful negotiations in New York between Indonesia and Australia on a status of forces agreement, the first elements of INTERFET, under the command of Major General Peter Cosgrove, landed in East Timor on 20 September. Despite some tense confrontations, there was no direct conflict with the numerous Indonesian units in the territory. Within three weeks, a large part of the full complement of over 9,000 troops from eighteen nations were in complete occupation of East Timor. In addition to 4,500 Australians, the force included significant detachments from South Korea, Italy, Canada, Thailand, Jordan, New Zealand, the Philippines and the United Kingdom, and the commitment of battle-ready British Gurkhas contributed significantly to its early impact. The US provided vital logistics, supplies and intelligence, as well as a small number of specialist personnel.

The anticipated clash with elements of the former militias did not materialize, but INTERFET found many other tasks to perform. These included assisting an international relief effort in a territory so devastated that few buildings retained their roofs, investigating suspected war crimes, and helping with the repatriation of refugees and deportees returning from Indonesia. The return of Xanana Gusmão on 21 October gave the independence movement new direction, even while it raised the longer-term problem of locating legitimate authority in the post-Indonesia era. The image of Australian troops, weapons at the ready, protecting Gusmão as he delivered his first public speech in Dili since 1975 will long resonate in regional memories. Meanwhile in Jakarta, Abdurrahman Wahid replaced Habibie as president, the former's handling of the Timor issue probably the main cause of his political demise. At the same time, the MPR (People's Consultative Assembly) ratified the ballot result and on 25 October 1999 finally relinquished Indonesia's claim on East Timor. Australia now had a new regional neighbour.

The INTERFET operation quickly restored a measure of security to East Timor. Reporting to the UN Security Council on 4 October, the Secretary-General recommended that a new authority be constituted to deal with the next transitional stage in the territory's development. On 25 October, the Security Council (in Resolution 1272/1999) resolved to establish a UN Transitional Administration in East Timor (UNTAET) with executive, legal and administrative responsibility for the territory, and thus with the most comprehensive of mandates (United Nations 1999d, 1999e). UNTAET incorporated three components: an administrative component (including an international police contingent mandated at 1,640 officers), personnel responsible for humanitarian assistance and relief work, and a military component (mandated at 9,150 troops, with actual numbers deployed of around 8,000). Not since the formation of the UN administration in Cambodia had the world body assumed so many responsibilities for a given population (Downie 2000).

While the initial deployment of INTERFET was an undoubted success, it marked only the beginning of an indefinite security commitment by Australia to East Timor. The military arm of UNTAET made the final transition to security responsibilities on 28 February, and the Australian troop presence was progressively reduced to 1,500 personnel, with the senior Australian officer, Major General Mike Smith, acting as deputy to the force commander, Lieutenant General Jaime de los Santos of the Philippines. Although internal pacification was readily accomplished, East Timor continued to experience threats to its security. The bulk of the Australian contingent was deployed on the western border, and had to deal with a series of infiltrations by former militias, which culminated, during a period of heightened tensions, in the killing of a New Zealand soldier on 24 July. UNTAET forces were enhanced as a response. At the same time the attempt to repatriate refugees displaced to West Timor and held there under militia control resulted in a number of tense incidents at the border crossings. The inability of Indonesia to maintain security in West Timor was vividly underlined by the killing of three UN workers in September 2000, with militia members suspected of committing the crime, despite Indonesian undertakings to disband and disarm all such formations in Indonesian territory. There was also the matter of funding these undertakings. INTERFET and its associated operations cost Australia nearly A$1 billion, and a special taxation levy was announced (but later rescinded) to defray this sum.

The impact of the commitment

The impact of the East Timor commitment had nothing less than a profound effect on many aspects of Australia's security and defence posture. Australia–Indonesia relations were placed on a new footing, past and future regional engagement became the subject of vigorous debate, and defence priorities were re-ordered. Perhaps the most obvious impact, however, was the dispute it engendered regarding whether the government's performance in 1999 amounted to a triumph or a disaster.

Precisely what reasoning had informed Australian policy in the run up to the East Timor ballot became a matter of dispute in the months that followed (Parliament of the Commonwealth of Australia, SFADTRC 2000: 174–90). One school of thought maintained that the government had acted for the best motives and had performed well in a testing time of crisis. Certainly this was the view of the UN Secretary-General himself, who visited Australia in February 2000 specifically to thank the government and the people for their role in helping East Timor in the aftermath of the UNAMET ballot. An opposing school held that the disaster of September 1999 was foretold and anticipated, but regarded as 'the massacre we had to have' in that only such an outcome could guarantee international intervention in the territory, which was always going to be the precondition for establishing an independent East Timor (Kevin 2000; compare Maley 2000b). The latter view undoubtedly overstates the extent of Australian influence over events. The former view, given what policy makers knew about developments on the ground, assumes that they discounted the possibility of the worst-case scenario of an attempted 'ethnic cleansing' of the territory. Nor were the differences between these schools necessarily partisan, though Paul Keating, after a quiescent period largely out of the public eye, attacked John Howard for acting for partisan reasons, as well as for irresponsibility in 'writing an incoherent letter to an interim president who had no authority to make this decision and letting it happen without peacekeepers' (SBS Television 2000).

It may be supposed that neither the UN nor the Australian government believed that, with the issue the subject of intense international scrutiny, the Indonesian government or its instruments would actively and brutally sabotage the realization of the UNAMET programme (Martin 2001: 71). Policy makers seemed to have believed that the vigorous and persistent pressure from Australian interlocutors had eventually had some effect. And it should be noted that, as a result of an Australian approach in late February, US Secretary of State Madeleine Albright agreed to raise directly with General Wiranto the question of military encourage-ment for the militias, thus securing US interest in conditions in the territory at an early stage (Lyons 1999b: 27). Nevertheless, in his retrospective account of the crisis, Downer asserts that it was 'against the backdrop of Indonesia's loss of control of the situation on the ground' (Downer 2000: 7) that the intervention by INTERFET was organized. This view indicated a reluctance, even after the event, to identify the Indonesian military as the main culprits.

In July 2001 DFAT published an account of East Timor policy that did little to resolve these outstanding questions. The study (discussed more extensively in Chapter 6) shows that the Australian government knew of the direct TNI sponsorship of the militias and their programme of intimidation, and had little confidence in Australia's capacity to convince Jakarta of the need to take its mandate to provide security in East Timor seriously. It does not however explain why the government did not then anticipate a 'worst-case' scenario or indeed plan for that eventuality. It does show, in the absence of such a plan, that the INTERFET operation was a masterpiece of military improvisation (DFAT 2001).

Australian decision-making during the preparation for the ballot needs to be seen in the context of several major constraints. First, the independence movement was adamant throughout that the opportunity for the ballot should be exploited, irrespective of the risks to the population. In light of the events of September 1999, a delay or abandonment of the ballot would almost certainly have been used as an opportunity to eradicate the independence forces, just as it would have produced an upsurge of protest from the population. Second, given that Indonesia refused to countenance an international security force, a peace-keeping operation (either at the time of the May agreement or at a later date) would have required UN Security Council legitimation upon the basis of a full interventionist 'chapter 7' mandate. It also would have depended upon some specific nations being willing to provide such a force. Neither was at all likely in the circumstances of early or mid-1999. If Australia had lobbied at the UN or elsewhere for such a force, Indonesia would have had reason to prohibit any further Australian role in UNAMET, thus losing for the operation resources and personnel without which it could not have functioned. By the same token, the volunteering of Australian forces would have been similarly represented. It is this reasoning that may have informed the reluctance to press for a peace-keeping force that was reportedly expressed by DFAT Secretary Ashton Calvert in his conversation with the United States Assistant Secretary of State, Stanley Roth, in late February (Lyons 1999b: 27). The considerable obstacles that lay in the way of organizing the INTERFET intervention, even in the desperate circumstances of September 1999, are illustrative in retrospect of the impossibility of such a task and of the basis of the government's assessment. Third, it can now be confidently asserted that even if a more stringent security regime had been part of the May agreement (requiring, for example, Indonesian troop reductions and cantonment), any such reassurances or undertakings on security were most unlikely to be observed (Martin 2001: 72).

Relations with Indonesia took a wholly new course with the intervention, a topic that is considered at length in Chapter 7. Even the prime minister was forced to concede that Australia's standing in Jakarta would never be the same as in the past (Dodson 2000). In particular, Australian intervention in East Timor was seen as a possible harbinger of future interference in Indonesia's internal affairs, especially in connection with West Papua.

If there was uncertainty in Indonesia regarding Australia's intentions in the region, this was not only a consequence of the nation's role in UNAMET and INTERFET, but also a reaction to the very public debate that the INTERFET intervention had sparked. While Australian forces were committed to Timor with the undoubted expectation that there would be loss of life, the success of the operation led to statements from political and military figures that seemed to imply a broader if indeterminate commitment to similar undertakings in the future. For a short period, the 'Howard doctrine', by which this position came to be known, depicted Australia as playing 'deputy' to the US in keeping the regional peace (Lyons 1999a).

According to the government's account, the objectives of the East Timor intervention were threefold. First a perennial problem in Australia–Indonesia bilateral relations was being addressed. This claim was accurate to the extent that the perception of Indonesia's human rights record in East Timor had certainly hindered a more favourable public assessment of that country for a generation. Second, and in light of the fact that the UN still held Indonesian occupation to be illegitimate, a new status for East Timor would remove perhaps the major obstacle to Indonesia playing a positive role in the world. Third, the intervention was a response to the very strong public reaction in Australia to the violence and suffering experienced by the East Timorese in the aftermath of the ballot.

Were these stated objectives reached? The evidence suggests that only the third of these was achieved, at the cost of palpable apprehension on the part of Indonesia. But while the public-opinion factor was undoubtedly important, behind these objectives lay other goals and calculations, and measured against these less public objectives, Australian policy is at least more explicable, if not more obviously successful. The most important – indeed, a factor that is hard to overemphasize – was the assuaging of Australian guilt for the long complicity in Jakarta's policy of repression and integration. A human rights disaster had unfolded on Australia's doorstep, and not only was it ignored but Australia also helped to train the very forces responsible. In addition, the East Timor intervention was a policy in keeping with the 'new interventionism', as demonstrated in Kosovo and the Anglo-American air war against Iraq, though of course played very much in a minor key. It can also be argued that Australia's intervention was in part born of the confidence generated by its strong economic performance during the Asian economic crisis. Australia's economic performance generated a new self-belief, probably excessive and evanescent, in the resilience and value of Australia's institutions and values. This factor in turn dovetailed into a wider notion that decisive action of this kind would generate respect and prestige in the region. For too long, according to this view, Australia was a supplicant in the capitals of Asia, the Timor commitment changing perceptions of the nation's commitment to fundamental values.

On 21 September, the day after INTERFET began its intervention the prime minister used the parliamentary debate on East Timor as an opportunity to outline some 'home truths' regarding Australia's position in the region. Though not so outspoken as the putative 'Howard doctrine', this statement represented the most distinctive and considered contribution by the prime minister to foreign policy discourse since he assumed office in 1996. The first of these truths was that foreign policy needs to be based on a clear sense of 'national interest' and 'values'. The national interest requires Australia to pursue relationships on the basis of mutual interest and to recognize, 'where they exist, differences in values and political systems'. Second, Australia occupies 'a unique intersection – a Western nation next to Asia with strong links to the United States and Europe' – and therefore commands 'unique assets': 'We have stopped worrying about whether we are Asian, in Asia, enmeshed in Asia or part of a mythical East-Asian hemisphere. We have got on with the job of being ourselves in the region. In turn, the region has recognised that we are an asset and have a constructive role to play in it' (Parliament of the Commonwealth of Australia, *Debates, House of Representatives* 1999: 10029). The assets listed include the ANZUS and Five Power security alliances, as well as bilateral defence cooperation programmes. However, the alliance with the US was then identified as a separate (third) truth, and was described as functioning 'very effectively', having helped deliver a significant US contribution in this instance. Adequate defence resources were the fourth truth, and as the prevailing security climate was 'uncertain', these resources were apparently insufficient, and additional expenditure was thus foreshadowed. The fifth and final truth was the need to take account of 'the values of the Australian community'. The inference to be drawn from this sentiment was that policies designed to improve Australian relations with Indonesia and the region should not compromise those fundamental values.

Returning to the issue of Australia's regional assets, John Howard contrasted his approach with that of commentators who maintained that under his tenure Australia would be excluded from regional frameworks and thus would never be accepted in Asia. This underestimated Australia's capacities and institutions, he argued, especially as demonstrated by the nation's positive performance during the Asian economic crisis:

> our economic, military and other credentials are respected and give us a capacity to help and constructively participate in the region. Just as we were in a position to assist our neighbours during the Asian economic crisis, so also on East Timor we have shown that we have the capacity under the United Nations to work with our regional partners in putting together a multinational peacekeeping force. It is an example of both our commitment to the region and our capacity to make a constructive and practical contribution to its affairs.
>
> (Parliament of the Commonwealth of Australia,
> *Debates, House of Representatives* 1999: 10031)

On this understanding of Australian foreign policy, the Timor commitment was consistent with the national interest in two respects: Australian forces were being used in the service of international institutions and with Indonesian consent to assist the East Timorese to realize the choice they made in an internationally supervised ballot, and these forces, by suppressing violence, were restoring regional order and ending uncertainty. But the issue of whether Australia's putative 'assets' were entirely welcome in the region was not regarded as problematic. Moreover, the enhanced military preparedness that would allow Australia to embark on a similar intervention in the future might conceivably be seen as a threat rather than a positive contribution to regional order, and was certainly represented as such by Australia's critics. Indeed, Malaysia's prime minister, Dr Mahathir, was forthright in his criticism of Australia's regional designs, though other criticism expressed in

Southeast Asia was more muted (Stewart 1999). However these developments are to be interpreted, Australia's willingness to employ military force marked the end of the policy of 'regional engagement', principally by way of participation in multi-lateral institutions and the practice of consensus diplomacy. Australia was now to occupy a different place in the regional order.

Finally, the East Timor experience had a powerful impact on security perceptions. Australian forces acquitted themselves well during the crisis of 1999, but the experience revealed limitations in military capability and shortages of appropriate equipment. As a result the 2000 Defence White Paper committed the government to significant increases in expenditure over a ten-year period. For the first time, the White Paper indicated that 'lower level operations', including peace-keeping, were the next most important priority for the ADF after the defence of continental Australia. This was taken to imply that other features of the East Timor experience might recur (Department of Defence 2000: 39). Regarding East Timor, the White Paper confirmed that Australia would be underwriting the new nation's security for years to come (Department of Defence 2000: 37). A week before the document was released to the public, the defence minister announced a A$26 million aid programme to help train and equip an East Timorese defence force, the core of which is drawn from the guerrillas of the former resistance (Garran 2000). Future relations with independent East Timor will not necessarily be harmonious as a result of this commitment or even in light of the A$150 million of aid promised by the government in 2000 over a four-year period (AusAID 2001). The most contentious bilateral issue will remain the exploitation of the resources of the Timor Sea.

From 'Timor Gap' to 'Timor Sea'

In the first week of March 2003, in just over an hour in the House of Representatives and around two hours in the Senate, the Australian Commonwealth Parliament ratified the Timor Sea Treaty. This process required amendments to some 12 Commonwealth Acts, as well as the passing of other supporting legislation. Parliamentarians received the necessary papers minutes before the bills were read, though the Treaty was the subject of extensive hearings by the Joint Standing Committee on Treaties between July and October 2002. Despite this haste, it is fair to say that the Timor Sea Treaty will have the greatest impact on Australia's relations with the new nation of Timor-Leste, a relationship, it should be recalled, in which the Commonwealth government has invested about A$3.9 billion from 1999.

The Parliament considered the Treaty legislation at the last possible moment before an agreement by Phillips Petroleum to supply LNG from the Timor Sea to Japanese power companies was due to lapse if legal certainty on the ownership of the resources could not be established. Critics of the legislation were forced to acknowledge that it was supported by the government in Dili which had already passed the Treaty through the East Timor parliament, but this did not prevent Greens senator, Bob Brown, from offering the following assessment:

The East Timorese are being subjected to extraordinary, improper, unfair, unethical duress in this matter by the Howard government and by the corporations . . . The reserves we are talking about are wholly within East Timor's legal seabed limits.

(Parliament of the Commonwealth of Australia,
Debates, Senate, 6 March 2003: 9220–1)

Senator Brown was subsequently expelled from the chamber for using the term 'blackmail' in connection with the government's policy. The Democrats expressed similar concerns. Labor criticism was more muted, and was largely concerned with Foreign Minister Alexander Downer's handling of the negotiations with East Timor in late 2002. A leaked transcript of Downer's exchanges with Prime Minister Mari Alkatiri at a meeting on 27 November depicted the minister as impatient if not overbearing. As a result of this meeting, Alkatiri was reported as being unwilling to accept telephone calls from Downer, and in early March Prime Minister Howard himself intervened with his East Timorese counterpart to secure his acceptance of Australia's terms.

At issue in the March debate was not the government's somewhat cavalier attitude to parliamentary process, but rather its refusal to ratify the Treaty without East Timor accepting an 'International Unitisation Agreement' regarding the exploitation of the Greater Sunrise field, most of which lies outside the area covered by the Treaty. Though the two issues were not necessarily linked it was the government's strategy to treat them as a package. In order to understand the issues at stake it is necessary to review the record of negotiations on seabed resources in the Timor Sea since 1999.

Australia's East Timor commitment of 1999 revived the issue of the resources of the Timor Sea, according to some commentators a major factor in Canberra's policy on Timor as early as 1975. The agreement negotiated between Australia and Indonesia on the exploitation of the seabed resources in the area between East Timor and Australia – the 'Timor Gap' – which was signed in December 1989 and came into effect in February 1991, was in more than one sense a provisional agreement. It was provisional both in the limited time span it anticipated (initially 40 years), and also in that it provided no definitive delimitation of the seabed boundary but instead established an interim regime for the exploitation of seabed resources pending such a delimitation. The crucial area of concern was the seabed zone designated 'Area A' (Bergin 1990; Kaye 1994). The area in question comprised that area of the seabed where the claims of both of the states were in conflict, essentially because Indonesia regarded the median line between the two countries as defining their border whereas Australia maintained that the 'Timor Trough' lying some 80 kms off the southern coast of the island was such a significant geophysical feature that it should be regarded as a division between two separate continental shelves. In this zone revenues from resource exploitation were to be split 50:50, and management structures were established to facilitate such exploitation. Revenue sharing commenced in 1998 as the Elang/Kakatua field began production.

With the extinction of Indonesian claims to sovereignty, new arrangements were required for what was now an area of active resource exploitation. Accordingly, on 10 February 2000, Australia entered an agreement with the UN authority in the territory, UNTAET, whereby 'all rights and obligations under the Timor Gap Treaty previously exercised by Indonesia are assumed by UNTAET, acting on behalf of Indonesia', an arrangement that would continue until independence (Australian Treaty Series 2000). This agreement was without prejudice to the territorial claims of the nascent state, which, it soon emerged, the CNRT (the Timorese resistance parties then still in coalition) wished to renegotiate on the basis of a line of equidistance between the two countries. This negotiation strategy was supported by the UN and especially by UNTAET's Director of Political Affairs, Peter Galbraith, who pushed for a definitive territorial delimitation to be negotiated by independence. At this time East Timorese spokesmen, and particularly senior FRETILIN figure Mari Alkatiri, expressed the view that a final territorial settlement would give East Timor most of the resources of the 'Gap' and thus a large and dependable income for some years into the future (McKee 2000).

Given that it had taken some ten years for Australia and Indonesia to arrive at the compromise of the Gap Treaty, it was not surprising that little progress could be made on this question, and instead attention became focused on the status of post-independence resource exploitation under existing contracts. In July 2001, after protracted negotiations involving members of the East Timorese transitional cabinet, José Ramos-Horta and Mari Alkatiri, in company with Peter Galbraith, a provisional 'Timor Sea Arrangement' was agreed, its provisions to be embodied in a future treaty between Australia and independent East Timor. The Arrangement replaced 'Area A' in the former treaty with Indonesia with a new 'Joint Petroleum Development Area' (JPDA) – though the area was defined in identical terms – with East Timor to receive 90 per cent of the hydrocarbon revenues generated therein, instead of the previous 50 per cent. The other areas in the 1991 treaty were abandoned. The arrangements also included an annex defining a delimitation of the respective proportional ownership of the Greater Sunrise field which straddles the JPDA and the area defined as Australian as a result of the 1972 seabed agreement with Indonesia. Australia was also to offer East Timor financial support of A$8 million (from 2005) to assist with the development of petroleum resources.

As in 2000, this agreement was without prejudice to territorial claims. At prevailing prices East Timor was thereby promised a revenue stream estimated at A$6.5 billion over 20 years, with Australia to receive about $1.5 billion. But the promise of this benefit was not received with uniform acclamation. In East Timor, some NGOs and parliamentarians were dissatisfied that the new country was expected, in effect, to persist with conditions that were the product, as they perceived it, of a corrupt and unequal division of resources that should belong in their entirety to the new nation. At the same time business interests in Australia emphasized the urgent need for uniform taxation and other financial arrangements for the area, given the requirement for commercial certainty without which petroleum companies would not find the large start-up costs required for gas and oil extraction.

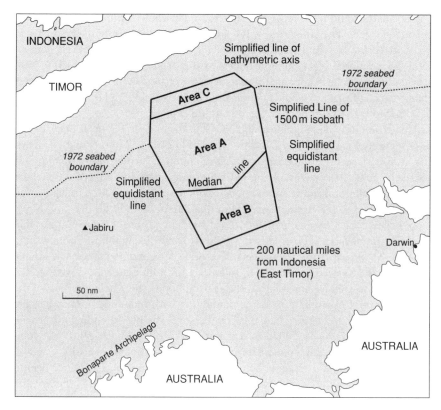

Figure 1 Timor Gap Zone of Cooperation, 1991.

Source: Parliament of the Commonwealth of Australia 2000: 77.

AREA A: Joint control by the Contracting States of the exploration for and exploitation of petroleum resources, aimed at achieving optimum commercial utilization thereof and equal sharing between the two Contracting States.

AREA B: Australia shall make certain notifications and share with the Republic of Indonesia Resource Rent Tax collections arising from petroleum production.

AREA C: Indonesia shall make certain notifications and share with Australia Contractors' Income Tax collections arising from petroleum production.

Source: Department of Foreign Affairs and Trade 1991.

Discontent in East Timor was encouraged by PetroTimor, a company partly owned by Oceanic Exploration of Denver, Colorado, which had been granted exploration concessions by Portugal in the Timor Sea in March 1974. PetroTimor later brought a case against the Australian government and those oil and gas companies who were exploiting the resources of the Gap, on the basis that they had assigned to themselves rights and revenues that did not properly belong to them. This case was subsequently rejected by the full bench of the Australian Federal Court in February 2003. But in 2002, PetroTimor, by suggesting that legal action might overturn the 1991 Treaty, encouraged some Timorese to believe that a new treaty would have to be negotiated which would grant the nation much enhanced rights. The latter view was held partly because most of the resources in question were to be found on East Timor's side of the median line, but also because some international legal opinion held that the principles under which a fresh agreement would be negotiated (in part given the change in the international legal climate since the 1980s) would enlarge East Timor's seabed rights, at the expense of both Australia and Indonesia (La'o Hamutuk 2002b).

This position, while popular in the NGO sector in East Timor, is perhaps less than securely founded. Firstly, in this calculation of East Timor's seabed rights, Indonesia's claim to 'archipelagic' status is discounted. An alternative opinion was offered by Professor Vaughan Lowe of Oxford University, but subject to trenchant criticism by other maritime specialists (Oceanic Exploration 2002). Indeed, if full weight is given to this archipelagic claim, the lateral boundaries that are drawn more-or-less coincide with the boundaries of 1991. In any negotiation or arbitration involving Indonesia's claims, Jakarta would be hardly likely to insist on anything less than boundaries thus determined. This raises a second and absolutely crucial point. For the 'Gap' to be enlarged, Indonesia must ultimately be a party to the negotiation, as well as Australia. And this would open the whole question of the renegotiation of Australia's maritime boundaries with Indonesia, an issue, as the foreign minister indicated, that the government was not intending to broach (Greenlees, *The Australian* 2002). As a senior DFAT official said at the 2002 Joint Standing Committee on Treaty hearings, when asked about the possible revision of the 1972 Australia–Indonesia boundary in connection with a definitive delimitation of the maritime boundary with East Timor, 'it is an agreed boundary and we would expect it to stay where it is' (Parliament of the Commonwealth of Australia, Joint Standing Committee on Treaties 2002).

Meanwhile, the likelihood of East Timor receiving additional seabed territory as a result of some form of adjudication was considerably lessened by the decision of the Australian government, in March 2002, to withdraw any issues of maritime boundary dispute resolution from the compulsory procedures of the International Court of Justice and the International Tribunal for the Law of the Sea. Although the government argued that this change had been under consideration for some time, and that in any case negotiated agreement of issues such as boundaries were much to be preferred to settlements by arbitration, the connection with the Timor Sea was readily apparent (Triggs and Bialek 2002b). The response of the East Timor government was to label this expedient an 'unfriendly' action.

Nevertheless, on the first day of independence, the Australian and East Timorese prime ministers signed a new treaty, the 'Timor Sea Treaty', which embodied and elaborated the provisions of the 2001 interim arrangement (Australian Treaty Series 2002). This included an annex which determined that the share of the Greater Sunrise field located in the JPDA was 20.1 per cent, with the remainder assigned to Australia. At a later function at the former market building in Dili, reconstructed with Australian aid, Prime Minister Howard was greeted by a large crowd of demonstrators, organized by the East Timor Socialist Party (PST), waving placards complaining of Australia's theft of Timor's resources. At the same time as the Treaty was signed, there was an 'Exchange of Notes' setting out the rules that would prevail until the Treaty was ratified by both parties. Once again, both the Notes and the Treaty reiterated the principle that these provisions did not diminish the territorial claims of either party.

How much had changed since the agreement with Indonesia in 1991? On the one hand, the terms of the 2002 Treaty can be interpreted as more advantageous to East Timor than to Australia. While the revenue split for the old 'Area A' was 50:50, the division of the revenues for the 'Joint Petroleum Development Area' is 90:10 in favour of the new state. The management structures also give East Timor an enhanced role, with the country providing a majority of members of the Joint Commission, whose approval would be necessary, for example, for the construction of a pipeline to land production at an Australian destination – an option with great potential advantages to the Northern Territory and for which the government in Darwin had been lobbying vigorously.

On the other hand, the Treaty, by providing for a practical resources regime, removes any urgency for a definitive delimitation of national rights to the seabed. According to some legal opinion it also amounts to a significant 'encroachment' on East Timor's rights, thus possibly weakening Dili's case at any future negotiation. And East Timor would only stand to benefit from the improved arrangements if the Treaty was ratified; in the absence of ratification by both parties the provisions of the 2000 arrangements would continue to apply, with East Timor's additional entitlement held in an escrow account. While the parliament in Dili ratified the treaty in 2002, though not without strong opposition from some non-government parties (including the Democratic Party), by the end of the year the appropriate legislation had still not been drafted for the Australian parliament to consider. The context for this delay appeared to be the fact that Dili and Canberra could not agree on the full details of the provisions of the IUA that would specify the pro-portion of ownership of resources in oil and gas fields that straddle the borders of the JPDA. Especially at issue here was the exploitation of the estimated 10 trillion cubic feet of gas (worth as much as A$30 billion) located in the Greater Sunrise field, a reservoir three times as large as the Bayu-Undan field, the largest to be exploited to that time. It appeared that Canberra was delaying ratification of the 2002 Treaty in order to press the unitization issue. The details that have emerged of the negotiations conducted between Downer and Alkatiri in November 2002 support this judgement. For their part, the Dili government was unhappy with any unitization process which, though undertaken ostensibly without prejudice to definitive territorial claims, was based upon the 1991 boundaries which East Timor held in dispute.

While it was clear, as DFAT officials testified to the Joint Standing Committee on Treaties, that there was no 'technical' linkage between the Timor Sea Treaty and the IUA, decoupling them would have removed the pressure to agree to the latter. For their part, the East Timorese were endeavouring themselves to link the negotiation of permanent seabed boundaries to the IUA by arguing for the introduction of a new 'joint authority' to handle the exploitation of Greater Sunrise. The Australian position was to stick to the May 2002 proposal for a split of the revenues, on the basis that such a joint authority would lead to an unravelling of the exploitation regime established by the Treaty. The leverage Australia possessed derived from the fact that East Timor desperately needed income, and with Canberra's ratification of the Treaty not only would the development of the Bayu-Undan field be delayed, but whatever extraction finally went ahead would be subject to the limitations outlined in 2000, with much of East Timor's potential income frozen. Downer was prepared to concede to the establishment of a Joint Maritime Commission to examine seabed rights, but was absolutely insistent that no changes would be made to Canberra's linkage of the Treaty and the IUA. Referring to one of Alkatiri's international advisors he is claimed to have said, 'That Morrow is very aggressive. Well he has met his match with me. We won't agree to a JDPA for Greater Sunrise. . . . Let me give you a tutorial in politics – not a chance' (Crikey.com 2003). It should be recalled that his chief interlocutor at this meeting was the head of government of a friendly sovereign power.

The reasons for the Australian government adopting the apparently conciliatory 90:10 formula can only be a matter of speculation (McKee 2002). It may derive from generosity mindful of East Timor's plight, or amount to an implicit recognition of the compelling nature of East Timor's claims, or be intended as leverage in order to increase the chances of major infrastructure being sited in Australia, or even represent a pragmatic judgement that generous revenues for East Timor will lessen the new nation's calls on Australian aid. Indeed, some legal authorities have suggested that notwithstanding the provisional and non-prejudicial nature of the Treaty, this concession may still weaken Australia's claims at any eventual negotiation of a permanent border. Facilitating the cutting of an advantageous deal on the IUA for Greater Sunrise must, however, have been a consideration.

While the Senate was still debating the Treaty, Downer was on his way to Dili to sign the IUA following its ratification at a special meeting of the East Timorese cabinet. In view of their previous exchanges, Alkatiri must have derived some satisfaction from the fact that he was able to extract a final sweetner as the price of closing the deal. Australia agreed to a further US$1 million a year for at least five years, and US$10 million per year once exploitation of Greater Sunrise begins (ABIX 2003). It should be kept in mind that the latter figure is around 15 per cent of the Dili government's budget. However, perhaps as a *quid pro quo*, reductions announced in the 2003 budget of 24 per cent in Australian overseas aid to East Timor reduced somewhat the net benefit of the arrangement.

It has been contended by some commentators that the relatively favourable terms Australia obtained in 1989 involved a *quid pro quo* for Canberra's recognition of Indonesia's sovereignty as reflected in the negotiation of the Timor Gap Treaty. These terms were certainly advantageous to the extent that by 1989 it was clear that significant gas and oil reserves lay in the joint area, whereas there were no known reserves to be found in the other seabed areas covered by the Treaty. Indeed, it was maintained even in 1975 by Ambassador Woolcott (in a cable to Canberra on 17 August 1975) that such resources were likely to be discovered in the 'Gap' and, given Portugal's resistance to the negotiation of any seabed agreement, Indonesian sovereignty over East Timor would therefore be of benefit to Australia (Walsh and Munster 1980: 200; Way 2000: 314). Nevertheless, in 2002 the first agreement between Australia and the newly independent East Timor amounted to a reaffirmation of the essential features of the 1991 Treaty, despite its unedifying and unhappy history. In the process, the former altruistic approach to East Timor appears to have been eclipsed through the application of a narrowly pragmatic calculus.

While it is too simplistic to reduce the story of the Australia–East Timor relationship to a struggle for control of hydrocarbon resources, their mutual relations continue to be marred by differences over resource issues which remain a source of resentment in the new state. Given that the exploitation of the oil and gas resources of the Gap will exhaust themselves within 30 years, it is difficult to interpret Australia's strategy as other than playing for time (and revenue), conjoined to the judgement that Australia's involvement will produce a more stable business climate than would otherwise be the case. And East Timor's position, whatever the posturing, seems to amount to an implicit acceptance of that strategy in the light of the fact that an Australian involvement will provide continuing protection for these resources which otherwise East Timor would not have the capability to defend. However, José Ramos-Horta, having discussed this point with Alexander Downer in October 2002, was repudiated by Alkatiri when he was sufficiently forthright as to articulate such a compact openly. But this will be the effect of the recent treaty ratification. And it should be recalled that East Timor's security situation remains precarious. As the UN Security Council was informed in a debate on 10 March 2003, the capacity of the government of East Timor to deal with disorder is still weak, and further resources need to be devoted to the provision of law and order. For this reason, plans to reduce the size of the peace-keeping force in the new nation were to be suspended for the time being and the UN meanwhile would retain ultimate control of the police force.

Conclusions

In the context of political transition and economic vulnerability in Indonesia, the failure of Jakarta's policy in East Timor led Australia to orchestrate and participate in the deployment of a major and continuing UN intervention in the region. While the emergence of East Timorese independence raised acute questions within Indonesia on the political role of the military, for Australia it helped to renew the debate on the desirability of, and modalities appropriate for, Asian engagement. Given the coalition government's skepticism regarding the role of the UN, it is ironic that in 1999 the Australian government was to make an unprecedented contribution to global peace enforcement, thus winning the unstinting praise of the UN Secretary-General expressed on his trip to Australia at the beginning of 2000. And it is noteworthy that Australia's first act of official diplomacy with the newly independent nation was to return to the perennial issue of seabed resources.

6 Australia's East Timor

The official version and its critique

As has been argued, the decision to support the movement for self-determination in East Timor that culminated in the INTERFET intervention in the territory in September 1999 was undoubtedly the most significant foreign policy innovation of the John Howard coalition government in Australia. It led to the largest commitment of Australian military forces overseas since the Vietnam war, and transformed the nation's security relationship with its largest neighbour, Indonesia. As a result, the foundation was laid for a defence and development relationship with East Timor which is bound to continue well into the new century and that has already had important security implications for regional order.

The East Timor commitment stimulated unusual and intense public interest in Australia. Newspaper and other media coverage of the issue was extensive. The most courageous, determined and acute reporter working on East Timor was John Martinkus, whose reporting on the issue began in 1994 when, as he has related, most newspaper editors did not consider it newsworthy (Martinkus 2001). His account of the events within the territory from 1997 to the INTERFET intervention, published in 2001, is both a personal story but also informed by deep knowledge of the personalities and forces involved. It will come to be regarded as emblematic of the deep engagement of some Australian commentators with the East Timor issue.

In the interests of a better appreciation of the roots of Timor policy, DFAT published, ahead of the normal release date for such materials, an extensive compilation of documents on Australia's policy covering the period 1974–76 during which the decolonization of the territory was ultimately frustrated by Indonesian invasion (Way 2000). This material has been extensively analyzed earlier in this book. In the light of the vociferous public debate on the reasons for and success of the policy of intervention, this volume was followed by a lengthy official study of Australian decision-making from 1998 to 2000 (DFAT 2001). The study in question is organized chronologically, and was written by a team of foreign affairs officers with access to all the relevant documents. A close analysis demonstrates both that the official narrative has yet to catch up with the revolution in Australia's regional relations that has occurred as a result of East Timor, while also revealing that some of the major criticisms of the government's conduct in 1999 have some foundation in the assumptions evidently made by policy makers at the time.

History in the official account

Given the immense burden of history attached to the East Timor issue, it is extraordinary that the official account perpetuates the extremely selective not to say distorted version of events current in government pronouncements during the long period in which Canberra was in denial. East Timor's political awakening and the events of 1975 prior to the invasion are discussed without any reference to the Indonesian campaign of destabilization which is so well documented as to be incontrovertible. Without that campaign, differences between the indigenous political parties may never have developed so much as to lead to conflict. The declaration of independence of 28 November by the FRETILIN administration is discussed in the same paragraph as the Balibo declaration of 29/30 November by the pro-Indonesian parties, then in West Timor, proclaiming integration into Indonesia as though these occurrences were in any sense equivalents, an impression reinforced by the comment that 'neither proclamation achieved any recognition on the part of the international community' (DFAT 2001: 2). As some of the participants later testified, the 'Balibo declaration' was prompted and orchestrated by Indonesian military intelligence. By contrast, following the visit to Africa by FRETILIN leader, Mari Alkatiri, in November, some 25 governments had pledged to recognize the new state once it was established (Jolliffe 1978: 215–16). In the text, Indonesian forces only make an appearance from 7 December with the landings at Dili, whereas (again as is thoroughly documented) they began crossing the western border in mid-September and by the following month were supported by naval and air units. Amongst the earliest casualties inflicted by these forces was Greg Shackleton and his Australian media colleagues, the one fact about Timor's history that is probably the best known by Australian readers but receives no acknowledgement. The major study of this event from Des Ball and Hamish McDonald is ignored in the official account (Ball and McDonald 2000). And it was published before the appearance of the definitive study by Jill Jolliffe (Jolliffe 2001).

Perhaps the least satisfactory statement in this chapter is the remark, in connection with the early and middle 1990s, that 'the most fundamental problem in East Timor continued to be the oppressive military presence far beyond that needed for security. This resulted in a climate of fear and tight control in which the maintenance of security overrode the objective of creating a peaceful and normal environment' (DFAT 2001: 9). This reads like nothing so much as Paul Keating's assessment of the Dili massacre of 1991 which, even in 2000, he maintained 'was the result of an appalling lapse of control by individual security forces on the ground in Dili rather than deliberate policy instructions from Jakarta'. This episode raised for Keating 'the deeper question of why the Indonesian authorities maintained such an intense military presence in East Timor' (Keating 2000: 129). Given the events of September 1999 it is quite extraordinary that DFAT's drafters could not resolve the issue that was such a puzzle for Keating. As is so well documented, the climate of fear was an absolutely necessary feature of Indonesian policy, although there is also good evidence that the Dili massacre was in part the consequence of political struggles within the military command. In its absence freedom of association and expression would have made it apparent to any observer that the Indonesian occupation was rejected by the great majority of the population (as can readily be inferred from the results of the August 1999 ballot). It has been argued that the Dili massacre was a result of differences between military factions, but, as opposed to the Keating interpretation, these were differences that existed at the highest level.

The brief section of the initial chapter on Australia's role is profoundly misleading. Without being a 'party principal', the text asserts, 'effort was made from the outset to play as positive and constructive a role as possible to encourage an orderly and peaceful decolonisation process' (DFAT 2001: 10). This is written as though the controversy that was rekindled with the speech of February 1999 of Shadow Foreign Affairs spokesman Laurie Brereton on Whitlam's Timor policy had never occurred. The debate on this issue focused on the question of whether the Australian government, and especially Prime Minister Whitlam, inadvertently or deliberately encouraged Indonesian annexation, the outcome of which, as is abundantly clear, was 25 years of misery. Neither interpretation reflects well on the Australian role and both are inconsistent with an objective of 'orderly decolonisation'. Nevertheless, Foreign Minister Peacock did make clear, as the chapter notes, that with the question of the invasion before the UN Security Council in December 1975, Australia publicly supported the proposition that Indonesia should withdraw and the decolonization process should be resumed. Thus, as is pointed out, Ralph Harry, the Australian representative at the United Nations, argued before the Security Council that steps should be taken to allow the East Timorese to undertake a genuine act of self-determination. But as the historical material discussed in Chapter 2 shows only too well, behind the scenes Australia's principal effort was being devoted towards quite a different end. As Harry observes in a cable to Canberra of 9 December regarding the deliberations ahead of the Security Council vote:

> Our immediate diplomatic problem and task has been to do what we can to reduce the pressure on the Indonesians, [Duncan] Campbell's skilled and pertinacious negotiation in the Fourth Committee has kept the 'ASEAN plus' group together and a relatively mild resolution seems to be emerging which will (A) avoid condemnation of Indonesia (B) avoid recognition of the so-called democratic republic (C) link withdrawal of forces with the programme of self-determination. The Indonesians have been given time to restore order [sic] and to set in train their plans for organizing the act of self-determination [sic].
>
> (Way 2000: 617)

With this and related material now openly available it is tendentious in the extreme to ignore it.

The background to Australian engagement

On the events of 1998 the DFAT book is correct to point to the statement of (newly promoted) President B. J. Habibie on 9 June that he was prepared to consider a new form of special status for East Timor as the factor that broke the logjam on the East Timor issue. Habibie's intervention provoked extensive and renewed interest in East Timor including, as is noted, in the foreign policy machinery of the European Union, at the United Nations and (a fact not mentioned in the book) in the United States Congress where, by this time, there was an influential East Timor lobby. In the context of revived negotiations between Portugal and Indonesia, it also stimulated an upsurge in independence sentiment in East Timor itself. These developments, and a review undertaken by DFAT of East Timorese opinion on possible future arrangements for the territory which showed there was little trust of Indonesia's intentions and modalities, comprised the background for the letter of Prime Minister Howard to Habibie, delivered on 19 December. In the months prior to the writing of the letter, according to the book, Foreign Minister Alexander Downer and others had endeavoured to convince Foreign Minister Ali Alatas, who on the reported views of other members of the administration in Jakarta was a key policy player, of the need for dialogue with the leaders of the East Timorese and of the need to consider some future alternative to an autonomy package for the territory. Alatas was resistant to the idea of a referendum to determine East Timorese opinion and when supplied with the findings of the DFAT survey of East Timorese opinion was 'privately dismissive' of the exercise (DFAT 2001: 28).

The foreign minister was an important policy actor in the events of 1999 and the key Indonesian interlocutor for Minister Downer, but the book is undecided on his position, and it is difficult not to conclude that this reflects some confusion on the part of Australian policy makers. Informed readers will most likely associate Alatas with the airborne celebration of the Timor Gap Treaty, or with his doorstop interview pleading, on the eve of international intervention, for more time for Indonesian forces, now acting under a newly introduced martial law mandate, to restore 'order' in Dili. With what kind of figure (and regime) was Australia's foreign affairs machinery dealing? This is a question that a study of this kind might be expected to answer.

In fact, no clear judgement of Alatas is offered. It is claimed that he was 'long associated with more liberal views on East Timor within the Indonesian Cabinet' (a claim considered in Chapter 3 of this study), though not sufficiently liberal as not to describe Australia's policy shift in a public interview as 'very premature' and thus unhelpful (DFAT 2001: 46, 36). Of his conversion to accepting in late January 1999 the necessity of consulting East Timorese opinion, the text records that Alatas 'moved effortlessly and professionally to discard the long-held position of "no referendum" to now advocate the virtues of a democratic approach' (DFAT 2001: 41).

However, the volume records that in February 1999, in conversation with Downer, he denied categorically that the Indonesian armed forces were supplying arms to the militias (DFAT 2001: 62). In April, he told Ambassador McCarthy that reports about the Liquiça massacre (when around 60 people were killed in the vicinity of the town's church by a pro-autonomy mob organized and armed by the TNI) had been 'exaggerated' (DFAT 2001: 64). And he was a key participant in the April Bali summit when Habibie and his ministers rejected outright a request from Prime Minister Howard that international peace-keepers ought to have a role to play in the upcoming ballot process (DFAT 2001: 78–9). Now the book's main contention (to be discussed further below) is that there were close and evident links between the TNI and the militias. The inescapable conclusion is either that Alatas was a mere cipher or, if he was a major policy actor, then he was one of those principally responsible for the September disaster. If Alatas was an executor of 'a more democratic approach', it is difficult on the evidence presented here to distinguish such an approach from its opposite.

To what effect was Australia's diplomatic effort with Alatas and his colleagues on East Timor? Overall, the official account asserts that not only was Australia a directly concerned party but that 'the Government recognized that it had only a marginal capacity to influence the approaches of those who were' (DFAT 2001: 31). Nevertheless, the Indonesian reaction to the Australian change of policy signaled by the Howard letter was a development significant enough to receive adverse comment from a number of public figures in Indonesia, including Alatas himself, a point reinforced by the later testimony of various of the policy actors (Anwar 2000: 18–24).

The following chapter of the official study considers the domestic and international reaction to Habibie's agreement, announced on 27 January 1999, that if special autonomy was unacceptable to the East Timorese, then he would recommend renouncing Indonesian sovereignty. A point that emerges in this chapter is the evident lack of a clear commitment from the Indonesian side to a meaningful act of choice on the part of the East Timorese. The Habibie government was ostensibly proffering alternatives, but was unwilling at this stage to concede that a direct referendum would be necessary to ascertain the opinion of the East Timorese themselves. Australia's response was to encourage as great an international profile for the East Timor question as was possible in the circumstances, though efforts to re-establish an Australian consulate in Dili were rebuffed, and the Indonesian government was not receptive to Australian suggestions that a greater role be given to the ICRC. This presence was not to include a peace-keeping force, calls for which were described by Prime Minister Howard in February as 'premature' (DFAT 2001: 45). In a comment evidently aimed at statements from Shadow Labor Party Foreign Affairs spokesman, Laurie Brereton, the book notes that at this time 'there were recurring public calls for Australia's response to include the deployment of a peacekeeping force, notwithstanding that at that time, the Indonesian Government continued to resist the notion of *any* UN presence' (DFAT 2001: 44). In the event, of course, such a force was required, though only after so much damage had been done that the UN Security Council was prepared to support, and Jakarta forced to accept, such a force. It is certainly arguable that no such support would have been forthcoming in the circumstances prevailing until the ballot, and that an attempt to have the UN consider such a force might well have jeopardized the whole ballot process.

Nevertheless, the book evidently seeks to convey the clear impression that Australia's policy makers were preparing for such a worst-case scenario. The announcement by Defence Minister John Moore, on 11 March 1999, that Australia would have two full army brigades forward deployed at 28-day readiness by the end of June is noted in the context of the increasing number of Australians and other foreign nationals in East Timor (DFAT 2001: 52). There is also a comment on the meeting between Dr Ashton Calvert and US Assistant Secretary of State Stanley Roth in February, at which the issue of peace-keepers was discussed. The debate that occurred was the subject of a record leaked to the press that suggested that Australia was opposed to such an expedient. According to that account as interpreted by the media, Roth maintained that peace-keepers were necessary whereas Calvert preferred to attempt to bring the parties together by 'adept diplomacy' and thus avoid overt conflict (Lyons 1999b: 27). But 'this is simply not so' according to the text:

> It was recorded clearly that Roth agreed that Australia's approach would not preclude peacekeeping and that it would serve to keep a wide number of options open. Calvert had told Roth that Australian planners had been giving close attention to the possibility of a worst-case scenario in East Timor that included an international military response involving Australian troops. Calvert explained to Roth that Australia's preferred approach was first and foremost for the international community to work in concert to avoid the need for recourse to a worst-case response, noting Indonesia's opposition at that time to an international presence of any kind and sensing no apparent international appetite for large scale UN intervention.
>
> (DFAT 2001: 52)

In case the reader has missed this passage, a similar statement is made later in the book:

> The Government's approach to the East Timor transition never precluded peacekeeping or some other form of international military presence . . . The Government gave detailed consideration to worst-case scenarios in East Timor and was closely involved in contingency planning for an international response involving Australian troops. Australia consistently expressed a willingness to be involved in any UN transitional arrangements for East Timor, including the military component of such arrangements.
>
> (DFAT 2001: 85)

The casual reader of these passages might conclude that the government was indeed planning for Australian participation in a peace-keeping (or peace-enforcing) force, should one prove (in the 'worst-case scenario') necessary. Such a reader might then regard the INTERFET peace-keeping operation as a vindication of the government's far-sightedness and criticism of its handling of the situation as ill-informed if not vindictive.

But what 'international military response involving Australian troops' was actually the subject of the planning in question? The evidence on the public record now demonstrates that there were two such exercises (Australian National Audit Office 2002: 27–30). The first involved what was referred to in some quarters as 'UNAMET 2', that is, planning for operations to secure the territory with an international force that – under the direction of an augmented UNAMET – would assume progressively wider responsibilities following a ballot in favour of independence. Australian planners cooperated with the security staff at the United Nations to develop the essentials of such an operation, and also discussed this operation with their United States counterparts. This plan did not assume a post-ballot cataclysm, though it did foresee a range of public order and safety issues as Indonesia disengaged from the territory. The second exercise, codenamed 'Operation Spitfire', was essentially an evacuation exercise requiring the rapid insertion of force elements to collect and protect UNAMET and other international personnel (many of them Australian citizens) in order to withdraw them from the territory. The official account refers to this operation as 'contingency evacuation measures' announced on 6 August (DFAT 2001: 114). The assumption here was that the UN might then call on Australia for assistance under conditions where disorder had broken out between the parties in the territory and where the TNI and the Indonesian police did not have the capacity or the will to intervene. On the aftermath of the ballot Operation Spitfire was in effect reduced in scale and used as the framework for the evacuation, with Indonesian approval, of UN personnel as well as of refugees from the UNAMET compound in Dili and also from Baucau from 6 September. While these evacuations were in progress, military planning staff were busy transforming Spitfire into 'Operation Warden', considered and approved by the Chief of the Defence Force's Strategic Command Group on 7 September. Operation Warden became the Australian component and the leading element of INTERFET. But it was by now an expanded peace-keeping operation with an international component. The fullest treatment of these issues to appear so far is to be found in Bob Breen's volume, *Mission Accomplished, East Timor* (Breen 2000).

If the first was planning for a 'peace-keeping' exercise, then it was under conditions assumed to be far from the 'worst-case', as was clear from the fact that no 'UNAMET 2' force was on the horizon at the end of August. The second did assume something like the 'worst-case' but it was manifestly not a peace-keeping operation. And neither were in planning as early as February, when the Calvert–Roth exchange took place. In short, the planning that was worst-case was not for peace-keeping, and what peace-keeping planning had been done did not make worst-case assumptions. There was no planning of the kind of operation that became INTERFET and to imply otherwise is positively misleading.

Assessing the situation in East Timor in 1999

Perhaps most indicative of the failure of the official account to consider the possibility of policy failure is that part (chapter 4) of the DFAT study which considers the phenomenon of the militias. During 'the first months of 1999', the study asserts, 'a pattern emerged of militia violence and intimidation against independence supporters, with extensive TNI collusion' (DFAT 2001: 55). Though the TNI's 'real attitude' was 'difficult to gauge', by March there was 'evidence of a dual policy' on the part of the military, lip service to neutrality, but in reality support for integration (DFAT 2001: 57). And the instrument fashioned by the TNI for that end was the militia. By this time John Martinkus had filed many stories (some of which languished unpublished) which had identified only too clearly the individuals and groups involved. The sixth chapter of his book, based in part on interviews with militia leaders Cançio Carvalho, Eurico Guterres and João Tavares conducted at the time when they were threatening to 'sacrifice' the lives of Australian pressmen in the interests of defending integration, is required reading on this topic. At this point the DFAT study tries to develop a distinction between these militia formations and other types of quasi-official paramilitaries:

> Initially . . . the militia resembled the older style paramilitaries: rough and ready squads intended to provide the security authorities with some extra muscle. But the new militia proved to have a different agenda. Rather than being hired security help, they became the armed instruments of interest groups committed to preserving the status quo. Doing the bidding of others, they became caught up in a zero-sum political contest that locked them into a course of action from which they would be unable to turn back. For the militia, the democratic choice between autonomy and independence ultimately became a fight to the death.
>
> (DFAT 2001: 58–9)

The imprecise not to say erroneous thinking revealed in this quotation is disturbing. If it is granted that the TNI were stationed in East Timor to realize and defend integration, that is, a position to be identified as 'the status quo', then they were the very 'interest groups' that controlled and used the militia. Accordingly, the assistance these irregular forces rendered prior to the UNAMET phase was of the same character as the part they played during the preparations for the ballot. And as to the conflict they were engaged in being 'zero-sum', this was only the case because their masters deemed it so and required and permitted them to vent their frustrations (with very few fatalities among the militia themselves) on the general population.

If the militia were the creatures of the TNI, then the precise way in which they were managed remained, for Australian policy makers, 'impossible to determine'. And who was ultimately in charge of the operation could not be definitively established. According to the text, what remained unclear to the Australian government was the extent to which this TNI orchestrated campaign was 'sanctioned by, or ordered from, Jakarta', an issue further obscured by the existence of a 'second chain of command' in the hands of the Special Forces (DFAT 2001: 61).

Having affirmed what was even at the time the mainstream media interpretation of events in the territory, the text does not take time to explain why or to what end the 'rogue element' theory was advanced by the Australian foreign minister and others to explain the appearance of TNI–militia complicity. The chapter devoted to the militias closes with the findings of investigations made by Australian officials of the violent incidents that occurred in the final month of the negotiation of the agreement to stage the ballot. The summary view is offered that 'the Liquiça and Dili killings [in April 1999] . . . reinforced Australia's assessment that TNI was doing far less than it was capable of in ensuring security' (DFAT 2001: 70). This statement is puzzling to say the least. If the TNI's approach was in accordance with the 'dual policy' discerned in March, then the killings at this time were utterly in accordance with its policy which was not to enhance but to undermine security. There is no evident reason for this major inconsistency. It may be supposed that the latter position might have been the view taken at the time, and that the assessment that there really was a 'dual policy' in operation was only made later, though retrospectively applied to the account of the thinking in the Australian policy bureaucracy offered in this book.

Habibie's acceptance of independence as an alternative to autonomy, announced on 27 January (ironically by Information Minister Yunus Yosfiah, widely believed to be responsible for the death of Greg Shackleton and his colleagues at Balibo in 1975), required commitment to a strict timetable. The choice between the alternatives was to be placed before the new People's Consultative Assembly (MPR) due to convene (according to the existing quinquennial schedule) in late August, following the June national elections. But an agreement was required for mechanisms to assess the East Timorese position, and the negotiation of this agreement between Portugal, Indonesia and the United Nations proved tortuous and time consuming. The DFAT account records the consistent support the Australian government offered to facilitate a popular consultation in the territory. When a UN advance planning mission led by Francesc Vendrell visited Australia in March the government pledged a A$20 million support package, including the facilities and services of the Australian Electoral Commission and the use of Darwin as a logistics base. But attempts to organize a reconciliation meeting in Australia between the various Timorese factions were blocked by Indonesia, and in the absence of any similar mechanism in the territory itself there were no means for the population themselves to express a view regarding the shaping of the consultation process.

Neither did the convening of the Commission on Peace and Stability at a meeting chaired by General Wiranto on 21 April offer any resolution to the security problem. The farcical nature of the proceedings was apparent from the fact that the two representatives of the pro-independence parties who attended, Manuel Carrascalão and Leandro Isaac, were under protective custody, and Carrascalão's son had been murdered in a militia attack on the family compound in the centre of Dili four days previously. A symbolic surrender of militia weapons occurred following the meeting. As the book notes, 'they were later handed back to the militia' (DFAT 2001: 70).

With the agreement due to receive the final assent, Prime Minister Howard requested a summit meeting with President Habibie to discuss the precarious security situation in the territory. At the Bali meeting, as has subsequently been revealed, Howard's appeal for an international peace-keeping presence was rejected. However the DFAT volume argues that the discussions produced a positive result in that after difficult negotiations the Indonesian side accepted an augmented number of UN CIVPOL (civilian police) in the projected UN presence and also approved the establishment of an Australian consulate in Dili.

In the event, the May agreement to establish the UN mission was deeply flawed, as the Indonesian authorities alone were to be responsible for the maintenance of security. Wiranto's Commission on Peace and Stability was given a role in developing a code of conduct which was no reassurance whatever. And these flaws were part of a deliberate design on the part of Habibie and his ministers, as the DFAT volume records:

> Security arrangements for the ballot remained the most problematic aspect of the negotiations and came to a head as the negotiations drew to a close. By the 21 to 23 April Tripartite Talks, Indonesia had watered down the draft security agreement originally put to it. Indonesia deleted from the draft provisions relating to disarmament of militia, early TNI withdrawal, cantonment and a training role for UN CIVPOL. There was no disarmament or security enforcement role given to UN CIVPOL and the agreement did not specify how many UN CIVPOL would be allowed. Inclusion of any reference to UN CIVPOL in the agreement was nevertheless a hard-won concession, one about which the UN had been extremely pessimistic in March and still feared the Indonesian Cabinet might reject.
>
> (DFAT 2001: 86)

In short, this study is quite unequivocal that Australia committed police and military personnel to a consultation process in an environment where it was clear that those responsible for security were committed to its sabotage. It is difficult not to conclude that Habibie's unrealistic timetable allowed Indonesia to exert pressure on all of the interested parties – the UN, Portugal, and not least the East Timorese (as well as Australia) – to accept security and other arrangements that were manifestly and deliberately flawed.

From UNAMET to INTERFET

On the tasks facing UNAMET once it was established in East Timor, the DFAT study underlines the very unsatisfactory nature of the security situation and recounts the Australian contribution to the exertion of pressure on the Indonesian authorities to take their responsibilities seriously. From the first, the Australian assessment was not positive. The Indonesian government's Task Force for the Implementation of the Popular Consultation in East Timor was prone to voice unwarranted criticism of UNAMET. Despite the presence of Xanana Gusmão (let out of prison for the purpose), a meeting of the Commission on Peace and Stability failed to produce an agreement on disarmament, and attacks on UN personnel and property at Maliana, Viqueque and Liquiça all demonstrated the lack of neutrality of the security forces and their disinterest in ensuring a fair ballot. In Jakarta, Ambassador McCarthy and his staff made repeated representations to the Indonesian government, and following the violence at Maliana the prime minister wrote to President Habibie with a personal appeal to improve the security situation (DFAT 2001: 103). In an extraordinary act of military diplomacy (an account of which subsequently appeared in the Australian press) on 21 June, the vice chief of the Australian Defence Force, Air Marshal Riding, visited two senior Indonesian commanders in Jakarta to confront them with evidence of the TNI's covert support for the militias.

> He noted that in Australia's assessment, TNI had provided support to the militia by legitimising and decriminalising militants and failing to prevent or punish their activities. Further, TNI had failed to provide basic protection to peaceful and law-abiding supporters of independence and TNI protection of and support for the militia had prevented the police from maintaining law and order effectively.
>
> (DFAT 2001: 99)

The Indonesian response was to send a large cabinet level delegation to Dili, led by Alatas, to indicate its commitment to the proper conduct of the consultation.

Despite dire warnings from the UN expressing concern regarding the deterioration in the security situation which forced delays in the electoral registration process and then in the convening of the consultation, the Secretary-General never exercised the power that had been given him by the Security Council to abandon the ballot altogether. As the campaign to convince the electorate got under way, violent incidents again occurred. Even in the face of the militia rampage in Dili on 26 August which claimed the lives of at least two East Timorese and during which Indonesian police were utterly and deliberately inactive, the ballot was not aborted. Through the last weeks of UNAMET, Australian officials continued their representations, Foreign Minister Downer visiting Jakarta and Dili in late July, meeting Habibie, Wiranto and others and also holding talks with Xanana Gusmão. A particular problem that confronted the government was the fact that 'Australia became the target of a sustained campaign of criticism and misinformation' (DFAT 2001: 110) over acts by Australian personnel that allegedly demonstrated bias in favour of the pro-independence movement. Nevertheless the ballot proceeded, with an official Australian delegation led by former deputy prime minister, Tim Fischer, amongst the many international observers. Fischer subsequently published an account of his experiences (Fischer 2000).

The story of the upheaval that followed the decisive ballot result has been told many times. The DFAT study underlines the deliberation that lay behind it, at least as far as it applied to the international personnel on the scene:

> It was clear that the post-ballot violence had not been a spontaneous reaction to the outcome of the ballot. Vital infrastructure and essential services were not destroyed in the mayhem but rather turned off and on again, as with electricity, water and communications at UNAMET headquarters. There were clear goals behind the violence, the principal one being to rid East Timor as quickly as possible of any foreign presence, including the media, humanitarian workers and UNAMET staff.
>
> (DFAT 2001: 129)

Australia's response to this disaster was prompt and decisive, though the study does not advert to the sense of panic which prevailed when early statements from members of the policy community in Washington suggested that the US might not support an intervention. With Habibie refusing to countenance an international peace-keeping force ahead of the MPR's vote on East Timor's status (not now due until October) and an organized programme of deportations giving rise to a humanitarian disaster of monumental proportions, Prime Minister Howard took a personal role in contacting his foreign counterparts to urge such a force and in leading by example in volunteering a sizeable Australian contingent. Following the UN Secretary-General's agreement that Australia should lead a peace-keeping contingent, Chief of the Army, General Hickling, visited a number of his regional counterparts to secure local allies. As has been noted, the providential scheduling of the Auckland APEC leaders' meeting provided another venue for Australian diplomacy, with Downer helping to convince regional foreign ministers of the need for a peace-keeping initiative and the prime minister working with President Clinton to gain Indonesia's assent to the intervention.

The DFAT official study acknowledges the effort and expense devoted to mounting the INTERFET operation. Not only was the rapid initial commitment of Australian troops – growing to around 5,500 at peak deployment – vital for its success, but the provision of extensive Australian logistics and in-kind assistance allowed INTERFET to deploy quickly and with a strong international component. The figure of approximately A$740 million is cited as an estimate of the overall cost. Meanwhile, Australian diplomacy with regional interlocutors led to a strengthening of the Asian component of the intervention force (Breen 2000).

Despite Habibie's unconditional acceptance of the force, three days of tortuous negotiations at the United Nations were necessary before a status of forces agreement could be reached. The study acknowledges the cooperation of Indonesian local commanders during the insertion of the force but also enumerates the number of very tense incidents involving troops and militia that could easily have escalated. In Jakarta the Agreement on Maintaining Security was abrogated with the Indonesian Foreign Ministry specifically criticizing Australia's policy in East Timor as the source of mutual discord; *Antara* (the official Indonesian newsagency) 'ran lurid but inaccurate stories alleging gross brutalities committed by Australian INTERFET troops' (DFAT 2001: 145), and there were a series of major demonstrations outside the Australian Embassy at one of which shots were fired at the building. These profoundly mixed signals are noted in the DFAT study without comment. Australia's role in the humanitarian effort is also discussed, with airdrops of supplies to remote areas beginning three days before the INTERFET landings began, and the national contribution to the humanitarian programme in the territory amounting to A\$37 million in the 1999–2000 financial year. A further A\$7.6 million was provided for the relief of refugees in West Timor.

This commitment to East Timor's reconstruction continued with the advent of UNTAET, which assumed final authority for the security of the territory in February 2000. Of the 1,270 CIVPOL committed by mid-2000, 80 were provided by Australia. Of the 8,000 personnel in the UNTAET security force, 1,500 were Australian, with Major General Mike Smith serving as the initial force deputy commander, and with Australian and New Zealand troops discharging the most demanding task of guarding the Western border. One New Zealand soldier died in July in a clash with infiltrating militia and a Nepalese soldier was killed the following month, a fact illustrating the continued security problems that confronted the force. In addition to Australia's various contributions to East Timor's humanitarian and development needs, an aid package totaling a further A\$150 million and focused largely on capacity building projects was announced in mid-2000.

Martinkus and Breen largely succeed in telling in a comprehensive fashion the stories, respectively, of the Timorese and of the intervention force. In their different ways they are both model accounts. But despite their unrestricted access to the documents and the policy makers, the drafters of the DFAT study omitted some issues that have been the subject of strong public interest in Australia and in the region. What is missing from the DFAT survey? The allegation that Australia was withholding intelligence material from the United States (Ball 2001), an allegation that surfaced following the suicide of an Australian intelligence liaison official in the United States, is not acknowledged, though the foreign minister in his speech at the launch of the volume adverted to this issue. On that occasion he said that he had obtained

> a written assurance from the Director-General of ONA [Office of National Assessments] confirming on behalf of all Australian intelligence heads that Australia maintained close and constant contact with the US in the intelligence field during the crisis, as was the case with policy areas, and held nothing back that would normally be shared between the two countries.
>
> (Downer 2001)

Another aspect of INTERFET that is neglected concerns the fact, now a part of the public record, that it was a good deal more than a peace-keeping operation, given the very uncertain security environment in which it was to be active and the unpredictable reaction of the very large contingent of TNI troops still present in the territory. From some perspectives this was the most significant lesson of the episode, showing that even if peace-keeping is to be the most important future task for the ADF (or other militaries in the region) advanced war fighting capability may still be necessary (Dickens 2001).

A disappointing aspect of the DFAT official volume is its failure to discuss the administrative dimension of policy making. Australia devoted considerable bureaucratic resources to the East Timor issue from 1998, with departments and agencies from across the government and the intelligence services forming working groups to consider policy options, evaluate intelligence and react to contingencies. The Australian office at the United Nations was especially busy. Many officials, members of the military and public servants worked very long hours. Though the interdepartmental East Timor Policy Group established on 17 September in the Department of the Prime Minister and Cabinet (and known as the Taylor Committee afters its chair) is mentioned, none of the prior bureaucratic effort receives much attention, despite a great deal of information about it being in the public realm.

Conclusions

What overview of the Australian policy processes emerges from the official study? It is clear that the Australian government energetically supported a consultation process, including committing Australian police, military and civilian personnel to an environment where it was believed that those responsible for security were actually intent upon its sabotage. Fortunately not one of the many Australian citizens involved were harmed, though if they had been perhaps this official account would not have appeared, given that in their public utterances the government always rejected the likelihood of the worst-case scenario. But there were certainly many East Timorese fatalities, and Australia must therefore be regarded as having contributed to their fate (Maley 2000a). The best that can be presumed is that Australia's policy makers and executors believed that pressure from interested members of the international community, including Australia, would lead to an improvement in the security situation. The study is also clear, despite the apparent efforts of its drafters, in showing that policy makers made no preparations for a 'worst-case' outcome, though the rapid adaptation by the military of the plans that had been made was little short of miraculous and is to their enduring credit.

This lack of preparation is culpable given, as the DFAT volume acknowl-edges, that by March 1999 the militias were assessed to be the creatures of the TNI. What policy makers expected they would do when, as always looked likely, their campaign for autonomy was so decisively frustrated is not recorded. Finally, though it is evident that representations were made repeatedly, energetically, and at the highest level – including by the prime minister himself – to prevent the September disaster, there is no discussion of the reasons why the Australian government and its officials were so far astray in their assessment of their capacity to persuade those responsible. If they consistently believed that this capacity was 'marginal' (DFAT 2001: 31), then – in a further crucial issue ignored by the DFAT drafters

– they must have regarded others as having more influence. From the evidence of this book, it is difficult to conclude other than that this was a major failure of policy, or advice, or both. The decision by the Australian government to pursue an interventionist policy in East Timor undoubtedly had a major impact on regional order, but the inference to be drawn from the official account is that this outcome was as much a product of accident as the result of well-informed design.

7 Outcomes

Peace-keeping lessons, security dilemmas, bilateral tensions

In many respects, the decision of the Australian government first to volunteer forces for an international intervention in East Timor and then to assume the role of coordinator of a United Nations-sanctioned 'coalition of the willing' was in sharp contrast to past Australian policy on the territory and also to its previous approach to regional and bilateral diplomacy. This judgement has been a major theme of this book so far.

The East Timor experience has had a powerful impact on Australian regional policy, on military doctrine and on the national security outlook as well as on Canberra–Jakarta relations. For the first time, Australia fulfilled the role of 'lead nation' in a multinational coalition, operating under UN auspices but largely free of international direction. This action, moreover, was performed in territory previously occupied and administered by Indonesia. Australia's role as a major source of funding and support for the new East Timor Defence Force has entailed a continuing commitment to East Timor, including to the new nation's domestic security and economic development. This chapter will concentrate specifically upon the military and security aspects of the commitment as well as on its impact on relations with Indonesia, issues that have become closely inter-linked in the post-September 11 world.

Shaping INTERFET

Australian experience with peace operations in East Timor can be considered under three broad categories – leadership of the multinational INTERFET (International Force East Timor) mission, managing the transition to the PKF (peace-keeping force) role of UNTAET (United Nations Transitional Administration in East Timor), and participating as a major partner in UNTAET. Most attention will be focused here on INTERFET, given Australia's role as the lead nation in the international coalition.

The INTERFET formula depended upon the existence of a lead nation, not excessively constrained by the political requirement to involve many other partners in order to guarantee the overall legitimacy of the mission. When the UN Security Council on 15 September 1999 authorized (in Resolution 1296/1999) the establishment of a multinational force to restore peace and security in East Timor, there was no agreement on its national leadership. For practical and political reasons – relating to political will as well as to the availability of troops and supplies – Australia assumed that leadership.

Almost all military campaigns of any consequence conducted in the twentieth century have been coalition operations, and with the rise of the doctrine of intervention since the end of the Cold War, the inevitability of coalition operations has become almost an axiom in planning for the use of military force. But the assembling of the INTERFET coalition was not an easy task and underlines the limited and even contradictory commitment to intervention that is characteristic of contemporary global politics (Cronin 1994). It may be assumed that all intervention coalitions will be intended to build peace and security in a disordered environment. The actual operations of the forces involved will, however, be conducted under political restraints the most important of which – aside from the avoidance of a more general conflict – will be to take no steps that would threaten the cohesion of the coalition. And all contributing parties will still be guided by their own distinct national interests which can be expected to outweigh the requirements of the local coalition commander.

All these potential limitations were in evidence in the record of INTERFET. Once the Indonesian government had signalled its willingness to accept an international force in East Timor, it was apparent that the incorporation of significant regional representation would serve to assuage Indonesian concerns and facilitate cooperation with the TNI. The Australian and the Thai governments were especially active in soliciting contributions for the force. It should be recalled that at this point it was not clear whether the East Timorese 'militias' would offer resistance to the intervention or even indeed whether TNI regular troops, who in the theatre numbered around 15,000, would assist or oppose the operation. The latter possibility was not a remote contingency. By that time Jakarta had appointed a martial law commander who was endeavouring to replace the existing contingents with Army Strategic Reserve (Kostrad) personnel whose loyalty, as he candidly explained to Australian military liaison officers, could be relied upon.

At the forefront of the regional commitment were the Thais, who in providing troops that had recently been on exercises with Australian forces greatly facilitated the common INTERFET effort (Ryan 2000b: 45–54). However in negotiations with Australia it was made explicit that the Thai commitment would only be possible if its expenses could be defrayed, and would be constrained by the importance of maintaining bilateral relations with Indonesia. The Philippine government was motivated by similar concerns, and the non-combatant status of the engineering and medical units ultimately dispatched to INTERFET was underlined by their official designation as a 'Humanitarian Task Force'.

The early decision by the Republic of Korea to offer a battalion-size force was helpful in building the political momentum of the coalition. Given their numbers and their capacity to operate independently, the Koreans were capable of providing security for a significant stretch of territory, but as the government in Seoul evidently did not wish to see any casualties they were assigned a specific area of operations in the eastern-most part of East Timor. The least helpful contribution was made by Malaysia. After initially announcing a major commitment, Kuala Lumpur contributed some 30 staff officers, commanded by a Brigadier General. They were competent and professional soldiers who enjoyed cordial relations with the remainder of the international force, but their activities were undermined by remarks by the Malaysian prime minister, Dr Mahathir, who alleged that the intervention was part of an Australian strategy to weaken and divide Indonesia. Beyond the immediate region, contributions to the INTERFET force were made by France, Italy, Canada, Jordan, Kenya and the United Kingdom, as well as by New Zealand. The US role in providing logistics and intelligence, though low profile, was vital (Dee 2001; Ryan 2000a).

In distributing his forces, therefore, the commander was constrained by political and diplomatic sensitivities. The 'lead nation' model, however, did place at his disposal a sufficient number of reliable forces to secure the main military objectives. Overall, the effect was to restrict the deployment of forces into the border theatre to Australian, New Zealand and UK units who then were required to deal with militia infiltrations and the prospect of death or injury.

At that stage constrained by constitutional and legal requirements, Japan facilitated the launch of INTERFET by providing a fund of US$100 million especially to assist in meeting the expenses of less-developed coalition members. Potential INTERFET partners were also reassured by a statement by the Australian prime minister that the costs of contributing nations would be covered and initial logistics support would, wherever possible, be provided. While the force numbers mandated by the UN were raised, and INTERFET ultimately received offers of infantry in excess of its eventual needs, some specialist units remained in short supply, and some national contingents were present as much for diplomatic objectives as for operational requirements.

Despite all of the above constraints, INTERFET force cohesion was maintained and its principal goal of restoring security in the territory was achieved. But as the coalition was not really tested by actual combat, it cannot be presumed that in a more exacting and hostile environment (as for example became the case in Somalia) it would have functioned so effectively.

The UN mandate specified a 'unified command structure', possibly with the precedent of the intervention in Haiti in mind (Ryan 2000b: 34–66). In practice, Australia reassembled its DJFHQ (Deployable Joint Force Head Quarters) in Dili which then controlled the operation. Liaison with other national force components was maintained not by the presence of their representatives at that HQ but in a somewhat ad hoc but nevertheless effective fashion involving personal contacts, frequent joint briefings, and visits by Major General Cosgrove to other contingents. Again, in more adverse circumstances these command procedures may not have worked so well, with Australia perhaps facing diplomatic pressure to avoid casualties or limit specific deployments. As it was, there were many stories in the Indonesian mass media which were to an extent retailed in other parts of Southeast Asia detailing alleged Australian arrogance, aggression and brutality. Any actual fighting would have been sure to have elicited heightened criticism that would have had a powerful domestic political impact.

INTERFET: the formula for success

INTERFET's relative success can be attributed to the rapid insertion of over-whelming force in a context where the political ground had been very carefully prepared.

In late 1998, the Australian military had conducted (with UK, US, Canadian and New Zealand participation) an exercise at DJFHQ, 'Exercise Rainbow Serpent', that simulated a peace enforcement exercise in a regional country (Breen 2000: 3). However, prior to the August 1999 ballot, while there were steps taken in Australia to raise force readiness there were no specific plans for an operation of the size and character of INTERFET. As has been previously indicated, two scenarios were given extended consideration. Military planners had been directed to prepare either for participation in an international force that, it was assumed, would progressively take charge of security in the territory following Indonesia's abandonment of its claims, or for the requirement to evacuate international personnel if order broke down suddenly and irretrievably (Australian National Audit Office 2002: 27–30). In retrospect, and given what was known about conditions in East Timor and especially about the 'militias', failure to plan for peace-keeping was a significant oversight on the part of the Australian government, a point considered in Chapter 6.

In the event, the INTERFET plan of action had its origins in the latter scenario, 'Operation Spitfire', which was altered to add more combat power and a greatly strengthened logistics component and was re-named 'Operation Warden'. Evacuation required the rapid seizure and securing of appropriate landing sites and port facilities to which international personnel would then be transported either by helicopter, by wheeled vehicles or by small ships. As there could be no safe assumptions regarding the security conditions in the territory, the force would have to be sufficiently numerous and well-armed to deal with any possible antagonist, including elements of the TNI (and possibly even naval and air units).

This strategy was retained in the INTERFET operation, though with an important modification. Major General Cosgrove flew to Dili one day ahead of the initial deployment to meet directly with his Indonesian counterpart, Major General Kiki Syahnakri, to explain his intentions and arrange an orderly transfer of responsibilities. Upon advice from liaison officers already in Dili, he then abandoned the plan to insert the first contingents by helicopter as this tactic might have resulted in a hostile reaction from TNI forces guarding the Dili airport (Breen 2000: 23–9). The first special forces arrived by C-130 which left them initially exposed, but this manoeuvre was successful in building an atmosphere of cooperation, at least at the landing zone.

It should be recalled that even after Indonesia accepted the need for an intervention force, there were demands both that the force itself should be entirely drawn from the region, and that it should only be lightly armed. When Major General Cosgrove made it plain that he would be arriving with armour and would be using the airfield even at night to permit a rapid build-up of forces, the magnitude of the reversal they had received must have dawned on many Indonesian officers. Even though Indonesia was relinquishing the territory it took three days of solid negotiation in New York before the Indonesian representatives would accept a status of forces agreement for East Timor.

There were some occasions, even after the first forces were successfully inserted, when INTERFET might yet have been threatened. Two Indonesian T-209 submarines were detected shadowing the INTERFET fleet and its anti-submarine capabilities had to be employed to protect the transport of supplies (amongst which fuel was crucial) and also personnel. At one point contact was lost with one of the vessels, and the possibility of an attack had to be considered. Only when the TNI naval command were contacted with credible information on the activity of the submarines were they withdrawn (Dickens 2001). Similarly some Indonesian military aircraft adopted potentially hostile tactics.

Once the initial landing sites were secured and the capital subject to intensive patrolling to deal with any remaining militia members, the INTERFET command then pursued an 'oil spot' strategy (Ryan 2000b: 70; Bostock 2000). Baucau, East Timor's second city, was occupied to provide an alternative airport. The western border region was secured by armour transferred by landing craft, forces were then inserted on the southern coast region by air and sea, and finally the Oecussi enclave was occupied. At each stage a rapid build up of forces supported by air mobility prevented possible antagonists from taking the initiative while simultaneously delivering a powerful and positive message to the population that security had been established.

The conclusion drawn by Major General Cosgrove and others was that 'high end capability' was an absolutely essential element in any intervention of this type. Without extensive anti-submarine capability, the Australian fighter force forward deployed and on standby, heavy armour in Darwin available for insertion, and the Aegis class cruiser USS Mobile Bay to provide battle space surveillance, the force may have lacked credibility and may even have invited opposition from adventurist elements. Major General Cosgrove subsequently asserted that in operations of this kind the lesson to be learned was that whereas forces trained for combat could be extended to undertake peace enforcement and building tasks, the reverse was not possible. If lead nation coalitions are to recur in the future, they can only be successfully conducted if the command has at its disposal a full suite of capabilities (Cosgrove 2000).

Frequent and visible patrolling served to reassure the population, who then cooperated with the force to isolate and control the militias, such cooperation then building the foundations for the longer-term political objectives of the intervention. Within four days of the initial landings, a full battalion of troops supported by armoured personnel vehicles had arrived in Dili by sea. Within six days extensive patrolling in force cleared the capital of militia members. The decision was taken to use armour as an integral part of the force, with 113 M113A1 APCs, and 29 ASLAV vehicles finally deployed (Bostock 2000). The conventional wisdom in peace-keeping operations is to avoid, where possible, the use of armour in order to stay in direct contact with the population. The INTERFET forces found, however, that not only did their tracked vehicles give them mobility in the difficult terrain but that the militias were overawed and dispirited by the presence of armour.

Once initial security was established, larger patrols with full equipment were replaced by smaller (typically four-person) units whose presence on the streets and in the villages quickly reassured the population. As the word spread that the militias had been vanquished, civilians began to return from hiding in the hills and bush. Any suspected militia members remaining in the vicinity of INTERFET forces were then quickly identified and detained.

In these operations the judgement of junior officers was crucial, and the resolution of problems greatly facilitated by the presence of language specialists amongst the coalition personnel. At the tactical level, there were continuous consultations between INTERFET and the TNI, with Australian liaison officers attached to Major General Kiki Syahnakri's command. Later, after a firefight on the western border the result of conflicting map information, a procedure was developed to defuse any possible border incidents. However the potential always existed for conflict and more serious incidents were narrowly avoided.

From the initial deployment, INTERFET forces were under orders to demand identification of any doubtful personnel using the roads. In an incident that might have erupted into a major firefight, with incalculable consequences, personnel manning an INTERFET checkpoint in Dili prevented the passage while their identity was established of a large convoy of vehicles transporting elements of TNI territorial Battalion 745 en route to the border. The party was led by a group on motorcycles not dressed in uniform and carrying weapons. The convoy refused to respond to requests in *Bahasa Indonesia* for identification and through their night vision equipment the INTERFET personnel could see that weapons were being aimed directly at them (Breen 2000: 44–7). The decision was taken to allow the vehicles to pass, though some individuals in the convoy were clearly militia members. It has since been established that Battalion 745 was responsible for a number of murders and extensive looting as it made its way down the length of the territory and exited to West Timor (*Christian Science Monitor*, 13 March 2000).

Until the TNI began to withdraw in large numbers there were many other incidents in which INTERFET forces were threatened by armed TNI and militia members travelling in trucks, and there were also instances of TNI personnel in the streets discharging their weapons. TNI destruction and looting did not stop with the arrival of INTERFET, and when some members of the international force identified sites where, apparently, torture and murder had occurred, tensions between the forces grew. The steady discipline of the coalition force prevented any of these potential confrontations from descending into direct combat. The lesson was drawn that an intervention force must have not only precise rules of engagement but the strictest controls on behaviour.

At the earliest stage the INTERFET command decided, as a result of numerous requests, to transport a party of local and international journalists equipped with satellite communications to Dili. From the end of the first day, the conduct of INTERFET was therefore under the closest scrutiny. This was at a time when security was yet to be established, as the murder of one journalist and the detention of another demonstrated. Any violent incident was bound to be the subject of immediate media publicity and analysis. Decisions taken by junior officers and

NCOs might well have had an immediate effect, not merely upon the conduct of the operation but even on the coherence of the coalition itself. The importance of recognizing the impact of the media was later stressed by Major General Cosgrove himself:

> In my day, as a junior leader, my decisions had an immediate impact on my troops and the enemy. In today's military operations the decisions of junior leaders still have those immediate impacts, but modern telecommunications can also magnify every incident, put every incident under a media microscope, and send descriptions and images of every incident instantly around the world for scores of experts and commentators to interpret for millions of viewers and listeners. Thus the decisions of junior leaders and the actions of their small teams can influence the course of international affairs.
>
> (Cosgrove 2000)

Once again the lesson appeared to be the need for clear and coherent rules of engagement and completely reliable discipline.

Once in occupation, INTERFET's operations against the Timorese 'militias' entailed the use not only of military capacity but also of powers of arrest and detention, functions that can only be discharged in cooperation with the civil power. From the first day of deployment, INTERFET forces were confronted with civil tasks. One of the requirements of the UN mandate for the force was to provide assistance to UNAMET, but as this mission was not empowered with any authority for the territory or population, and given the complete dissolution of the Indonesian administration, government effectively did not exist in the territory. INTERFET forces detained suspected militia members but there were no gaols to hold them nor legal process to adjudicate their suspected crimes. Scenes of murder and torture were discovered, and in the tropical conditions forensic work had to be hurriedly undertaken in order to record the evidence. INTERFET's capability to perform these important tasks depended largely upon ad hoc arrangements. While FRETILIN was clearly the dominant political movement, there was no systematic attempt to organize a local administration. Fortunately the force rapidly established relations of trust and cooperation with the population, and many problems were overcome on the basis of good will. In more demanding circumstances, this vacuum of authority might well have proved a contentious issue. If there had been significant complaints regarding the conduct of the force in discharging these duties, the coherence of the coalition might have been placed under strain.

As security was established, INTERFET's civil role extended to what might be termed the exercise of information operations. The force had to develop a capacity to project the message to the population that they had the ability and authority to protect them and to deal with any future threats. Sending this message involved the use of leaflets, posters, radio broadcasts and other forms of communication. Within a month of arriving in the territory, INTERFET had published the first issue (in three languages) of a broadsheet newspaper, *New East Timor*, and distributed copies in every locality. In an environment where all basic services were absent and most infrastructure destroyed, this was no easy task (Beasley 2002; Blaxland 2002). The importance of this work and the modest resources available to perform it led to the conclusion that the Australian Defence Force lacked specialist civil–military operations capability, and that in any future coalition operations such capability was a major requirement.

Despite these achievements, assuming the lead nation role stretched Australia's logistics capability to breaking point. Part of the problem derived from the sheer volume of demands on the logistics train. Despite agreeing to provision their forces with basic necessities, some national contingents arrived with virtually no supplies. With the force composition still being determined as the first elements arrived in what was then regarded as a potentially hostile theatre, there was little time to shape or change plans.

In addition, Australian logistics had been designed to support Australian formations rather than to provision and support a multinational force. Quite apart from their occasional needs for some specific items of equipment which were not of the Australian standard, these forces were to be reimbursed for part of their expenses, and thus required the Australian logisticians to account for the value of provisions supplied. It took some time to develop the techniques necessary to perform this task (Australian National Audit Office 2002: 52–88). Notwithstanding the difficulties of the theatre, some national contingents took these accounting requirements to extreme lengths. One contingent even claimed compensation from Australia for a shipment of supplies that was late arriving in their area of operations. The lesson to be drawn is for potential 'lead nations' to have their logistics systems appropriately equipped and to communicate to other coalition contingents their precise responsibilities.

The UN assumes direct responsibility for security

Given that PKO operations cannot be launched speedily, there may well be further instances of these operations replacing multinational missions. The Timor experience showed clearly that such transitions require the early identification of the force commander, and proper resourcing of a command headquarters, accompanied by appropriate planning and preparation. In the East Timor case there were significant problems in these areas.

As has been noted, the INTERFET HQ was, to all intents, an Australian command structure. UNTAET, including its security component, was authorized by the Security Council on 25 October 1999, but the UN Department of Peacekeeping Operations (DPKO) devoted most of its energies to the formation of a civil authority for the territory, a priority understandable in light of the absence of government noted above. The UNTAET force commander was only appointed on 30 December and did not arrive in East Timor until 25 January 2000 (de los Santos and Burgos 2001). In his absence INTERFET was forced to formulate a handover plan which began to be implemented when the eastern most sector of the territory was handed on to UN security authority on 1 February. While the force HQ was designed to be staffed by 200 personnel, only 75 had arrived by

23 February when the final elements of INTERFET were withdrawn, and many of the remaining positions were never filled. Those staff who were in post had had no experience of working together and lacked even basic equipment.

These problems of transition were exacerbated by the absence of clear lines of authority. A UN force commander is answerable to the SRSG (Special Representative of the Secretary-General) who is in overall command of the mission. In the East Timor case the initial force directive was supplied by the Under Secretary General, DPKO, and the SRSG did not promulgate a force directive specifically for the mission until 8 May (Smith and Dee 2003: 125–8). Moreover the force commander did not stay long enough in the theatre to lay a strong foundation for the successful operation of the UNTAET military force. Fortunately, at other levels the command structure proved sufficient resilient to cope. Here the Australian deputy commander, who had spent part of 1999 at UN headquarters dealing with the Timor issue, played a major leadership role.

Other problems encountered showed that a force mix to reflect the diverse tasks entailed by complex peace operations (including air support, a maritime component, intelligence capabilities, and communications) is essential to their success. The transition to full UNTAET responsibility for security was achieved on 23 February 2000. By that time the situation had stabilized to the extent that, beyond the western border, the actual security work required of the military forces was mostly routine. Contingents took the opportunity to perform useful community work (sometimes in collaboration with national NGOs) or undertake engineering and repairs to infrastructure. In mid-2000, however, a series of militia infiltrations tested defences on the central and southern borders, and two UNTAET peace-keepers were killed. Air assets contracted by UNTAET proved inadequate and the ADF transferred helicopters to East Timor to provide mobility and surveillance (though retaining direct Australian control over their use in operations). Though East Timor is an island nation UNTAET possessed no maritime force and thus was never able to interdict any hostile infiltrations by sea.

The UNTAET experience also demonstrated the problematic nature of intelligence in a multinational context. While INTERFET was able to use Australian intelligence assets, UNTAET, though it contained a Military Information cell, did not devote sufficient resources to intelligence gathering or assessment (Smith and Dee 2003: 135). Neither did UNTAET pursue a sustained policy on information operations which could have helped counter militia infiltrations.

In peace operations an engineering capability is vital, and as its employment to restore infrastructure and communications is bound to have a powerful humanitarian, social and political impact, it should be adequately resourced and its management conducted in cooperation with the civilian elements of the mission. The UNTAET engineering component was severely stretched. Some of the national engineering contingents while containing competent personnel were from nations where many restrictions existed on the use of equipment and the availability of supplies. Though the Australian engineering contribution to UNTAET was modest, Australian units performed well due to their more generous provisioning.

Finally the mission also demonstrated deficiencies in the UN system of logistics, supply and reimbursement. Problems with UN logistics are not a new issue, and recommendations as to changes in the system are included in Lakhdar Brahimi's *Report of the Panel on United Nations Peace Operations* of August 2000 (Brahimi 2000). On the view of the first deputy force commander, 'the current UN logistics system is unsatisfactory for the conduct of military operations, and more so those in a harsh environment over tenuous lines of communication. The current system lacks detailed planning and is too centralized, too slow, and not sufficiently responsive to the force commander's requirements' (Smith and Dee 2003: 141). Specific problems in East Timor included the provision of inadequate aircraft, a major problem in the supply of rations which took six weeks to resolve, and a poorly maintained telecommunications system that forced military forces to use their own radio equipment.

On the question of UN reimbursement to national contingents, the Australian experience with UNTAET is instructive. UN reimbursements are based upon the personnel and equipment provided by the contributing nation as agreed with the UN. There are set rates for personnel and lease rates for equipment. It took some time for the UN DPKO to come to an agreement with Australian Defence officials regarding the types of equipment appropriate for the Australian contingent, and a final Memorandum of Understanding was not exchanged until August 2001. The sum to be reimbursed for Australian expenses was around one-fifth of the actual expenses as estimated by the Department of Defence. Even this reduced reimbursement was slow to arrive, with payment of less than half of the agreed disbursement for the first year of deployment (to February 2001) arriving by October of that year (Australian National Audit Office 2002: 46–8).

At independence, those of UNTAET's functions that were not assumed by the new government were devolved to the successor mission, UNMISET, which was established with a mandate for the two-year period from independence. Though no longer in charge of the administration of the territory, the mission included a still substantial international security force of around 3,853 personnel (with a possible 5,000 mandated), as well as a civilian police component of 730 (United Nations 2002). About 1,000 members of the ADF were assigned to UNMISET, and as the mission retained ultimate authority for the maintenance of security through 2003, the Australian commitment remained significant.

The impact on Australian defence of the East Timor experience

The East Timor experience has been the subject of an intense domestic debate regarding the future directions of Australian defence. Even before September 11, it was argued that in the post-Cold War environment, military doctrine and training should reflect such new roles as peace-keeping and dealing with 'new generation' security issues such as trans-national crime and terrorism, as opposed to the old emphasis upon securing the defence of continental Australia (Dupont 2001).

The impact of the East Timor experience on the Australian security outlook has been significant. While it is held that Australian forces performed well during the crisis of 1999, especially given the immensely difficult logistics involved in inserting and supporting a multinational force (with no prior experience of working together) in a potentially hostile theatre, the commitment revealed a potential lack of capacity. As a result, the 2000 Australian Defence White Paper committed the government to significant increases in expenditure over a ten-year period. Such expenditure increases were already expected, given the problem of block obsolescence in much defence equipment. What was unprecedented in the White Paper was the clear statement that, after the defence of continental Australia, 'lower level operations', including peace-keeping, were the next most important priority for the ADF, and that other features of the East Timor experience might recur (Department of Defence 2000: 39). As has been already noted, the White Paper also underlined the strategic primacy of Indonesia, and affirmed that Australia's security would be threatened by 'adverse developments' inside Indonesia, whether internally or externally generated (Department of Defence 2000: 22). It should be recalled that this text was published before September 11 and the Bali bombing of October 2002.

On East Timor, the White Paper signalled nothing less than a continuing security commitment:

> Australia will seek to develop an effective defence relationship with [independent] East Timor . . . East Timor faces formidable security challenges. Our aim will be to provide, with others, an appropriate level of help and support for East Timor as it builds the capabilities and national institutions that it will need to ensure its security and thereby contribute to the security of its neighbourhood.
>
> (Department of Defence 2000: 37)

This commitment should be seen in the context of Australia's A$26 million military aid programme announced in late 2000, which was intended to help train and equip an East Timor Defence Force (ETDF), the core of which was drawn from FALINTIL (Garran 2000). As this was the guerrilla resistance army that was for a generation the Indonesian military's most dogged opponent, this commitment might be seen to inject something of a potential irritant into future relations with Indonesia (presuming the continued domestic political importance of the TNI).

Australia's support for the ETDF, though of significance in political terms, was of minor financial importance when compared to the overall cost of the East Timor policy adopted by the government from 1999. According to the 2000–01 federal budget, the total cost to Australia of the Timor deployment and associated aid and other expenses was almost A$3 billion, and if the expenditure for INTERFET is added the figure rises to around A$4 billion (see Table 1).

The point has been made by some critics that a more balanced pattern of expenditure might produce a better result. The long-term security and stability of East Timor will only be guaranteed by economic development and good

Table 1 Net cost to Australia of East Timor

	1999–00 A$m	2000–01 A$m	2001–02 A$m	2002–03 A$m	2003–04 A$m	Total[a] A$m
Expenses						
Defence						
Australian Defence Forces (ADF)	731	922	736	669	675	3002
Tax exemption ADF personnel in East Timor	62	23	23	23	23	92
Non-Defence Australian Federal Police	26	25	26	26	27	104
Aid	75	40	40	35	35	150
Safe haven provision for evacuees	21	–	–	–	–	–
Quarantine and inspection	–	2	2	2	2	8
Revenue						
Defence						
UN reimbursement	18	114	106	76	76	372
Net cost of East Timor	**897**	**898**	**721**	**679**	**686**	**2984**[a]

(a) Total cost over *four* years from 2000–01
Source: Commonwealth of Australia 2000.

governance, whereas the priorities of the Australian government have been overwhelmingly military (Ball 2002).

Nevertheless, East Timor has had a profound impact on the Australian security outlook. Some of the equipment and other shortcomings apparent as a result of the experience of INTERFET are being rectified, and Australian military doctrine now expressly anticipates participation in new coalition operations in the region as a possibility for which there should be preparation. However, the shift from late 2001 to the focus on terrorism has diverted attention and resources from a thorough assimilation of the Timor experience.

Dilemmas of peace-keeping

Each of the three phases of the Timor experience posed, though to different degrees, the classic peace-keeper's dilemma of being required both to establish and maintain order while simultaneously laying the foundation for nation building, tasks that may come into conflict (Suhrke 2001). Much has been written on the dimensions of this dilemma as reflected in the conduct of the UNTAET administration

(Beauvais 2001; Chopra 2002; Gorjão 2002). But in the military and security fields it was also in evidence.

In the relatively brief INTERFET phase, restoring security was the most urgent priority and this goal could only be realized by the international force. There were neither warring parties nor an administrative structure in existence so the tasks to be accomplished were uncontroversial albeit difficult, and INTERFET exercised the complete monopoly of force. Initially FALINTIL received the force as liberators, and discipline was maintained to restrain acts of vigilantism against suspected militia members. INTERFET brought Xanana Gusmão to Dili and he made his first address to the population on 22 October. But INTERFET was required to disarm all combatants, and if its orders were to be taken literally, this included the resistance. When this became a possibility, there were several incidents only defused by tactful diplomacy. Eventually it was decided not to require FALINTIL to disarm provided the force remained in its cantonments, and some force leaders were also then employed as scouts and guides on the western border. FALINTIL was clearly to be the core of any future East Timorese defence force, and their previous role had made the ballot and political independence possible. But the failure or inability of the UN to deal comprehensively with this issue necessitated in-theatre improvisation.

This problem became more acute during the tenure of UNTAET. Many FALINTIL members remained in their cantonments and discontent spread as promised supplies and international assistance failed to arrive. It was not until July 2000 that the UN administration tackled the problem, funding a study of security options that eventually led to the creation of an East Timor Defence Force and the recruitment of some FALINTIL veterans to fill its first battalion. It was fortunate for public order that, in general, FALINTIL members did not become more assertive in advancing their claims for recognition and compensation, given the support they might have enjoyed amongst the general population in the event of a clash with UNTAET military forces or police. The latter were the formal possessors of the exclusive right to exercise force, but the former were widely held to be the legitimate national combatants. Nevertheless some aberrant FALINTIL factions were involved in disorder in various locations including in Baucau as well as in connection with the dissident CPD-RDTL (*Conselho Popular pela Defesa da República Democrática de Timor Leste*: Popular Council for the Defence of the Democratic Republic of East Timor) and post-independence veterans' organizations remain a main focus of discontent with the Alkatiri government. And the formation of the defence force has itself become a source of political friction given the perception that its membership has been selected partly on the basis of political criteria.

Meanwhile, as has been noted, Australia has become involved as a major patron of the East Timor Defence Force and thereby may be drawn into domestic political disputes. It is conceivable that this force, relatively well provisioned and trained in an impoverished environment, may become political actors in some future crisis caused by government incapacity or failure. Australian involvement in issues of law and order as well as security deepened in August 2003 with the announcement that funding of A\$40 million would be extended to East Timor over a four-year period to train the police force. In East Timor, as in Cambodia and Kosovo, insufficient thought has been given to what foundations would be needed to maintain order and security at the conclusion of international intervention (Kondoch 2001; Caplan 2002). In late 2002, urban rioting as well as violent incidents in the border regions, both of which tested the security component of UNMISET, indicated that these problems have continued into the post-independence era.

In January 2003, a group of about 15 former militia infiltrated across the border and attacked two villages, killing six East Timorese. There were further incidents the following month. Appeals were made by East Timorese government spokespersons for Australian formations in the UNMISET force to take a special role in meeting this challenge. UN security forces went on the offensive against the infiltrators, but with a porous border and apparent sanctuary in West Timor the problem could not be dealt with at its source. After a review of the deterioration in the security position, the UN Security Council decided (in resolution 1473) on 4 April 2003, to slow the anticipated drawdown of UNMISET forces and also to reconfigure the police component to provide the capacity to deal more effectively with such problems (United Nations 2003). UNMISET was established with a mandate for the two-year period from independence, but it remained to be seen whether East Timor would be able to take full responsibility for all security tasks according to that schedule. Security in East Timor is clearly an equation in which Indonesia remains one of the key terms.

Australian perceptions of the problem of regional order

Overall, Australian policy must be situated within the evident weakness of regional order. Though the precise character of the regional security order is disputed, its most important indigenous component is ASEAN. Since the 1970s Australian foreign policy makers have accorded ASEAN major status as a security (and also as an economic) interlocutor, and when a region-wide economic organization was contemplated by Australian policy makers in the later 1980s, the ASEAN 'norms' and especially the emphasis upon consensus were adapted as the organizing principles for APEC. ASEAN's failure as a regional security institution either to detect the growing East Timor crisis or to act to remedy the problem before international intervention became a pressing need has been noted in Chapter 4. Its aspiration, therefore, to craft 'regional solutions to regional problems' was not realized in the East Timor case.

There can be little doubt that this failure of regional security structures was a major consideration in crafting the Australian reaction to the crisis. In response, the government developed a novel understanding of Australia's regional role. This was implicit in the prime minister's claim that Australia was both a western and a regional country, and thus occupied a special status, being able to bring Western as well as global forces to bear on regional problems (Brenchley 1999: 24). This outlook has had an enduring legacy, with policy makers now more strongly inclined to seek security within existing bilateral treaty arrangements or in cooperation with like-minded states. Although the East Timor experience led to an affirming of the role of the United Nations in sanctioning intervention, post-September 11 developments and especially the war in Iraq introduced a tension for Australia between this role and the obligations of the US alliance. In this regard it is significant that the Australian led and initiated intervention in the Solomon Islands which began in July 2003 was grounded in an accord with other South Pacific states and legitimated by an act of the parliament in Honiara rather than launched under United Nations sponsorship. It also reversed a considered position taken in 2000 to the effect that, whatever the law and order problems manifest in the Solomon Islands, Australia would not send personnel there for fear that any commitment would become open-ended.

Australian relations with Indonesia

As has been argued, the decision by the Howard government to overturn the bi-partisan legacy of support for Indonesian annexation of East Timor was the most significant development in Australian policy towards the Asia Pacific region and especially towards Indonesia since the Vietnam war. The result was a major realignment of relations with Jakarta. Just at the time, therefore, when Australian policy makers were contemplating the lessons learned and dangers posed by a major military foray into the region, they also had to confront a deterioration in that bilateral relationship that has the greatest impact on Australia's security outlook.

Australia–Indonesia relations took a wholly new course from September 1999. Up until that time there were expectations that the emergence of democracy in Indonesia, especially in the context of Australia's US$1 billion contribution to the IMF relief package provided as a response to the regional financial crisis, would put relations with Jakarta on an entirely new basis. Australian support for the infrastructure necessary to stage the 1999 parliamentary elections was indicative of the awareness that the progress of democratic consolidation was vital for Australia's national interests. But this support counted for very little in the balance as against what was widely represented in the Indonesian media as Australia's 'arrogance' and 'betrayal' over East Timor. This perceived hostility stirred passions. A vehicle carrying the Australian ambassador was shot at in Dili. After the defence minister stated that all bilateral defence contacts with Indonesia were suspended, Indonesia announced on 16 September that the 1995 bilateral Agreement on Maintaining Security would be abrogated. The agreement was then dismissed by the government as of little consequence, but its demise marked the end of a defence relationship painstakingly constructed from the 1960s. As the INTERFET operation began, demonstrators gathered outside the Australian embassy and there were violent incidents. And President Wahid himself described Australian policy as 'infantile' (Hill and Manning 1999; Bhakti 1999).

Despite strenuous diplomatic efforts, including a visit to Jakarta by Foreign Minister Downer in February 2000, relations with Indonesia remained in an awkward phase. Ironically, President Abdurrahman Wahid was personally very familiar with Australia and was also extremely fond of overseas travel, yet he could only be tempted to visit the country in the twilight of his presidency. It was therefore something of a surprise that Prime Minister Howard was invited to meet his successor, Megawati Sukarnoputri, immediately upon her taking office, though this development did not necessarily translate into closer cooperation on such key issues as people smuggling. The latter issue still remained unresolved when Howard staged his second visit to Indonesia in February 2002. By this time, though, post-September 11 global security issues brought the two leaderships closer together.

Finally, Australian intervention in East Timor was seen as a possible harbinger of future interference in Indonesia's internal affairs, especially in connection with West Papua. Despite strenuous denials from the Australian government, this suspicion was encouraged by statements from Colin Powell, shortly after being nominated by President-elect, George W. Bush as the new US Secretary of State. In remarks he made during confirmation hearings, he signalled a new scepticism of humanitarian interventions, and indicated that more reliance would be placed on allies, specifically referring to Australia's decision to 'take the lead' regarding Indonesia (Alcorn 2001). These remarks found an attentive audience in Jakarta.

Uncertainty in Indonesia regarding Australia's intentions in the region was a consequence not only of the nation's role in UNAMET and INTERFET, but also a reaction to the wider public debate that accompanied the East Timor commitment. The apparent success of the operation led to statements from political and military figures that seemed to imply a larger if indeterminate commitment to similar undertakings in the future. As has been noted, the 'Howard doctrine', by which this position came to be known, depicted Australia as playing a role as 'deputy' to the US in the region and thus a potential agent of interference in Indonesia's internal affairs (Lyons 1999a).

As has already been discussed, on the government's view the objectives of the East Timor intervention were threefold. First, a perennial problem in Australia–Indonesia bilateral relations was being addressed. It was incontrovertible that the perception of Indonesia's human rights record in East Timor had been an obstacle to a more favourable public assessment of that country for all the years since 1975. Second, and in light of the fact that the UN still held Indonesian occupation to be illegitimate, a new status for East Timor would remove perhaps the major obstacle to Indonesia playing a positive role in the world, commensurate with its size and potential. Third, the intervention was a response to the very strong reaction in the Australian public to the devastation wrought in the territory. But the key message derived from the intervention was, in the words of the prime minister, that foreign policy must take account of 'the values of the Australian community', and therefore that Australia should not seek 'a good relationship with Indonesia at all costs or at the expense of doing the right thing according to our own values' (Parliament of the Commonwealth of Australia, *Debates, House of Representatives*, 21 September 1999: 10029).

The East Timor experience also had a powerful impact on security perceptions both in Australia and in Indonesia. As has been noted, the 2000 Defence White Paper explicitly underlined the strategic primacy of Indonesia, and stated that Australia's security would be threatened by 'adverse developments' inside Indonesia, whether internally or externally generated (Department of Defence 2000: 22). This suggestion undoubtedly raised apprehensions regarding the possibility, however unlikely in reality, of some form of Australian 'intervention' in Indonesian affairs. Further, given Canberra's continuing security commitment to East Timor, Australia was now committed to the protection and development of a country the birth of which constituted Indonesia's greatest policy reversal in all of its history as a nation.

In this context it should be acknowledged that the message of the intervention for the wider Southeast Asian region was decidedly mixed. Some ASEAN states participated in the INTERFET operation, but there were also some expressions of dismay and distrust at what was presented as the humiliation of Indonesia and its armed forces by an external power (Cotton 2000). In retrospect, this shift in policy is in part testimony to the weaknesses and limitations of those multi-lateral institutions that had been the preferred mechanisms for the stabilization of regional order prior to the 1997 regional crisis. The Keating and Evans' legacy was thus largely discarded.

September 11, the Bali bombing and echoes of East Timor

Aside from the United Kingdom, Australia has been the most enthusiastic of the allies of the US in the war against terrorism. Australian troops served in Afghanistan and Australian naval units and aircraft were stationed in the Persian Gulf. Later, Australia participated directly in the Iraq war. While for a period this was a remote commitment, as the focus of the war shifted to other regions it became in part a contest on the nation's doorstep, impinging on relations with Indonesia and even involving East Timor.

The arrest of members of groups linked to al-Qaeda in Singapore and Malaysia, and evidence of al-Qaeda support for Abu Sayyaf in the Philippines drew the attention of US policy makers to Southeast Asia. Evidence of an al-Qaeda connection in Indonesia was identified, including the existence of a secret terrorist training camp in Sulawesi and funding for the fundamentalist Jemaah Islamiyah (JI), an organization committed to the creation of a pan-Islamic state in the archipelago. According to the Singapore government, the spiritual leader of this group was an Indonesian Islamic cleric and schoolmaster, Abu Bakar Ba'asyir (International Crisis Group 2002).

While it was difficult to determine the size and influence of this group, there are many militant Islamic organizations in Indonesia. For long the most prominent of these was Laskar Jihad, whose supporters openly collected funds on Jakarta's streets and whose volunteers traveled to Maluku to engage in the communal fighting there. The erstwhile leader of Laskar Jihad fought in Afghanistan in 1988 and 1989, studied in Pakistan, and admitted to receiving support from Islamic organizations abroad including Abu Sayyaf, though he denied ever having cooperated with al-Qaeda or Osama bin Laden. In 2002, Laskar Jihad was one of the organizations that became of concern to Washington.

US Deputy Secretary of Defense, Paul Wolfowitz, specifically criticized Indonesia for its lack of resolve in dealing with the terrorist issue. It is certainly true that the government did not speak with a consistent voice on the issue. No sooner did President Megawati Sukarnoputri return from her first meeting in Washington with President Bush where she endorsed the war against terrorism than her vice-president, Hamzah Haz, bitterly criticized US policy towards the Islamic world.

Whether the US assessment was correct or not, the prospect arose of some form of US pressure on the Indonesian government to participate more actively in the campaign against terrorism. And in dealing with Indonesia the US clearly expected and assumed close cooperation from Australia. However Indonesia was in the throes of a difficult and protracted process of democratization. Megawati came to power only after her predecessor was threatened with impeachment, her hold on the office was weak and her government – which was seeking to implement simultaneously a large number of reform measures – lacked capacity. Islamic parties continued to be a major part of the political landscape. They supported Megawati, whose political movement is mostly secular, but it was no secret that many of their members were unhappy that the country's leader was a woman. Cooperation with the US campaign might not only force her from power but could well further destabilize the political system. And if Australia was seen to be playing a role, this would create havoc in bilateral relations.

These developments provide the context for the visit of Prime Minister Howard to Jakarta in February 2002. Aside from the theatrics of the visit, its most substantive result was a memorandum of understanding on terrorism. The memorandum related specifically to intelligence sharing and cooperative efforts on international manifestations of terrorism. Though this may have been crafted to help the Indonesian government, it raised the prospect, in so far as it might relate to the activities of such groups as Laskar Jihad, of some role for Australia in Indonesia's 'internal affairs', the perennial bugbear of many Indonesian intellectuals. Further, in so far as the Indonesian side might regard separatists in Aceh, Papua and elsewhere as having connections with international terrorism, it might also entail requests from Jakarta to share intelligence on these organizations. In short, both developments might inflame those domestic publics concerned at the direction taken by the bilateral relationship. During the Howard visit the groundwork was laid for a regional conference on people smuggling convened in Bali and also for trilateral consultations with Indonesia and East Timor on economic and border questions. Once again the Timor issue was a major item on the agenda of Australia–Indonesia relations.

Initially, the Indonesian government was reluctant to take practical measures to assist in the campaign against terrorism. It was revealed in the US press that only pressure to suspend aid finally moved the Indonesian government to seek to locate and freeze the assets of terrorist suspects (*Asian Wall Street Journal* 2002a). It also emerged that the perpetrators of an aborted plot to bomb the US embassy in Jakarta were permitted to leave the country in July 2001, even though the Indonesian police had been advised of their activities. But members of the Bush administration later modified their view to suggest that the best way to achieve their anti-terrorist objectives in Indonesia was through the re-establishment of cooperation with the Indonesian military. However, such cooperation lay under Congressional interdiction as a result of the outrages of the Indonesian military in East Timor in 1999, and the failure (thus far) of the perpetrators to be brought to justice. Department of Defense officials then devoted their efforts to overcoming or circumventing this obstacle, including exploring the possibility of offering Indonesia counter-terrorism training under the provisions of the programme approved by Congress in December 2001. These efforts produced at least modest results, with some terrorist suspects being quietly transferred to US jurisdiction.

The terrorist bombing in Bali on 12 October 2002 in which 202 people were killed – 88 of them Australians – increased international pressure on the Indonesian government. The fact that three bombs were detonated simultaneously in Bali and one in Sulawesi (at the Philippine consulate in Menado) and that Australians were apparently targeted seemed to indicate that al-Qaeda was involved. However the Indonesian government only began to take measures to constrain the activities of JI after the United Nations took the decision to add the organization to its consolidated list of al-Qaeda-related terrorist entities. Ba'asyir was then detained for questioning by Indonesian police (a step urged on President Megawati by George Bush himself in mid-September), though initially on suspicion of connections with past sectarian violence (*Jakarta Post* 2002b). Later he was implicated in the Bali events. Even this cautious response received a mixed reaction from Muslim figures, who also expressed anxieties that new anti-terrorism legislation would be used to constrain critics of the government.

It is clear that in the period prior to the Bali bombing, the Australian government was in receipt of intelligence suggesting that Australian nationals or their property in Southeast Asia were potential targets for terrorist attack. In response to this intelligence the Australian diplomatic mission in Dili was closed for a week in September 2002, the building and other facilities were placed under armed guard, and some embassy staff members were repatriated. In December, there were riots in Dili which resulted in the deaths of two people and the destruction of a number of properties including the house of the prime minister. Though these events were apparently unconnected with regional terrorism, Australian-owned property, including a supermarket and a hotel, were looted and burned. Evidence emerged that former militia based in West Timor played a part in this incident. Shortly afterwards several armed bands infiltrated across the border, killing villagers and causing widespread alarm. There were claims that the individuals responsible, also former militia, were armed and trained by TNI officers (Jolliffe 2003). Foreign Minister José Ramos-Horta complained that the international security force of UNMISET (United Nations Mission of Support in East Timor – the successor to

UNTAET) was not sufficiently responsive to this threat and made a specific plea that Australian members of the force be mobilized to deal with it. This raised the prospect once again of a direct confrontation between Australian forces and elements of the TNI.

Just at the time when unprecedented cooperation with Indonesian police was yielding a surprising degree of success in identifying and arresting the Bali bombers, remarks by Prime Minister Howard on 1 December 2002 that Australia reserved the right to take pre-emptive action in the region to counter terrorist threats once again stirred apprehensions that Australia was seeking to control events in the region (Howard 2002; Baker 2002). In attempting to deal with these apprehensions, the foreign minister, Alexander Downer, though he stressed that pre-emption was very much a last resort would not rule out that expedient if it would save Australian lives (Downer 2002). This episode demonstrated just how far Australia's approach to the region had changed since 1997. While the context for these remarks was the Bali bombing, for some Southeast Asian audiences it was another item in a narrative that began with the Howard letter to Habibie of December 1998 regarding the future of East Timor. Nevertheless, it should not be forgotten that the personal and institutional linkages binding the two nations are complex and extensive (Hardjono 1992; Sulaiman *et al.* 1998) providing at least the potential for a more positive albeit more honest relationship.

Conclusions

By any conventional standards the Australian military strategy pursued during the East Timor intervention was a success. Security was rapidly established, there were only a handful of casualties and most of these the result of accidents rather than exchanges of fire, and the East Timorese population did not sustain any collateral damage. In occupation the security force developed good relations with the population, and transferred its responsibilities successfully to UNTAET. Though the civil and political record of UNTAET was decidedly varied in its degree of success, popular dissatisfaction with its slow progress in some areas did not prejudice the security situation. The territory was able to undertake a ballot to choose a constituent assembly in almost completely peaceful circumstances. The UN has now begun handing on security duties to its local counterparts in a generally cooperative atmosphere.

Given the reservations on the part of many nations regarding the UN's possible responsibilities as an agency of intervention (as can be seen in criticisms of even the modest proposals made in the Brahimi Report), international coalition strategies of the future may well adapt the approach taken in East Timor. As Alan Ryan has argued, for such a coalition strategy to be successful, the lead nation must be able to exercise strong control, command and intelligence systems must be effective, and a degree of regional cooperation is essential for coalition legitimacy (Ryan 2002). None of these measures will be sufficient, however, without a common peace enforcement doctrine, the evolution of which is currently on the global agenda (Thakur 2001). And Australia may well be more cautious in the future in participating in such coalitions, for though the East Timor exercise may be judged a success many perils were only narrowly avoided and the defence establishment was stretched to its limit to accomplish the task.

In the context of the debate on possible non-traditional roles of military forces, the East Timor case clearly illustrates the connection that may develop between participation in complex peace operations and dealing with new sources of trans-national violence. Australia's commitment to East Timor, which is likely to be long term, has arisen as a result of participation in a peace operation which is now at the phase where institutions are being constructed for the newly independent nation. As a result of poverty as well as of the social strains that resulted from the traumatic violence of 1999, East Timor will remain vulnerable to disorder and perhaps even state failure for some time to come. This vulnerability and lack of state capacity also renders East Timor open to the activities of trans-national terrorism, whether linked to dissident military personnel inside Indonesia or to fundamentalist militancy. In September 2002 (and prior to the Bali bombing), as a result of intelligence received of a possible terrorist plot, the Australian military mobilized members of its peace-keeping forces to guard civil and military facilities in Dili. In participating in the peace-building exercise in East Timor, the Australian military has also to prepare for the contingency, in the circumstances of the post-September 11 era, that its personnel and facilities in the country may become a target for international terrorism. In order to deal with the latter issue, Australia and East Timor in August 2003 entered into a counter-terrorism arrangement. In the new global environment, old and new security challenges to the regional order may thus be seen to coalesce. The Bali bombing is a striking example of this phenomenon.

8 Conclusion

Independent Timor-Leste in a regional and global context

The endpoint of the process begun with the momentous events of 1999 has been the creation of a new East Timorese state. It was formally recognized as independent on 20 May 2002 and admitted to the United Nations as the one hundred and ninety-first member on 27 September of the same year. It remains the East Timorese view that independence was actually achieved in 1975 (hence the constitution prescribes in Article 2 that the anniversary of independence falls on 28 November), albeit only acknowledged internationally in 2002. However this issue may be interpreted, it is a state deeply engaged with Australia and finding its way in the context of a still unsettled regional order. This final chapter seeks an overview of these events. It argues that the independence of East Timor (now officially Timor-Leste) can only be understood with reference to the conjunction of a range of national, regional and international narratives.

At first sight, it would appear that East Timor's trajectory from 1999 to the present can best be located within two narratives, one global and one regional. The first is the rise of interventionism on humanitarian grounds as a policy of the United Nations; the second is the re-evaluation of Australia's approach to the Southeast Asian region, in the aftermath of the Asian financial crisis and the lack of regional coherence manifest in the performance of ASEAN. While, as the analysis in earlier chapters has shown, these factors were undoubtedly important and even determining, their operation must nevertheless be seen in the context of the failure of the Indonesian policy of 'integration' and of the almost paradoxical tenacity over the past 25 years of the Luso-Timorese identity. This chapter therefore attempts to establish a more complete context for the recent political history of East Timor, paying particular attention to the contrast that emerges between regional and global forces and trends. To this end, an overview of the main arguments of this book will be set in a wider international and historical context in order to account for the specific trajectory taken by East Timor towards independence. In particular the UN, having functioned as the legitimizing agency for the expulsion of Indonesian authority, then found itself in the position of nation builder, with major consequences for the emerging political order.

East Timor as a Lusophone identity

For the purposes of this chapter, the first of the narratives to be considered will be the Lusophone. While Timor-Leste possesses a rich tradition of indigenous social and political identities (which indeed played a part in the formation of the FRETILIN government in 1999), it was only with the arrival of the Portuguese that the territory came to be conceived as a single entity. Though there had been a Portuguese presence in the Timor area since the middle of the sixteenth century, it cannot be said that the European impact left a sizeable footprint before the end of the nineteenth century (Boxer 1960). However the appearance of the Portuguese brought into being a creolized Luso-Timorese elite, the Topasses, who seem to have constituted the most powerful political force on the island through the seventeenth century and who dominated the most important commodity trade, the sandalwood trade. Visiting Lifau, then the chief Portuguese settlement in 1699, William Dampier found only three Portuguese in residence (Dampier 1981: 176). Having been forced to leave Lifau by a rebellion, the Portuguese re-established their capital in Dili in 1769. Writing in 1861, Alfred Russell Wallace observed that the Portuguese presence on the island was so small and the Portuguese officials so indolent that it could hardly be claimed that the territory was under colonial control:

> The Portuguese government in Timor is a most miserable one. Nobody seems to care the least about the improvement of the country, and . . . after three hundred years of occupation, there has not been a mile of road made beyond the town, and there is not a solitary European resident anywhere in the interior.
>
> (Wallace 1869, reprinted 1987: 151)

Only after suppressing a major rebellion in 1912, and following the delimitation of the border with Dutch West Timor after arbitration in 1913, did the writ of the Portuguese extend over the entirety of the territory. On the basis of field work conducted almost exactly a century after Wallace, David Hicks found that though the Portuguese had attempted to graft the very limited personnel in their administration on to local political structures, this syncretism had not been a success (Hicks 1983). According to post-war data, there were only some 568 Portuguese on the island, and a mere 1,541 of the inhabitants had become sufficiently acculturated as to be granted *civilizado* (assimilated) status (Saldanha 1994: 77). By this time it was estimated that perhaps 30 per cent of the population could be described as of the Catholic faith.

At the time it was widely believed that the Indonesian invasion of 1975 would terminate this tenuous narrative. By his own account the young José Ramos-Horta was an admirer of Indonesia as a successful post-colonial nation, and there were significant ethnic and economic ties between the western and eastern parts of the island. In the early days of the invasion the Indonesians were assisted by a fifth column, though many of its most prominent members soon deserted them. And

Portugal did little to defend its former colonial subjects, in 1986 coming very close to forming an arrangement with Indonesia to abandon altogether its residual international claims over the territory. Nevertheless, in international law, Portugal remained the *de jure* administering power, and support for Timorese refugees in Portugal in practice assisted the political resistance.

In Timor itself, the tenuous Lusophone-Catholic narrative was sustained by a most unlikely source. The cruelty and rapacity of Indonesian rule prevented the development, to any extent, of loyalty to the Republic or of belief in its symbols and ideology. On the other hand, the Catholic Church increasingly functioned as a community of cultural refuge and as the only sphere independent of Indonesian manipulation. And amongst the guerrilla independence movement, the use of Portuguese was retained as a badge of resistance. East Timor in 1999 was in some respects more receptive of Portuguese culture than was the case in 1974. It is a matter of debate amongst Indonesianists as to whether the military state of the early 'New Order' era could have crafted a different approach to 'integration' but there can be little dispute that the original plan for subversion and invasion was the product of military factional rivalries at Suharto's court (McDonald 1980: 189–215). Many of the personnel involved had earlier been responsible for the 'Act of Free Choice' in West Papua, whereby in 1969 the territory had been transferred to the Republic. Given these circumstances, a narrative of peaceful integration is hard to conceive.

International reactions to the invasion of East Timor

Due to the position taken by the United Nations from 1975, Indonesian claims to sovereignty over East Timor never received uncontested international consent. Since 1975 East Timor was in effect an international ward of the United Nations. Indonesia acquired East Timor as a result first of a policy of subversion and then through outright military conquest. As a result of internal disorder and policy paralysis in Lisbon, Portuguese administration was effectively in abeyance from 27 August 1975. The independence of the Democratic Republic of East Timor was declared on 28 November 1975, by which time the success of Indonesian border incursions had clearly signalled Jakarta's ultimate intentions. Dili was invaded directly from the sea and air on 7 December, this invasion violating important principles and usages in international law, a fact the UN could never thereafter completely ignore. In particular, the denial of the right of self-determination contradicted both a major recognized feature of international law as well as a crucial operating principle of the various organs of the United Nations.

The international reaction to the Indonesian invasion reflected these transgressions. In 1975 and again in the following year the UN Security Council demanded an immediate Indonesian withdrawal so that an appropriate act of self-determination could take place. However, these resolutions were to a large extent empty gestures, since the Security Council never provided for punitive measures should they be ignored. While 1976 was the last occasion before 1999 when the Security Council considered the East Timor issue, it was a matter on which the

General Assembly debated annually until 1982. Similarly in these debates the right of the East Timorese to self-determination was affirmed, though with the passage of time with diminishing enthusiasm (Ramos-Horta 1987: 125–58). Even when the Assembly abandoned the issue, it remained a responsibility of the Secretary-General who sought a solution under his 'Good Offices' powers. Therefore, East Timor never quite disappeared from the UN agenda, and accordingly a majority of UN members never recognized Indonesian sovereignty.

Despite this international opprobrium, until the end of the Cold War, Indonesia's military occupation of East Timor was sanctioned and sustained by the United States and its allies. In the post-Vietnam climate, US Asia policy was determined largely by the intention to contain Vietnam without becoming directly involved militarily in mainland Southeast Asia. Indonesia, under the 'market friendly' New Order, was perceived to be a reliable potential client in the region. This perception was undoubtedly encouraged by the similar Australian assessment of the Suharto regime. The Indonesian president had informed the US administration that he was contemplating an invasion of East Timor, and the invasion was further discussed during the Ford-Kissinger visit to Jakarta in December 1975 (National Security Archive 2002a). The US side expressed 'understanding' for Indonesian concerns regarding the apparent radicalism of the FRETILIN movement, by then the government, but there must have been an awareness that an Indonesian intervention would then make the country dependent diplomatically and militarily upon the US (Hitchens 2001: 90–107). Once the invasion occurred the administration circumvented Congressional censure to maintain the supply of weapons to the Indonesian military, and specialist munitions and equipment made the difference in the war against the FALINTIL guerrilla army (Budiardjo and Liem 1984). At the UN, American action ensured that Indonesia would escape any consequences for its actions, and this strategy was supported by key allies including Japan and the United Kingdom. This situation prevailed until the early 1990s, by which time the changing global situation began to elicit a reassessment of US interests.

In the post-Cold War environment, Indonesia's humanitarian and human rights record was frequently a matter of international scrutiny. Abuses of human rights in East Timor became increasingly important as humanitarian concerns moved to the centre of international diplomacy, largely as a result of events in Europe. UN attentions were rekindled by the Santa Cruz incident of 12 November 1991. Aid donors, including the Netherlands and Canada, withdrew their support, and the international media turned its attention to other forms of malfeasance by the Suharto regime. In concert with the Catholic Church and others, the UN arranged meetings abroad of various East Timorese in an effort to encourage reconciliation. In this context, José Ramos-Horta met Indonesian Foreign Minister Ali Alatas for the first time at the UN in 1995.

By contrast, as has been illustrated in Chapter 4, there was little regional pressure on Indonesia to account for its human rights performance in the territory. In 1993 the Bangkok meeting of Asian nations affirmed only a severely qualified commitment to human rights standards, with some Southeast Asian regimes as well as China expressing the view that a singular focus on this issue might provide a pretence for interference in their domestic affairs (Tang 1995). It is partly for this reason that the 'Asian values' discourse emerged at this time, ostensibly on the grounds that the values thus identified – community, harmony, respect for authority – were more consistent with the indigenous cultures of the region. With a human rights disaster developing in their midst, the regional countries' calculated avoidance of the issue of rights left their governments without the means to critique Indonesia's performance.

Lobby and interest groups focused on the East Timor issue (and overwhelmingly supportive of the independence movement) influenced decision makers in key nations and in international institutions. The second international narrative in which the East Timor story is embedded concerns the extensive support that the resistance cause secured from sources abroad. Especially in Portugal and Australia, lobby groups informed by refugee networks kept attention focused on the issue. In the Lusophone world, members of East Timor's political diaspora were given status and access to resources, with the FRETILIN mission in Mozambique being accorded diplomatic status. In the 1990s this lobby activity extended to groups in the United States, the United Kingdom, and also in the Netherlands, Ireland and Austria. The US-based East Timor Action Network was especially effective in influencing members of the Congress to sever US aid to the Indonesian military and in publicizing the complicity of previous administrations in Jakarta's policy of invasion and military occupation (East Timor Action Network 2000).

As the internet became increasingly available as a tool for policy advocacy the various East Timor lobbies effectively saturated this medium, and the Indonesian government made very little attempt to counter its influence. With the extension of email to Dili, resistance members were able to feed information to this network to further raise awareness of their cause (Hill 2002). When global attention shifted to East Timor in the early months of 1999, the resistance account of the issue commanded information sources.

The regional financial crisis, itself a consequence of global developments, rendered the government in Jakarta uniquely vulnerable to international pressure. As long as Indonesia remained the key state of the region, and was in the hands of a leadership resolute in its determination to 'integrate' East Timor, little movement could be expected on this issue. The regional financial crisis exposed the weakness of the régime, and the need for it to turn to the International Monetary Fund for emergency finance eventually opened the way for external leverage to be applied. The extent to which the crisis was a local as opposed to an international narrative is disputed (Noble and Ravenhill 2000: 1–35; Winters 1999: 79–97), but it would not have occurred without the globalization of communications and financial flows. With the fall of Suharto, the logjam was broken.

Under international pressure, and now in the hands of a transitional political leadership of doubtful credibility, Jakarta was forced to turn to the UN for the negotiation of new arrangements for the increasingly restive territory. For their part, the East Timorese resistance responded to the Indonesian loss of nerve with renewed vigour, convening free speech meetings in the major centres which the security forces found difficult to constrain (Gunn 2000a). Once its future political disposition passed again to the forefront of the UN agenda and was thus internationalized, its past history could no longer be ignored.

Action according to the principle of humanitarian intervention, increasingly a norm of international society in the 1990s, then became a possibility. A third international narrative which had a vital bearing on the East Timor issue was the shift in international norms of sovereignty in the post-Cold War era. From its inception through to the early 1990s, the United Nations had affirmed the inviolability of state sovereignty save in circumstances where the actions of a state actor undermined global peace and security. Thus Indian intervention in East Pakistan, though it was a response to a major humanitarian and human rights catastrophe, was only saved from Security Council sanction by a Soviet veto. The grounds for a more expansive definition of security were laid in the 1980s, with the rise of human rights as a standard in the behaviour of states, both through the operations of the Conference on Security and Cooperation in Europe (CSCE), as well as by the extension and strengthening of the global human rights regime. From the crisis in Kurdish Iraq through Somalia to Rwanda, and facilitated by the end of the Cold War immobilism of the Security Council, humanitarian disasters then became recognized as grounds for intervention in the domestic affairs of states. Though there were other stated grounds for the intervention, humanitarian considerations were an integral element in the decision to authorize the insertion of INTERFET. UN Security Council Resolution 164/1999 noted the 'worsening humanitarian situation in East Timor' and expressed concern at reports of extensive human rights violations. Accordingly, it referred to the need to punish those responsible for such violations.

A further element in this narrative should be noted. The Security Council turned its attention to the East Timor issue shortly after considering the NATO intervention in Kosovo. The latter had entailed a debate in which, while the intervention had not been directly legitimated, nations unsure of the grounds for humanitarian intervention in this instance had nevertheless refrained from censuring it. As Peter van Walsum, the Security Council president at the time has argued, most nations considered that in the light of public opinion and of the Indonesian-led harassment of UNAMET, intervention was well nigh inevitable. For the Council to have failed, once again, to endorse an intervention might have so damaged the principle of state sovereignty as to open the way to major problems in the future (van Walsum 2002). For this reason, status quo states that otherwise might have sought to preserve Indonesian 'sovereignty' were therefore induced to support the intervention coalition. This is a further instance of specifically global developments having a powerful impact in East Timor.

Meanwhile the dominant image of East Timor was framed around Max Stahl's depiction of the 1991 Santa Cruz massacre. In an increasingly interconnected world, images have taken on vastly increased power. If there was one single image of East Timor that became definitive, it derived from Max Stahl's video of demonstrators being deliberately killed by the Indonesian military in the grounds of the Santa Cruz cemetery in 1991. There had been many other such incidents, but none had been recorded in this way. These images in their original form, and later used in a well-publicized film by John Pilger, became the most common images in the global awareness of East Timor. Others present at this incident were able to use these images to reinforce testimony given before the US Congress which was instrumental in persuading Congress to prohibit any further training of Indonesian military officers in the US through the official aid budget. Especially after the award of the 1996 Nobel Peace Prize jointly to Bishop Belo and José Ramos-Horta, this awareness fuelled a demand for intervention that was eventually realized in 1999.

The role of the resistance coalition

The resistance coalition, their status rooted in the brief experience of independence in 1975, were accorded the role in international discourse of chief articulators of legitimate East Timorese aspirations. The independence regime of 1975 had been exclusively a FRETILIN affair. The other major domestic political force, the UDT, had been defeated and expelled after a brief civil conflict in August. Some of its leaders then served the Indonesians, but others chose exile. Mari Alkatiri, Minister of State for Political Affairs in the independent government of 1975 and now prime minister, had conducted a diplomatic tour of Africa in November that had secured promises from a number of states for recognition once independence was declared (Dunn 1983: 274). FRETILIN's ideological and programmatic kinship with the Afro-Marxist FRELIMO in Mozambique was clear to all at the time (Hill 2002: 70–83). Independence was FRETILIN's key objective, and the symbols of independence, including the national flag and anthem, were those of the movement.

In the years following the Indonesian invasion, FRETILIN slowly transformed itself from a Marxist-Leninist resistance movement to the chief member of a broad national resistance coalition (Niner 2001: 15–30). The invasion radicalized the movement, and when it was reorganized in 1981 it took the name CRRN (*Conselho Revolucionária da Resistência Nacional*) and proclaimed itself as the exclusive representative of the East Timorese people. Fighting in the field under Xanana Gusmão, however, the local leadership soon recognized the need for cooperation with any elements favourable to the resistance, and contacts were initiated with UDT supporters at home and abroad. In 1987 Xanana resigned from FRETILIN and reorganized FALINTIL as a non-party resistance army, forming the CNRM (*Conselho Nacional da Resistência Maubere*) in an attempt to involve individuals outside the party. By 1989 these changes had been accepted by elites in the diaspora, and nationalism replaced the amalgam of Marxism, Afro-socialism and other ideas that had been the movement's ideology. The final act in this transition occurred in 1998 when the UDT in exile (in company with some other groups) formally entered the movement, now renamed the CNRT (*Conselho Nacional da Resistência Timorense*).

Despite this inclusive strategy, FRETILIN remained the mainstream of the independence movement. It retained its distinctive leftist approach and its most prominent members were individuals who had spent the years since 1975 in exile, often in Mozambique. Though from the late 1980s members of the 'clandestine resistance', mostly young students, bore the brunt of the resistance effort, the moral leadership of FRETILIN was not disputed (Pinto and Jardine 1997). Thus when circumstances finally permitted the East Timorese to exercise an independent political role, FRETILIN was poised within the CNRT to play the dominant part.

The Southeast Asian region and Australia

Against these various international trends, regional states, as has been shown, took no interest in the security dimensions of the Timor issue, though they were compelled to make a contribution as the momentum for international intervention grew in 1999. Variously described as a security community or a diplomatic community, the ASEAN organization has been a major component of regional order since its inception. From 1975 until the UNAMET ballot, ASEAN, in solidarity with Jakarta, took no steps to resolve the East Timor issue, despite the fact that the Indonesian invasion violated the group's espoused norms, including the pacific settlement of disputes and respect for sovereignty. At various times the governments of regional states actively obstructed the activities of their own citizens where these were intended to support the independence movement in the territory. This was the context for ASEAN's poor response to the crisis of 1999 (Inbaraj 1995). Only when the intervention received international legitimation did Thailand and the Philippines agree to contribute substantial numbers of troops, though on condition that they would not become combatants.

In the absence of a regional response to the crisis, INTERFET became an exercise dominated by Australia. East Timor's transition to independence would not have occurred without the commitment of the Australian government to lead an intervention force provided by a 'coalition of the willing'. This commitment reversed a quarter of a century of support for Indonesia, and can be interpreted as a consequence both of international as well as of domestic dynamics.

It has been argued in the chapters of this book that the decision of the Australian government first to volunteer forces for an international intervention in East Timor and then to assume the role of lead nation in a United Nations sanctioned 'coalition of the willing' was in sharp contrast to past Australian policy on the territory and also to its previous approach to regional diplomacy. For 20 years successive Australian governments had been uncritical supporters of the Indonesian policy of 'integration', and good bilateral relations with Jakarta were regarded as essential to the nation's security. In the early 1990s, even at a time when outside of Southeast Asia Indonesia was widely condemned for its handling of the East Timor issue, Australia's military cooperation with Indonesia developed and deepened. Despite the presence of a vociferous East Timor lobby, until 1997 the major political parties were in agreement that East Timor was off the foreign policy agenda.

The reasons for the change of policy in 1998–99 have been a major concern of this book. The initial focus on East Timor was as a result of President Habibie's announcement that a new approach would be taken towards the issue, which induced the EU countries, the US and the UN all to examine the problem anew. The involvement of the UN was especially important. Without the engagement of these major international actors, the Australian government would not have made its preference known for a negotiated solution to the East Timor issue. The commitment of personnel and funding to the UNAMET exercise gave Australia a major stake in its success. Retrieving the situation after the post-ballot mayhem became a major priority for the government, with public opinion supporting the most uncompromising action. Nevertheless, formal Indonesian assent was a necessary requirement. This was granted undoubtedly because of Indonesia's dependence at the time upon international financial assistance which determined the Jakarta government's particular receptivity to the warning delivered by President Clinton on the eve of the Auckland meeting of APEC.

The absence of an ASEAN response to the issue was interpreted by Australian policy makers as a sign of major deficiencies in the regional order. Accordingly, Australia has moved away from the strategy of regional 'engagement' back towards reliance upon its traditional security alliances, a trend accelerated by the events associated with September 11 (Cotton and Ravenhill 1997b, 2002: 3–9). It can also be argued that, to the extent therefore that the government was able to enjoy electoral advantage from pursuing a course of action distinct from the 'engagement' approach of its predecessor, the intervention may also have been partly impelled by calculations of partisan advantage.

The United Nations as state builder

Such were the factors that contributed to East Timor's eventual independence. But the particular shape taken by the emergent independent polity is only intelligible with reference to the United Nations, its character and its limitations. From October 1999, the United Nations acted as a midwife to the new state. While UN rhetoric was dominated by notions of participation and inclusivity, in the event its procedures privileged a particular group of East Timorese interlocutors while simultaneously obstructing grassroots opinion from assuming a significant voice. At the same time, the new administrators of the territory faced immense difficulties in locating East Timorese with sufficient skills to participate in the state building exercise.

The task of the UNAMET mission was to register the opinion of the East Timorese regarding their political future. With an exceedingly tight schedule – imposed by Indonesia's constitutional timetable – the inhabitants were to be given the choice of accepting or rejecting 'autonomy', the implied consequence of the latter option being independence. In an electorate in the countryside largely illiterate, the UN was required to nominate a visual symbol for the second option to place on the ballot paper. The symbol chosen was the CNRT flag, with the alternative to continued membership of Indonesia being thus presented as the narrative of the guerrilla resistance (East Timor Elections 2001). Attempts at convening 'third forces' were not successful, and Xanana Gusmão became the acknowledged figurehead of East Timor's independent future. Although the CNRT could hardly campaign openly – its premises in Dili being trashed and its public leadership pursued into hiding – the extent of the popular following for the cause it represented became clear with the 78.5 per cent vote (from a 98 per cent turnout) for independence in the August ballot (Fox 2000).

The international intervention that was organized in response to the mayhem that then occurred was designed to restore security and provide humanitarian relief. Civil authority was left in abeyance, and even those limited civil tasks that were discharged by INTERFET – including the identification and detention of militias and the forensic examination of apparent crime scenes – proceeded according to ad hoc arrangements. For a period of several weeks East Timor was not only without the apparatus of a state but also without its juridical foundation, given Indonesia's disputed original title. In effect, the INTERFET commander was an interim de facto head of state. With the formal abandonment on 25 October of any claims to Indonesian sovereignty, UNTAET was mandated to assume authority for the territory and manage its transition to full independence, although in practice INTERFET (assisted at this stage by a CIVPOL contingent) continued to exercise administrative authority in some regions.

Some members of UNAMET who remained in the region were re-assigned to the new administration, but its senior core, led by the Special Representative of the Secretary-General, Sergio Vieira de Mello, were veterans of the Kosovo occupation. Though there were some parallels in the UN roles in Eastern Slavonia and in Kosovo (and to some extent earlier in Cambodia), the challenges posed for the UN in East Timor were unique, since never before had responsibility been assumed to create a state from *terra nullius*. In East Timor the UN then wielded all legislative, executive and judicial power, while in Kosovo there was the acceptance of the fiction of residual Yugoslavian/Serbian sovereignty (Kondoch 2001).

By some standards, UNTAET was successful in the discharge of its mandate, with major civil disorder avoided, the foundations for a legal and administrative system established, and elections for a founding government conducted without incident. Despite the singular efforts of UN staff and volunteers in some of the districts, it was somewhat less successful in rehabilitating the infrastructure, re-establishing industry or dealing with the serious crimes of 1999. However, the transitional strategy adopted by the authority certainly had a profound impact on the shape of the emerging political system and especially on the fortunes of FRETILIN.

As many critics of UNTAET's administration have argued, de Mello was very slow to incorporate the East Timorese into the workings of his government (Beauvais 2001; Gorjão 2002). The model of administration brought to East Timor which derived from the UN DPKO was both centralized and bureaucratic. While the mission was still in the planning stages, an attempt by the CNRT to involve Timorese in its leadership was ignored (Suhrke 2001: 9–10). According to Jarat Chopra (who spent a period as a member of UNTAET), the fate of the system of district administration was indicative of the centralizing and hierarchical approach of the UNTAET leadership. Rather than respond to the breakdown of authority by rapidly dispatching (as had originally been planned) adequately supported district administrators to the countryside, UN volunteers, many of them formerly members of UNAMET, were designated as interim field officers, and though sometimes charged with considerable responsibilities were provided with quite inadequate resources. The first priority was given to the concentration of personnel in the capital, as is illustrated by the fact that in January 2000, while there were 174 professional officers in Dili, there were only 17 in the districts (Chopra 2002: 985–8). Ministries established in the capital then appropriated line authority for most local activities, thus severely limiting the role of district administrators. While it was envisaged that a district council (later designated a District Advisory Council) would be convened in each locality to permit the local community to exercise initiative, the announcement that such bodies would be constituted was not made until April, by which time resistance networks were in charge at the grassroots. Similarly, the UN administration strenuously resisted the implementation of the World Bank's US$35 million Community Empowerment Program because it would not be in a position to control the disbursement of the funds or the local bodies that would be formed to decide where money would be expended (Chopra 2000: 30–1).

Nevertheless, de Mello recognized that his mission required a link with the Timorese to legitimate its role. His strategy was to construct that link directly with his own office, partly on the grounds that the UN should maintain 'neutrality' regarding the contending political forces within the country. He cultivated a personal relationship with Gusmão, and in December 1999 established a 15-member National Consultative Council (NCC). Eleven of the membership were Timorese, of which the seven CNRT members were by far the most important. Three places (one of which remained vacant) were reserved for non-CNRT parties, which in the East Timor context meant that they had been former supporters of integration (United Nations 2000). The NCC's role was solely advisory, and within a few months even de Mello admitted that it did not sufficiently address East Timorese demands for participation. The NCC was then replaced in July 2000 with a 33-member National Council (ETNC), later expanded to 36. This was an exclusively East Timorese affair, with the largest group from the CNRT (ultimately ten members) and representatives drawn from various functional groups in the society. At the same time a 'Cabinet of the Transitional Government' (UNTAET 2000) was formed, with four of its members being East Timorese. In addition, an 'East Timor Transitional Administration' (ETTA) was established and the recruitment began of Timorese to staff it.

The institutions constituted in the July reform exercised only such powers as the SRSG cared to grant to them, and he retained ultimate legislative and executive authority. Gusmão was elected chair of the ETNC and the Timorese in the first Cabinet were Mari Alkatiri (Economic Affairs), Ana Pessoa (Internal Administration), Filomeno Jacob (Social Affairs) and João Carrascalão (Infrastructure). The Cabinet was expanded in October when Ramos-Horta became responsible for Foreign Affairs. Of these individuals, Alkatiri and Pessoa were leaders of FRETILIN from the political diaspora, Carrascalão the leader of the UDT, and Jacob a non-partisan member of the priesthood.

As was clear even in 1999, the CNRT was a body only given unity by its resistance to the Indonesian occupation. By mid-2000 the tensions between its constituent parts were plainly in evidence, and within months after its August conference it effectively ceased to exist. As the party most closely associated with the symbols and narrative of the guerrilla resistance, FRETILIN then emerged as the most important. The manner and character of UNTAET's discharge of its responsibilities became enmeshed in the emerging partisan political struggle, and when the Timorese members of the Cabinet threatened to resign in December 2000 on the grounds that most of the administration's funds and efforts seemed to be devoted to attending to the needs of the international staff, de Mello's priorities shifted to developing a 'transition timetable' for independence. In effect this required the creation of legitimate – that is, elected – East Timorese political institutions which in turn required the drafting of a constitution.

The process of drafting a constitution – an essential act in the establishment of state legitimacy – presented the UN with a major choice. It was well known that FRETILIN had already prepared a draft constitution which it expected to adopt once it assumed state power. This document was based on the constitution of Portugal, modified to an extent by the usage of Mozambique. It incorporated the position of a largely ceremonial presidency, with effective executive power being wielded by a prime minister chosen by majority vote of the legislature. It should have been clear to all – it was certainly apparent to the leadership of FRETILIN – that such a constitution would produce a FRETILIN government. The over-whelming popularity of Xanana Gusmão would make him the favourite candidate for head of state, but in this largely dignified role and having abandoned party affiliation, his effective power would be inconsiderable. He would still, of course, exercise considerable moral authority. Who, then, would lead the government? In terms of party seniority and international profile, Alkatiri's only real rival was Ramos-Horta, but he too had withdrawn from party affairs and in any case evinced no interest in exercising power. The party's senior leadership structures were dominated by a group of cadres many of whom had spent the Indonesian period in Mozambique, working in coalition with several prominent members of the guerrilla resistance, notably Lu'Olo (Francisco Guterres). When FRETILIN emerged from the constraints of the CNRT alliance, they chose the most senior member of the Mozambique group, Mari Alkatiri, as leader. A Portuguese-style constitution would thus inevitably deliver an Alkatiri government in which the diaspora would be the most important element.

Differences between Gusmão and Alkatiri go back to the 1980s, when Gusmão was endeavouring to build a broad nationalist front while many in the diaspora leadership of FRETILIN, including Alkatiri (then in Mozambique), were initially disinclined to abandon their ideological dominance of the resistance (Shoesmith 2003). While Gusmão's emphasis, given the immensity of the tasks confronting the new nation, was upon the need to promote unity, Alkatiri was more inclined to apply zero-sum and party political calculations to the construction of the political order. These contrasting perspectives were apparent to any casual observer and should have been a major consideration in de Mello's calculations.

UNTAET's strategy for the formation of the constitution was to entrust the task to a constituent assembly, to be elected in August 2001. This decision was taken in a context now dominated by partisan political differences. The CNRT was formally dissolved in June 2001, and shortly afterwards 16 political parties registered with the Independent Electoral Commission in order to contest the coming elections. The choice to elect a constituent assembly was made in the knowledge that this body would be dominated by FRETILIN with the party's by now fixed views of the outcome. It was also thought to be likely that the assembly would then exercise the option to reconstitute its membership as the new legislature, delivering office immediately to FRETILIN. At this point there were several schemes for involving the Timorese at the local level in the construction of the new political order. A commission was organized to convene meetings in the districts to consider constitutional issues, but this process did not lead to the drafting of a document. The campaign for the election was generally peaceful, but Alkatiri's statement that he would 'sweep the ground clean' after FRETILIN was victorious was far too redolent of the threats made by the militias in 1999. When disgraced former defence minister, Rogerio Lobato, reappeared in FRETILIN senior ranks (he had spent some years in prison in Angola for gem smuggling) there were concerns that this would open the way for corruption and malfeasance.

Following the election, FRETILIN's numbers – 55 of the 88 seats, and 55.37 per cent of the vote – fell just short of the number of votes required in the new Assembly (60) to pass the constitution (East Timor Elections 2001). With the support of the six elected members of the ASDT (the party of the first president, Xavier do Amaral), however, Alkatiri and his followers enjoyed a free hand. Despite the presence of a number of international advisers who pointed out ambiguities in the proposed document (including lack of clarity on the command of the armed forces) the Portugal/Mozambique model was adopted with few changes. When the draft was eventually completed, a 'socialization' exercise was then held to explain the contents to the population rather than to elicit suggestions for alterations.

There can be no disputing Mozambique's enormous assistance to the Timorese resistance in the past. However its development was dogged by the struggle between FRELIMO and the externally-supported RENAMO organization, which both exhausted the country and its population, and also stimulated the most doctrinaire trends in the governing movement. These events must have constituted a considerable influence upon the East Timorese then in residence, including Alkatiri. In the 1990s, the economy of Mozambique had been reshaped by the IMF/World Bank and its political system reconstituted after significant United Nations involvement (Newitt 2002). But with still immense problems of development and governance, it is surely problematic as a useful model for a state coming into existence in the twenty-first century.

With the narrative of independence now firmly in the hands of the émigré Mozambique faction, they emerged as the legitimized leaders of the state through the election exit-strategy prescribed by United Nations processes. Did the UN administration have any alternative except to endorse the FRETILIN machine under the control of the diaspora? In the later years of the Indonesian period, FRETILIN established a parallel local administration that seems to have enjoyed considerable popular loyalty. In the cities of Dili and Baucau a 'clandestine resistance' of student activists, also including East Timorese members of the civil service, supported the guerrilla forces with intelligence and resources, and skilfully mobilized to protest Indonesian rule. Though these organizations were disrupted by the events of September 1999 they were re-constituted to a considerable extent by 2000. The resources and influence of these indigenous political forces would have been augmented had the UN chosen to devolve power and finance to the districts as indeed some were urging it to do in the early part of that year. This may have tipped the balance against the diaspora politicians, who might well then have been forced to share power in the government of the emergent state. However, given the character of the indigenous political culture, it would probably have been unrealistic to expect a genuinely competitive politics to have emerged at this stage (Hohe 2002a, 2002b).

After the August elections, under pressure from de Mello, a coalition of a kind was negotiated between FRETILIN and the PD (*Partido Demokrático*) – the latter the political movement that was most associated with the former clandestine resistance – to form a transitional administration, with Alkatiri as chief minister. But the partnership was, at this late stage, most unequal. On independence the PD were given no role and FRETILIN alone occupied government, albeit in the company of some 'independent' figures, most of whom (including José Ramos-Horta and Roque Rodrigues) had long been associated with the party. Meanwhile, Gusmão had been elected to the presidency, though not without tensions between him and the party leadership coming out into the open.

In retrospect, UNTAET's calculations are quite comprehensible if understood within their full context. The East Timorese were not in any important sense the constituency of the mission. Rather, it was most responsive, as Astri Suhrke (2001) has argued, to the bureaucratic and consensus based procedures of the United Nations (a significant number of the member states of which are, of course, not democracies) and constructed according to the logic of peace-keeping and to an extent of humanitarian relief. Responsibilities for sustainable development and governance both required active East Timorese participation, but a bureaucratic and consensus based mechanism is not attuned to dealing with an inevitably politicized population and is also, for the most part, unlikely to cede its powers to the local inhabitants, such a transfer being necessary if these tasks are to be accomplished. These priorities are reflected in the crude statistics of the UNTAET mission. The total UNTAET budget for FY 2001 was $563 million, around ten times that of the budget of the government of Timor-Leste at independence. The biggest single item of expenditure was staff and related costs, but less than 1 per cent of the budget was spent on East Timorese staff. Four million dollars alone was spent on providing bottled water (imported from Indonesia) to all staff members (La'o Hamutuk 2001), money that would have been quite sufficient to restore Dili's sabotaged water supply. After exerting considerable patience, many East Timorese began to wonder whether UNTAET existed for their benefit or for purposes of its own. It is for these reasons that the exit strategy became the main preoccupation of the mission in the final year of its operations.

Despite the support promised by donor countries for the new nation, East Timor was nevertheless bound to be dependent upon international capital. East Timor's emerging leadership embraced, as a result, techniques for engagement with the regional and international economy which were in accordance with recognized international development strategies and consistent with the preferences of such major economic partners as Australia.

East Timor's economic predicament, being one of the poorest less-developed countries with little industry and a major unemployment problem, offers its leaders little room to manoeuvre. Given even modest government programmes and a civil service considerably smaller than existed in the Indonesian period, in its first year of operation the Timor-Leste government was only able to fund around three-quarters of its US\$77 million budget from its own revenues and from past international assistance. International aid provided the balance, and this pattern must continue or poverty and attendant social unrest will be the lot of the population. The proportion of aid needed to balance the budget is expected to rise in coming years. Whether by managing the funds of donors, or whether by being a source of development loans, the World Bank will undoubtedly exert a very strong influence upon East Timor's economic policies (La'o Hamutuk 2002a). Already the World Bank played a major role in drafting the initial 'National Development Plan' for East Timor. Of course the Bank is unlikely to support any activities contrary to the Washington consensus.

Longer term, perhaps within six years, East Timor could secure sufficient oil revenues not only to balance its budget but even to enjoy a modest surplus. This is to assume, however, the disposition of the oil resources shared with Australia in the 'Timor Gap' having been definitively established, that major oil and gas companies will invest the capital necessary to land those resources. This is unlikely without, again, a government committed to market consistent policies, including a functioning legal system. It is pressures such as these that have forced a leadership not yet completely divorced from its Marxist origins to signal its commitment to the market. This embrace of globalization, however, did not occur without tensions and struggles and is far from resolved. At the time of the August elections and later at independence, the PST (*Partido Socialista de Timor*) was the only party to espouse an explicitly anti-globalization platform, but elements of this position are popular amongst East Timorese intellectuals. During the transition to independence, even Alkatiri himself became associated with a move to renegotiate the whole Timor Gap agreement, despite the uncertain investment climate that would have been the consequence (Hill and Saldanha 2001; Aditjondro 2001; World Bank 2002). East Timor's status in the narrative of globalization is not completely assured.

The stability of the new political order

Timor-Leste's elite settlement is far from stable. Divisions within the political class along with government incapacity are already threatening public order. Before even a year of independence had elapsed, East Timor's government, brought to power in the manner described above, experienced a crisis of expectations. President Gusmão complained openly of the lack of application of cabinet members and parliamentarians to the immense national challenges. The East Timor international donors conference met on 10 December 2002 in the aftermath of demonstrations in Dili that saw two demonstrators killed and property, including the prime minister's house and an Australian-owned store and guesthouse, destroyed.

Accounts of these events varied, with many analysts pointing to the prevalence of youth unemployment especially in the capital, and also to the unpopularity of the police force, given the fact that some of its members were formerly employed by the Indonesian police prior to 1999. The seriousness of the unemployment problem cannot be overstated, but in this respect East Timor resembles other underdeveloped nations with high birth rates and very little industry. The particular restiveness of East Timor's youth can be attributed both to the legacy of UNTAET and the immobilism of East Timorese politics.

Many East Timorese came to observe and perhaps also to envy the first world lifestyle of UNTAET's numerous international personnel, the bulk of them concentrated in the capital. As has been argued, UNTAET's leadership was slow to address many of the problems left by the departing militias, initially administering the territory without directly involving Timorese personnel and spending lavishly on their own personnel while failing to reconstruct much of the infrastructure damaged or destroyed in 1999. The contrast between the UN lifestyle in Dili and the difficulties and discomforts experienced by the UN volunteers in the provinces must have been a further puzzling contrast. Belatedly recognizing the contribution of FALINTIL, the armed wing of the resistance, UNTAET then oversaw the creation of a well-provisioned Timorese national military force where member-ship was attained on the basis of non-transparent criteria. It is widely believed that the core of the new military are Gusmão loyalists, which some other members of the elite are attempting to counter by resourcing and supporting members of the police force. Demonstrations by disgruntled guerrilla veterans became a feature of life in Dili in 2002, adding to the sense of dissatisfaction with the government. There were also clashes between military personnel and police.

The Timorese became frustrated by the lack of resolve shown by their own leadership. Since independence in May 2002, the new government had been slow to deal with the many challenges facing the new nation. As has been noted, the most influential members of the cabinet are members of a group who spent the years since 1975 not in the resistance but abroad. Their ability to inspire and mobilize the East Timorese remains in doubt. The decision to impose Portuguese as the official language of East Timor was particularly unpopular, given the fact that few under the age of 50 speak it, and many of the *Bahasa Indonesia*-speaking youth consider that their sacrifices were crucial in forcing the Indonesian occupiers to accept an international ballot. Despite a clear majority for the ruling FRETILIN party, the effectiveness of the parliament was in dispute, taking a month break from its work in 2002 and failing to pass much needed legislation. There is no doubt that some individuals formerly members of the pro-Indonesian militias played a part in the violence of late 2002. However, the fact that demonstrators could be so easily mobilized and foreign property be targeted in their activities was a sign of the extent of popular dissatisfaction.

And there were other inchoate forces whose integration into the political structures of 2002 remained in doubt. In the Bacau region, the most organized of the groups of former independence guerrillas, the *Sagrada Família*, led by Cornelio Gama (usually known by his FALINTIL codename 'L-7'), espoused an idio-syncratic ideology of social justice and Timorese traditional beliefs. In an echo of the Southeast Asian past, a movement with the same name, informed by both Catholic and pre-Christian redemptionism, was amongst those popular millennial groups that disputed Spanish rule and ultimately contributed to the Katipunan independence revolt of 1896 in the Philippines (Ileto 1979: 37–92). In the border area the new government faced a challenge from an armed millennial group, Colimau 2000. The context for millenarianism in East Timor has not been sufficiently studied, but it may be conjectured that just as the sudden arrival (and abrupt departure) in other Austronesian societies of foreigners in possession of seemingly inexhaustible resources stimulated the formation of 'cargo' cults, some of which espoused quite specific political programmes (Worsley 1970), so something of the same processes may have been at work in East Timor. After there were reports that this movement and former militias were making common cause, a number of its members were arrested and detained by the government, though with doubtful legality. In short, an extremely diverse collection of political and social outlooks will have to be accommodated in the new republic if it is to achieve some measure of stability. The most important task remains to establish a connection between rural society on the one hand, and the diaspora elites and the Indonesian-influenced generation in the cities on the other. Without such a connection, the new state will be vulnerable to the kind of destabilizing forces in evidence in post-independence Papua New Guinea and the Solomon Islands. The Dili government also faces challenges from without, as has been noted in the previous chapter.

Conclusions

The particular circumstances of East Timor's political independence are the consequence of a conjunction of sometimes unlikely developments. In assessing their respective impacts, it is a striking fact that while East Timorese political independence is partly to be attributed to changing global narratives, even as late as September 1999 there was very little support within the Southeast Asian region for this trend. Timor-Leste is now seeking membership of ASEAN, and its everyday economy is reintegrating with that of Indonesia, but the character of its future development is very much dependent upon global capital and its institutions. At the very least, this pattern appears to indicate the limitations of Southeast Asian as opposed to global sources of regional order. On the other hand, Australian support and sponsorship have been an irreducible element in the independence narrative, to an extent reshaping if not also fracturing that order in the process.

References

References on East Timor

There is a very full bibliography (to 1995) in Carey and Bentley. This also contains an extremely useful chronology by John Taylor.

Bibliographical guides to materials on East Timor
Rowland, Ian (1992) *Timor. World Bibliographical Series vol. 142*, Oxford: Clio Press.
Sherlock, Kevin (1980) *A Bibliography of Timor*, Canberra: The Australian National University, RSPacS Aids to Research A/4.
Berlie, Jean A. (2001) *East Timor. A Bibliography*, Paris: Les Indes Savantes.

The most comprehensive *atlas* on East Timor is:
Durand, Frédéric (2002) *Timor Lorosa'e. Pays au carrefour de l'Asie et du Pacifique*, Bangkok: IRASEC.

Works on East Timor

Aarons, Mark and Domm, Robert (1992) *East Timor. A Western Made Tragedy*, Sydney: Left Book Club.
ABC (2000) 'Timor papers reveal Australia's dark secret', *7.30 Report*, 12 September. <http://www.abc.net.au/7.30/s175297.htm>
ABIX (Australia Business Intelligence) (2003) 'Government in secret Timor gas deal', *The Age*, 10 March.
Aditjondro, George (1994) *In the Shadow of Mount Ramelau: An Indonesian Intellectual Speaks Out*, Leiden: INDOC.
—— (1999a) *Is Oil Thicker Than Blood? A Study of Oil Companies' Interests and Western Complicity in Indonesia's Annexation of East Timor*, Commack, New York: Nova Science.
—— (1999b) 'East Timor. ABRI inc.', *Sydney Morning Herald*, 10 May: 13.
—— (2000a) 'Mapping the political terrain', *Arena Magazine*, April–May: 27–36.
—— (2000b) 'From colony to global prize', *Arena Magazine*, June–July: 22–32.
—— (2001) *Timor Lorosa'e on the Crossroad*, Jakarta: Center for Democracy and Social Justice Studies.
Alatas, Ali (1999) 'Ali Alatas looks back on 11 years of Indonesia's foreign policy', *Jakarta Post*, Jakarta, 2 November.
Amnesty International (2001) *East Timor: Justice Past, Present and Future*, London: Amnesty International, Report ASA 57/001/2001, July.
Anwar, Dewi Fortuna (2000) 'The East Timor crisis: an Indonesian view', in Bruce Brown

(ed.) *East Timor – The Consequences*, Wellington: New Zealand Institute of International Affairs, 18–24.

Archer, Robert (1995) 'The Catholic Church in East Timor', in Peter Carey and G. Carter Bentley (eds) *East Timor at the Crossroads: The Forging of a Nation*, London: Cassell, 120–33.

Arndt, Heinz (1979) 'Timor: vendetta against Indonesia', *Quadrant*, 23, December: 13–17.

Asian Development Bank, Trust Fund for East Timor (2000) *East Timor Rehabilitation and Development, Progress Report*, Manila: ADB.

Aubrey, Jim (ed.) *Free East Timor: Australia's Culpability in East Timor's Genocide*, Sydney: Vintage.

Ausaid (2001) *East Timor Update*, 17 January, AUSAID, Canberra.

Australian National Audit Office (2002) *Management of Australian Defence Force Deployments to East Timor*, Canberra: The Auditor-General Audit Report no. 38.

Australian Treaty Series (2000) 'Exchange of notes constituting an agreement between the government of Australia and UNTAET':
<www.austlii.edu.au/au/other/dfat/treaties/2000/9.html>
—— (2002) 'Timor Sea Treaty':
<www.austlii.edu.au/au/other/dfat/special/etimor/Timor_Sea_Treaty.html>

Ball, Desmond (2001) 'Silent witness: Australian intelligence and East Timor', *The Pacific Review*, 14, 1: 35–62.
—— (2002) 'The defence of East Timor: a recipe for disaster?' *Pacifica Review* 14, 3: 175–89.

Ball, Desmond and McDonald, Hamish (2000) *Death in Balibo, Lies in Canberra*, Sydney: Allen & Unwin.

Bartu, Peter (2000) 'The militia, the military, and the people of Bobonaro district', *Bulletin of Concerned Asian Scholars*, 32, 1–2: 35–42.

Beasley, Kent (2002) *Information Operations during Operation Stabilise*, Canberra: Land Warfare Studies Centre, Working paper 120, August.

Beauvais, Joel C. (2001) 'Benevolent despotism: a critique of UN state-building in East Timor', *International Law and Politics*, 33, 4: 1101–78.

Bergin, Anthony (1990) 'The Australian–Indonesian Timor Gap Maritime Boundary Agreement', *International Journal of Estuarine and Coastal Law*, 5, 4: 383–93.

Berlie, Jean A. (2000) 'A concise legal history of East Timor', *Studies in Language and Cultures of East Timor*, 3: 138–57.

Bhakti, Ikrar Nusa (1999) 'Howard sets back RI–Indonesia ties', *Jakarta Post*, 12 September: 4.

Birmingham, John (2001) 'Appeasing Jakarta. Australia's complicity in the East Timor tragedy', *Quarterly Essay*, 2: 1–87.

Blaxland, John (2002) *Information-era Manoeuvre. The Australian-led Mission to East Timor*, Canberra: Land Warfare Studies Centre, Working paper no. 118, June.

Bostock, Ian (2000) 'East Timor: An operational evaluation. By the book', *Jane's Defence Weekly*, 3 May: 23–7.

Bowers, Peter (1991) 'Hawke blundered on Timor, says Whitlam', *Sydney Morning Hearld*, 10 December, 1, 11.

Boxer, Charles R. (1960) 'Portuguese Timor: a rough island story, 1515–1960', *History Today*, 10, 5: 349–55.

Breen, Bob (2000) *Mission Accomplished, East Timor: The ADF Participation in INTERFET*, St Leonards: Allen & Unwin.

Brereton, Laurie (1999) 'Australia and East Timor', speech to the Queensland Branch of the AIIA, 4 February 1999.

Brown, Bruce (ed.) (2000) *East Timor – The Consequences*, Wellington: New Zealand Institute of International Affairs.

Budiardjo, Carmel and Liem Liong Soei (1984) *The War Against East Timor*, London: Zed Books.

Caplan, Richard (2002) *A New Trusteeship? The International Administration of War-torn Territories*, Adelphi Paper no. 341, London: IISS/Oxford University Press.

Carey, Peter (1995) 'Historical introduction', in Peter Carey and Steve Cox, *Generations of Resistance. East Timor*, London: Cassell, 9–55.

—— (1997) 'From Netherlands Indies to Indonesia – from Portuguese Timor to the Republic of East Timor/Timor Lorosae: two paths to nationhood and independence', *Indonesia and the Malay World*, 25, 71: 3–21.

Carey, Peter and Bentley, G. Carter (eds) (1995) *East Timor at the Crossroads: The Forging of a Nation*, London: Cassell.

Catholic Institute for International Relations and International Platform of Jurists for East Timor (1995) *International Law and the Question of East Timor*, London: CIIR/IPJET.

Chalk, Peter (2001) 'Australia and Indonesia: rebuilding relations after East Timor', *Contemporary Southeast Asia*, 23, 2: 233–53.

Cheeseman, Bruce (1999) 'Thailand pressed to take Timor reins', *Australian Financial Review*, 15 October.

Chesterman, Simon (2001) 'A Nation waits', *The World Today*, 57, 5: 25–7.

—— (2002) 'East Timor in transition: self-determination, state-building and the United Nations', *International Peacekeeping*, 9, 1: 45–76.

Chinkin, Christine M. (1993) 'East Timor moves to the world court', *European Journal of International Law*, 4, 2: 206–22.

Chinkin, Christine M. (1995) 'Australia and East Timor in international law', in Catholic Institute for International Relations and International Platform of Jurists for East Timor, *International Law and the Question of East Timor*, London: CIIR/IPJET, 269–89.

—— (1999) 'East Timor: a failure of decolonisation', *The Australian Year Book of International Law* 20, Canberra: Centre for International and Public Law, ANU.

Chopra, Jarat (2000) 'The UN's Kingdom of East Timor', *Survival*, 42, 3: 27–39.

—— (2001) 'The UN and East Timor, divided rule', *The World Today*, 57, 1: 13–15.

—— (2002) 'Building state failure in East Timor', *Development and Change*, 33, 5: 979–1000.

Chosum Ilbo (1999) 'Editorial: Korea should not send combat troops to East Timor', *Korea Focus*, 7, 5, 100–1.

Christian Science Monitor (2000) 'A brutal exit – Battalion 745': <http://www.csmonitor.com/atcsmonitor/specials/timor>

Clarence-Smith, W.G. (1985) *The Third Portuguese Empire 1825–1975. A Study in Economic Imperialism*, Manchester: Manchester University Press.

Clarence-Smith, W.G. (1992) 'Planters and smallholders in Portuguese Timor in the nineteenth and twentieth centuries', *Indonesian Circle*, 57, March: 15–30.

Clark, Roger S. (1995) 'The "decolonisation" of East Timor and the United Nations norms on self-determination and aggression', in Catholic Institute for International Relations and International Platform of Jurists for East Timor, *International Law and the Question of East Timor*, London: CIIR/IPJET, 65–102.

—— (1996) 'Public international law and private enterprise: damages for a killing in East Timor', *Australian Journal of Human Rights*, 3, 1: 21–39.

Clinton, William (1999) 'Statement by the President on East Timor', 9 September: <http://clinton6.nara.gov/1999/09/1999-09-09-statement-by-the-president-on-east-timor.html>

Cole-Adams, Peter and Alcorn, Gay (1999) 'Peacekeeping force in search of leadership', *Sydney Morning Herald*, 7 September.

Cotton, James (1999a) 'East Timor and Australia – twenty-five years of the policy debate', in James Cotton (ed.) *East Timor and Australia*, Canberra: Australian Defence Studies Centre/Australian Institute of International Affairs, 1–20.

—— (1999b) '"Peacekeeping" in East Timor: an Australian policy departure', *Australian Journal of International Affairs*, 53, 3: 237–46.

—— (2000) 'The emergence of an independent East Timor: national and regional challenges', *Contemporary Southeast Asia*, 22, 1: 1–22.

—— (2001a) 'Against the grain: the East Timor intervention', *Survival*, 43, 1: 127–42.

—— (2001b) '"Part of the Indonesian world": lessons in East Timor policy-making, 1974–76', *Australian Journal of International Affairs*, 55, 1: 119–31.

—— (2001c) 'Australia's commitment in East Timor: a review article', *Contemporary Southeast Asia*, 23, 3: 552–68.

—— (2002) 'The East Timor commitment and its consequences', in James Cotton and John Ravenhill (eds) *The National Interest in a Global Era: Australia in World Affairs 1996–2000*, Melbourne: Oxford University Press, 213–34.

Cribb, Robert (2002) 'From total people's defence to massacre: explaining Indonesian military violence in East Timor', in Freek Colombijn and J. Thomas Linblad (eds) *Roots of Violence in Indonesia: Contemporary Violence in Historical Perspective*, Leiden: KITLV Press.

Crikey.com (2003) 'Timor Sea Treaty Ministerial Meeting, 27 November': <http://www.crikey.com.au/politics/2003/03/06/20030306downertimor.html>

Cristalis, Irena (2002) *Bitter Dawn: East Timor, a People's Story*, London: Zed Press.

Daley, Paul (1999a) 'Australian troops for Timor', *The Age*, 27 February.

Daley, Paul (1999b) 'Soldiers flooding East Timor: a report', *The Age*, 18 March, 10.

Dampier, William (1981) *A Voyage to New Holland. The English Voyage of Discovery to the South Seas in 1699*, Gloucester: Alan Sutton.

Dee, Moreen (2001) '"Coalitions of the Willing" and humanitarian intervention: Australia's involvement with InterFET', *International Peacekeeping*, 8, 3: 1–20.

de los Santos, Jaime and Burgos, Arnulfo M.B. (2001) *Restoring Hope. Peacekeeping the East Timor Experience*, Manila: A M Cleofe Prints.

Department of Foreign Affairs, Republic of Indonesia (1977) *Decolonization in East Timor*, Jakarta: Department of Foreign Affairs, Republic of Indonesia.

—— (2003) 'The untold story of East Timor': <http://www.dfa-deplu.go.id/english/timtim.htm>

Department of Foreign Affairs and Trade (1991) *Treaty between Australia and the Republic of Indonesia on the Zone of Cooperation in an Area between the Indonesian Province of East Timor and Northern Australia*, Australian Treaty Series 1991 no. 9: <http://www.austlii.edu.au/au/other/dfat/treaties/1991/9.html>

—— (2001) *East Timor in Transition 1998–2000. An Australian Policy Challenge*, Canberra: Brown and Wilton.

Dickens, David (2001) 'The United Nations in East Timor: intervention at the military operational level', *Contemporary Southeast Asia*, 23, 2: 213–32.

Dodd, Mark (1999) 'Fears of bloodbath grow as militias stockpile arms', *Sydney Morning Herald*, 26 July.

Dodson, Louise (2000) 'Timor rewrote relations: PM', *Australian Financial Review*, 28 April.

Downer, Alexander (2000) 'East Timor – looking back on 1999', *Australian Journal of International Affairs*, 54, 1: 5–10.

—— (2001) Speech at the launch of *East Timor in Transition*, 17 July:
<http://www.dfat.gov.au/media/speeches/foreign/2001/010717_et.html>

Downie, Sue (2000) 'The United Nations in East Timor: comparisons with Cambodia', in Damien Kingsbury (ed.) *Guns and Ballot Boxes. East Timor's Vote for Independence*, Clayton: Monash Asia Institute, 117–34.

Downie, Sue and Kingsbury, Damien (eds) (2001) *The Independence Ballot in East Timor: Report of the Australian Volunteer Group*, Clayton: Monash Asia Institute, 2001.

Dunn, James S. (1983) *Timor: A People Betrayed*, Milton, Queensland: Jacaranda Press.

Dupont, Alan (2000) 'ASEAN's response to the East Timor crisis', *Australian Journal of International Affairs*, 54, 2: 163–70.

East Timor Action Network (ETAN) (2000) Background on East Timor and U.S. Policy East Timor Action Network, May:
<http://www.etan.org/timor/BkgMnu.htm>

East Timor Elections (2001) The Asia Society: <http://www.eastimorelections.org>

East Timor International Support Centre (1999a) 'Indonesia's death squads: getting away with murder': <http://www.easttimor.com/death_squads.htm>

—— (1999b) 'Indonesian-orchestrated savagery in East Timor':
<http://www.easttimor.com/savagery/indonesian_savagery1.htm>

East Timor Relief Association (1996) *It's Time to Lead the Way. Timorese People Speak about Exile, Resistance and Identity*, Melbourne: ETRA.

Escarameia, Paula (1993) *Formation of Concepts in International Law. Subsumption under Self-determination in the Case of East Timor*, Lisbon: Fundação Oriente.

Farrell, John Hunter (2000) *Peacemakers: INTERFET's Liberation of East Timor*, Rocklea: Fullbore Magazines.

Feith, Herb (1992) 'East Timor: the opening up, the crackdown and the possibility of a durable settlement', in Harold Crouch and Hal Hill (eds) *Indonesia Assessment 1992: Political Perspectives on the 1990s*, Canberra: Australian National University, Political and Social Change Monograph, 17: 63–80.

Fischer, Tim (2000) *Ballot and Bullets. Seven Days in East Timor*, Sydney: Allen & Uwin.

Fitzpatrick, Daniel (2000) 'Re-establishing land titles and administration in East Timor', *Pacific Economic Bulletin*, 15, 2: 152–60.

—— (2001) 'Property rights in East Timor's reconstruction and development', in Hal Hill and J. M. Saldanha (eds), *East Timor: Development Challenges for the World's Newest Nation*, Singapore: ISEAS, 177–92.

—— (2002) *Land Claims in East Timor*, Canberra: Asia Pacific Press.

Fox, James J. (ed.) (1980) *The Flow of Life. Essays on Eastern Indonesia*, Cambridge, Mass: Harvard University Press.

—— (2000) 'The UN popular consultation and its aftermath in East Timor', in Chris Manning and Peter van Dierman (eds) *Indonesia in Transition. Social Aspects of Reformasi and Crisis*, Singapore: ISEAS, 109–18.

—— (2001) 'Diversity and differential development in East Timor: potential problems and future possibilities', in Hal Hill and J. M. Saldanha (eds) *East Timor: Development Challenges for the World's Newest Nation*, Singapore: ISEAS, 155–73.

Fox, James J. and Soares, Dionisio Babo (eds) (2000) *Out of the Ashes. Destruction and Reconstruction of East Timor*, Adelaide: Crawford House.

Freney, Denis (1991) *A Map of Days. Life on the Left*, Port Melbourne: Heinemann Australia.

Fry, Ken (2003) *A Humble Backbencher. The Memoirs of Ken Fry MHR Fraser, 1974–1984*, Canberra: Ginnindera Press.

Garran, Robert (2000) '$26m fund for Timor rebel force', *The Australian*, 24 November.

Goldson, Annie (1999) *Punitive Damages* – feature film, New Zealand: Occasional Productions.

Gorjão, Paulo (2001a) 'The end of a cycle: Australian and Portuguese foreign policies and the fate of East Timor', *Contemporary Southeast Asia*, 23, 1: 101–21.

—— (2001b) 'The East Timorese Commission for Reception, Truth and Reconciliation: chronicle of a foretold failure?', *Civil Wars*, 4, 2: 142–62.

—— (2002) 'The legacy and lessons of the United Nations Transitional Administration in East Timor', *Contemporary Southeast Asia*, 24, 2: 313–36.

Grant, Thomas D. (2000) 'East Timor, the U.N. system, and enforcing non-recognition in international law', *Vanderbilt Journal of Transnational Law*, 33, i2: 273–97.

Greenlees, Don (1999) 'Row over Timor shift', *The Australian*, 16–17 January, 20.

—— (2002) 'Downer rules East Timor seabed border changes out of bounds', *The Australian*, 25 May, 12.

Greenlees, Don and Garran, Robert (2002) *Deliverance. The Inside Story of East Timor's Fight for Freedom*, Sydney: Allen & Unwin.

Gunn, G. C. (1997) *East Timor and the United Nations. The Case for Intervention*, Lawrenceville: Red Sea Press.

—— (1999) *Timor Loro Sae. 500 years*, Macau: Livros do Oriente.

—— (2000a) 'The Student Solidarity Council Movement in East Timor', in *New World Hegemony in the Malay World*, Lawrenceville: Red Sea Press, 253–66.

—— (2000b) 'From Salazar to Suharto: toponymy, public architecture, and memory in the making of Timor identity', in *New World Hegemony in the Malay World*, Lawrenceville: Red Sea Press, 227–52.

—— (2000c) 'East Timor and the U.N. ballot of 1999', in *New World Hegemony in the Malay World*, Lawrenceville: Red Sea Press, 267–81.

—— (2000d) 'Language, literacy, and political hegemony in East Timor', in *New World Hegemony in the Malay World*, Lawrenceville: Red Sea Press, 215–226.

Gunn, Geoffrey C. with Lee, Jefferson (1994) *A Critical View of Western Journalism and Scholarship on East Timor*, Manila: Journal of Contemporary Asia.

Gusmão, [José Alexandre] Xanana (2000) *To Resist is to Win! The Autobiography of Xanana Gusmão, with Selected Letters and Speeches*, Melbourne: Aurora Books.

Hainsworth, Paul and McCloskey, Stephen (eds) (2000) *The East Timor Question. The Struggle for Independence from Indonesia*, London: I.B. Tauris.

Hastings, Peter (1999) 'Timor – some Australian attitudes, 1903–1941', in James Cotton (ed.), *East Timor and Australia*, Canberra: Australian Defence Studies Centre/Australian Institute of International Affairs, 23–40.

Haywood, Anthony (2000) *In the Name of Justice: The Films of John Pilger*, Sydney: Random House.

Hicks, David (1983) 'Unachieved syncretism: the local-level political system in Portuguese Timor, 1966–1967', *Anthropos*, 78: 2–40.

Hill, David T. (2002) 'East Timor and the internet: global political leverage in/on Indonesia', *Indonesia*, 73, April: 25–51.

Hill, Hal and Saldanha, J.M. (eds) (2001) *East Timor: Development Challenges for the World's Newest Nation*, Singapore: ISEAS.

Hill, Helen (1978): 'The origins, ideologies and strategies of a nationalist movement in East Timor, unpublished MA thesis, Monash University.

—— (2001) 'Tales of the reconstruction', *Arena Magazine*, 54, September: 8–10.

—— (2002) *Stirrings of Nationalism in East Timor. Fretilin 1974–1978. The Origins, Ideologies and Strategies of a Nationalist Movement*, Otford: Otford Press.

Hitchens, Christopher (2001) *The Trial of Henry Kissinger*, London: Verso.

Hohe, Tanja (2002a) 'The clash of paradigms: international administration and local political legitimacy in East Timor', *Contemporary Southeast Asia*, 24, 3: 569–89.

—— (2002b) 'Totem polls: indigenous concepts and "free and fair" elections in East Timor', *International Peacekeeping*, 9, 4: 69–88.

Hunter, Ian (1999) 'Elite forces scouted island from April', *Sydney Morning Herald*, 11 October.

Inbaraj, Sonny (1995) *East Timor. Blood and Tears in ASEAN*, Chiangmai: Silkworm Books.

Indonesian Observer (2000) 'Document ordering Timor burning is valid', 4 January.

Inside Indonesia (1992) 'Getting away with murder', June, 30, 9–11.

International Court of Justice (1995) 'Case concerning East Timor': <http://www.dfat.gov.au/intorgs/timor/icjdir.html>

International Crisis Group (2002) 'Indonesia: implications of the Timor trials', Brussels: ICG: <http://www.crisisweb.org/projects/asia/indonesia/reports/A400643_08052002.pdf>

Jackson, Michael Gordon (2001) 'Something must be done? Genocidal chaos and world responses to mass murder in East Timor between 1975 and 1999', *International Journal of Politics and Ethics*, 1, 1: 45–72.

Jakarta Post (1999) 'TNI leaders "will not face international court"', 23 December.

—— (2000a) 'KPP HAM team to question Feisal over East Timor debacle', 4 January.

—— (2002b) 'Government told to consult Muslim figures to avoid backlash', 28 October.

Jardine, Matthew (1995) *East Timor: Genocide in Paradise*, Tucson: Odonian Press.

Jolliffe, Jill (1978) *East Timor: Nationalism and Colonialism*, St Lucia: University of Queensland Press.

—— (2001) *Cover-Up. The Inside Story of the Balibo Five*, Carlton: Scribe.

—— (2003) 'East Timor leaders fly to border down after likely militia raid', *Sydney Morning Herald*, 7 January.

Juddery, Bruce (1999) 'The Whitlam letter, Labor and Timor', *Canberra Times*, 9 March.

Judicial System Monitoring Program (2003) 'Indonesia' (6 January update): <http://www.jsmp.minihub.org/Indonesia/accusedindo.htm>

Kammen, Douglas (1999) 'Notes on the transformation of the East Timor military command and its implications for Indonesia', *Indonesia*, 67, April: 61–76.

Kartasasmita, Sabana (1998) *East Timor: the Quest for a Solution*, Singapore: Crescent Design.

Kaye, Stuart (1994) 'The Timor Gap Treaty: creative solutions and international conflict', *Sydney Law Review*, 16, 1: 72–96.

Keating, Paul (2000) *Engagement. Australia Faces the Asia-Pacific*, Sydney: Macmillan.

Kelly, Paul (1999) 'East Timor: it's not our fight to join', *The Australian*, 17 March, 13.

Kevin, Tony (2000) 'Our East Timor role not so noble', *The Canberra Times*, 3 May, 9.

King, Robert (2002) Submission #43, Parliament of Australia, Joint Standing Committee on Treaties 2002: <http://www.aph.gov.au/house/committee/jsct/timor/subs.htm>

Kingsbury, Damien (ed.) (2000) *Guns and Ballot Boxes. East Timor's Vote for Independence*, Clayton: Monash Asia Institute.

Kohen, Arnold S. (1999) *From the Place of the Dead. Bishop Belo and the Struggle for East Timor*, Oxford: Lion Books.

Kohen, Arnold S. and Taylor, John (eds) (1979) *An Act of Genocide: Indonesia's Invasion of East Timor*, London: TAPOL.

Kondoch, Boris (2001) 'The United Nations administration of East Timor', *Journal of Conflict and Security Law*, 6, 2: 245–65.

Krieger, Heike (ed.) (1997) *East Timor and the International Community. Basic Documents*, Cambridge: Cambridge University Press/Grotius Publications.

La'o Hamutuk (2001) 'Funding East Timor's reconstruction: an overview', *The La'o Hamutuk Bulletin*, 2, 1, April, part 1.

—— (2002a) 'East Timor faces post-UNTAET challenges', *The La'o Hamutuk Bulletin*, 3, 4, May, part 2.

—— (2002b) 'Timor oil', *The La'o Hamutuk Bulletin*, 3, 5, June:
<http://www.etan.org/lh/bulletins/bulletinv3n5.html>

Leaver, Richard (2001) 'Introduction: Australia, East Timor and Indonesia', *The Pacific Review*, 14, 1: 1–14.

Lee Kim Chew (1999) 'Politics behind Asean's inaction on East Timor', *The Straits Times*, 18 October.

Lennox, Rowena (2000) *Fighting Spirit of East Timor. The Life of Martinho da Costa Lopes*, London: Zed Books.

Lowry, Bob (2000) 'East Timor: an overview of political developments', in Chris Manning and Peter van Dierman (eds) *Indonesia in Transition. Social Aspects of Reformasi and Crisis*, Singapore: Institute of Southeast Asian Studies, 91–108.

Lyons, John (1999b) 'The Secret Timor dossier', *The Bulletin*, 12 October: 24–9.

McBeth, John (1994) 'Change in the wind: Jakarta may be rethinking its Timor policy', *Far Eastern Economic Review*, 6 October, 26.

McDonald, Hamish (1980) *Suharto's Indonesia*, London: Fontana/Collins, 189–211.

—— (1999) 'The Whitlam Documents: political failure on East Timor', *Sydney Morning Herald*, 6 March.

McDonald, H., Ball, D., Dunn, J., van Klinken, G., Bourchier, D., Kammen, D. and Tanter, R. (2002) *Masters of Terror. Indonesia's Military and Violence in East Timor in 1999*, Canberra: Strategic and Defence Studies Centre, ANU.

McDougall, Derek (2001) 'Regional institutions and security: implications of the 1999 East Timor crisis', in Andrew Tan and J. D. Kenneth Boutin (eds) *Non-traditional Security Issues in Southeast Asia*, Singapore: IDSS, 166–96.

McKee, Geoffrey A. (2000) 'A New Timor Gap', *Inside Indonesia*, 62, April–June: 18–20.

McKee, Geoffrey A. (2002) Submission #87, Parliament of Australia, Joint Standing Committee on Treaties 2002:
<http://www.aph.gov.au/house/committee/jsct/timor/subs.htm>

Mackie, Jamie (2001a) 'Australia and Indonesia', *Australian Journal of International Affairs*, 55, 1: 132–41.

—— (2001b) 'Future political structures and institutions in East Timor', in Hal Hill and J. M. Saldanha (eds) *East Timor: Development Challenges for the World's Newest Nation*, Singapore: ISEAS, 193–206.

Mackie, Jamie and Ley, Allison (1998) 'The East Timor issue: differing cultures, values and perceptions', in Anthony Milner and Mary Quilty (eds) *Australia in Asia. Episodes*, Melbourne: Oxford University Press, 82–110.

McMillan, Andrew (1992) *Death in Dili*, Sydney: Hodder & Stoughton.

Mahathir, Mohamad (1999) 'The West has mishandled East Timor', *Mainichi Daily News*, 11 October.

Maley, William (2000a) 'Australia and the East Timor crisis: some critical comments', *Australian Journal of International Affairs*, 54, 2: 151–61.

—— (2000b) 'The UN and East Timor', *Pacifica Review*, 12, 1: 63–76.

Martin, Ian (2001) *Self-determination in East Timor: The United Nations, the Ballot, and International Intervention*, Boulder: Lynne Rienner/International Peace Academy.

Martinkus, John (1991) 'Envoy must die to stop civil war', *Sydney Morning Herald*, 1 March, 1.

—— (2001) *A Dirty Little War. An Eyewitness Account of East Timor's Descent into Hell 1997–2000*, Sydney: Random House.

Maxwell, Kenneth (1995) *The Making of Portuguese Democracy*, Cambridge: Cambridge University Press.

Metherell, Mark and Skehan, Craig (1999) 'US threatens to deploy international intervention force', *Sydney Morning Herald*, 3 September.

Monk, Paul M. (2001) 'Secret intelligence and escape clauses. Australia and the Indonesian annexation of East Timor, 1963–76', *Critical Asian Studies*, 33, 2: 181–208.

Moore, Samuel (2001) 'The Indonesian military's last years in East Timor: an analysis of its secret documents', *Indonesia*, 72: 9–44.

Mubyarto, Soetrisno, L., Hudiyanto, Djatmiko, E., Setiawati, I. and Mawarni, A. (1991) In Pat Walsh (ed.) *East Timor: The Impact of Integration. An Indonesian Social-Anthropological Study*, Melbourne: Indonesian Resources and Information Program.

Murdoch, Lindsay and Riley, Mark (1999) 'Downer hints at military support', *Sydney Morning Herald*, 31 July.

Naipospos, Coki (1996) 'Change in Indonesia, chance for East Timor', *Inside Indonesia*, 48, October–December.

Nairn, Allan (1995) 'Out of East Timor', *The Nation*, 17–24 July.

—— (2000) 'U.S. support for the Indonesian military. Congressional testimony', *Bulletin of Concerned Asian Scholars*, 32, 1–2: 43–48.

National Security Archive (2002a):
   <http://www.gwu.edu/~nsarchiv/NSAEBB/NSAEBB62/>

—— (2002b) Memorandum of Conversation between Presidents Ford and Suharto, 5 July 1975, 12:40 pm–2:00 pm.
   < http://www.gwu.edu/~nsarchiv/NSAEBB/NSAEBB62/doc1.pdf>

Nettheim, Garth (1995) 'International law and international politics', in Catholic Institute for International Relations and International Platform of Jurists for East Timor, *International Law and the Question of East Timor*, London: CIIR/IPJET, 181–204.

Nicol, Bill (1978) *Timor. The Stillborn Nation*, Melbourne: Visa.

Niner, Sarah (2001) 'A long journey of resistance: the origins and struggle of CNRT', in Richard Tanter, Mark Selden, Stephen R. Shalom (eds) *Bitter Flowers, Sweet Flowers. East Timor, Indonesia and the World Community*, Sydney: Pluto, 15–29.

Oceanic Exploration (2002) Submission #77, Parliament of Australia, Joint Standing Committee on Treaties:
   <http://www.aph.gov.au/house/committee/jsct/timor/subs.htm>

Orr, Robert C. (2001) 'Making East Timor work: the United States as junior partner', *National Security Studies Quarterly*, 7, 3: 133–40.

Pangilinan, Rowena Rivera (2000) *The UN Peacekeeping Operations in East Timor: Highlights of the Philippine Participation*, Manila: National Defense College of the Philippines, Occasional Paper 3, 11, November.

Parliament of the Commonwealth of Australia (1983) *Official Report of the Australian Parliamentary Delegation to Indonesia, led by W.L. Morrison*, Canberra: AGPS.

—— (1983) Senate Foreign Affairs, Defence and Trade References Committee [SFADTRC], *The Human Rights and Conditions of the People of East Timor*, Canberra: Government Printer.

—— (2000) Senate Foreign Affairs, Defence and Trade References Committee [SFADTRC], *East Timor Final Report*, Canberra: Commonwealth of Australia.

Payne, Marise (2002) 'Democratisation in East Timor', *Australia Quarterly*, 74, 3: 21–5.

Pilger, John (1998) 'A land of crosses', in Jim Aubrey (ed.) *Free East Timor. Australia's Culpability in East Timor's Genocide*, Sydney: Random House Australia, 153–76.

Pinto, Constancio and Jardine, Matthew (1997) *East Timor's Unfinished Struggle. Inside the Timorese Resistance*, Boston: South End Press.

Pura, Raphael (1999) 'Conflict over East Timor may test Asean's loyalties', *Wall Street Journal*, 1 October.

Ramos-Horta, José (1987) *Funu. The Unfinished Saga of East Timor*, Lawrenceville: Red Sea Press.

—— (2001) *East Timor and the Region*, Singapore: ISEAS, 'Trends in Southeast Asia', 1.

Raymond, Robert (1964) 'Timor – sleeping island', *The Bulletin*, 29 February: 13–18.

Reyes, Alejandro (1999) 'Days of diplomacy', *Asiaweek*, 24 September.

Richardson, Michael (1976), 'East Timor: the war Australia might have prevented', *The National Times*, 19–24 July: 9–15.

Robinson, Geoffrey (2001a) 'People's war: militias in East Timor and Indonesia', *South East Asia Research*, 9, 3: 271–318.

—— (2001b) 'With UNAMET in East Timor – an historian's personal view', in Richard Tanter, Mark Selden and Stephen R. Shalom (eds) *Bitter Flowers, Sweet Flowers. East Timor, Indonesia and the World Community*, Sydney: Pluto, 55–72.

—— (2002a) 'If you leave us, we will die', *Dissent*, Winter: 87–99.

—— (2002b) 'The fruitless search for a smoking gun. Tracing the origins of violence in East Timor', in Freek Colombijn and J. Thomas Linblad (eds) *Roots of Violence in Indonesia: Contemporary Violence in Historical Perspective*, Leiden: KITLV Press.

Robinson, Ian (1994) 'The East Timor conflict', in Michael Cranna (ed.) *The True Cost of Conflict*, London: Earthscan, 1–24.

Roff, Sue Rabbitt (1992) *Timor's Anschluss. Indonesian and Australian Policy in East Timor 1974–1976*, Lewiston: Edwin Mellen Press.

Rothwell, Donald R. and Tsamenyi, Martin (eds) (2000) *The Maritime Dimensions of Independent East Timor*, Wollongong: Centre for Maritime Policy, University of Wollongong, Papers on Maritime Policy, 8.

Ryan, Alan (2000a) *From Desert Storm to East Timor. Australia, the Asia-Pacific and the 'New Age' Coalition Operations*, Canberra: Land Warfare Studies Centre, Study Paper 302.

—— (2000b) *Primary Responsibilities and Primary Risks. ADF Participation in the International Force East Timor*, Canberra: Land Warfare Studies Center, Study Paper 304.

—— (2002) 'The strong lead-nation model in an ad hoc Coalition of the Willing: Operation *Stabilise* in East Timor', *International Peacekeeping*, 9, 1: 23–44.

Saldanha, João M. de Sousa (1994) *The Political Economy of East Timor*, Jakarta: Sinar Harapan.

Saldanha, João M. de Sousa (ed.) (1995) *An Anthology: Essays on the Political Economy of East Timor*, The East Timor project monograph 3/95, Darwin: Northern Territory University, Series editor – Paul Webb.

Salla, Michael B. (1997) 'East Timor, regional security and the Labor tradition', in David Lee and Christopher Waters (eds) *The Labor Tradition in Australian Foreign Policy*, St Leonards: Allen & Unwin, 219–33.

Savage, David (2002) *Dancing with the Devil : A Personal Account of Policing the East Timor Vote for Independence*, Clayton: Monash Asia Institute.

SBS Television (2000) *Dateline*, 29 March, Sydney: <http://www.sbs.com.au/dateline/p9t2.htm>

Scheiner, Charles (2000) 'The United States: from complicity to ambiguity' in Paul

Hainsworth and Stephen McCloskey (eds) *The East Timor Question. The Struggle for Independence from Indonesia*, London: I.B.Tauris, 117–32.

Sebastian, Leonard C. and Smith, Anthony L. (2000) 'The East Timor crisis: a test case for humanitarian intervention', *Southeast Asian Affairs 2000*, Singapore: ISEAS, 64–86.

Shanahan, Dennis (1999) 'Brereton the bomb thrower', *The Australian*, 6–7 March, 25, 30.

Sharfe, Sharon, (1996) *Complicity. Human Rights and Canadian Foreign Policy: The Case of East Timor*, Montreal: Black Rose.

Sheridan, Greg (1999) 'Forget the ideology and prejudices – Whitlam is in the clear', *The Australian*, 5 March.

Sherlock, Stephen (1996) 'Political economy of the East Timor conflict', *Asian Survey*, 36, 9: 835–51.

Sherman, Tom (1999) *Second Report on the Deaths of Australian-based Journalists in East Timor in 1995*, Canberra: Department of Foreign Affairs and Trade, January.

Shoesmith, Dennis (2003) 'Timor-Leste: divided leadership in a semi-presidential system', *Asian Survey*, 43, 2: 231–52.

Singh, Bilveer (1996) *East Timor, Indonesia and the World. Myths and Realities*, Kuala Lumpur: APDR Consult.

Smith, Michael G. and Dee, Moreen (2003) *Peacekeeping in East Timor. The Path to Independence*, Boulder: Lynne Rienner/International Peace Academy.

Smith, Sue (2001) 'A handmaiden's tale: an alternative view of the logistic lessons learned from INTERFET', Canberra: Australian Defence Studies Centre, Working Paper 65, April.

Soares, Dionisio Babo (2000) 'Political developments leading to the referendum', in James J. Fox and Dionisio Babo Soares (eds) *Out of the Ashes. Deconstruction and Reconstruction of East Timor*, Adelaide: Crawford House, 57–78.

Soesastro, M. Hadi (1991) 'East Timor: questions of economic viability', in Hal Hill (ed.) *Unity and Diversity. Regional Economic Development in Indonesia since 1970*, Singapore: Oxford University Press, 207–29.

—— (2000) 'Indonesia as Australia's neighbour', in Chris Manning and Peter van Dierman (eds) *Indonesia in Transition. Social Aspects of Reformasi and Crisis*, Singapore: Institute of Southeast Asian Studies, 128–37.

Steele, Jonathan (2002) 'Nation building in East Timor', *World Policy Journal*, 19, 2: 76–86.

Stewart, Ian (1999) 'East Timor rebuffs the Asean way', *South China Morning Post*, 27 September.

Strohmeyer, Hansjörg (2000) 'Building a new judiciary for East Timor: challenges of a fledgling nation', *Criminal Law Forum*, 11, 3: 259–85.

—— (2001) 'Collapse and reconstruction of a judicial system: the United Nations missions in Kosovo and East Timor', *American Journal of International Law*, 95, 1: 46–63.

Subroto, Hendro (1997) *Eyewitness to Integration of East Timor*, Jakarta: Sinar Harapan.

Suhrke, Astri (2001) 'Peacekeepers as nation-builders: dilemmas of the UN in East Timor', *International Peacekeeping*, 8, 4: 1–20.

Tanter, Richard, Selden, Mark and Shalom, Stephen R. (2000) (eds) *Bitter Flowers, Sweet Flowers. East Timor, Indonesia and the World Community*, Sydney: Pluto.

TAPOL (1999a) 'Special UN troops to Timor in March, Dili very tense', TAPOL 1/3/99: <http://www.easttimor.com/html/timor_news1.htm>

TAPOL (1999b) *TAPOL Bulletin*, 7 June: <http://www.gn.apc.org/tapol/rp9906tni.htm>

Taudevin, Lansell (1999) *East Timor. Too Little Too Late*, Sydney: Duffy & Snellgrove.

Taudevin, Lansell and Lee, Jefferson (eds) (2000) *East Timor: Making Amends? Analysing Australia's Role in Reconstructing East Timor*, Otford: Otford Press.

References 175

Taylor, John (1991) *Indonesia's Forgotten War. The Hidden History of East Timor*, London: Zed Books.
Thakur, Ramesh (2001) 'Cambodia, East Timor and the Brahimi Report', *International Peacekeeping*, 8, 3: 115–24.
Tiffen, Rod (2001) *Diplomatic Deceits: Australian Media and Policy in East Timor*, Kensington: University of NSW Press.
Toohey, Brian and Wilkinson, Marian (1987) *The Book of Leaks*, Sydney: Angus and Robertson.
Traub, James (2000) 'Inventing East Timor', *Foreign Affairs*, 79, 4: 74–89.
Triggs, Gillian and Bialek, Dean (2002a) 'The New *Timor Sea Treaty* and interim arrangements for joint development of petroleum resources of the Timor Gap', *Melbourne Journal of International Law*, 3, 3: 322–63.
—— (2002b) 'Current legal development: Australia – Australia withdraws maritime disputes from the compulsory jurisdiction of the International Court of Justice and the International Tribunal for the Law of the Sea', *The International Journal of Marine and Coastal Law*, 17, 3: 423–30.
Trowbridge, Erin (2002) 'Back road reckoning. Justice in East Timor', *Dissent*, Winter: 101–13.
Turner, Michele (1992) *Telling East Timor: Personal Testimonies 1942–1992*, Kensington: UNSW Press.
UNAMET (1999a): <http://www.un.org/peace/etimor99/etimor.htm>
UNAMET (1999b): <http://www.un.org/peace/etimor99/Fact_frame.htm>
UNTAET (1999): <http://www.un.org/peace/etimor/etimor.htm>
UNTAET (2000) Regulations 2000/23–24
 < http://www.gov.east-timor.org/english/html>
United Nations (1999a) Press Release SG/SM/6922 12 March, New York: United Nations.
—— (1999b) Report of the Security Council Mission to Jakarta and Dili, 14 September: <http://www.un.org/peace/etimor/9926220E.htm>
—— (1999c) Resolution 1264 of the Security Council, 15 September: <http://ods-dds-ny.un.org/doc/UNDOC/GEN/N99/264/81/PDF/N9926481.pdf?OpenElement>
—— (1999d) Report of the Secretary-General on the Situation in East Timor, 4 October: <http://www.un.org/peace/etimor/sg1024.htm>
—— (1999e), Resolution 1272 of the Security Council, 25 October: <http://www.un.org/Docs/scres/1999/99sc1272.htm>
—— (2000) 'Report of the Secretary-General of the United Nations Transitional Administration in East Timor', 26 January: <http://ods-dds-ny.un.org/doc/UNDOC/GEN/N00/261/62/PDF/N0026162.pdf?OpenElement>
—— (2002) 'UNMISET Facts and Figures': <http://www.un.org/Depts/dpko/missions/unmiset/facts.html>
—— (2003) Press Release SC/7719, 4 April.
United States Senate (1992) *Crisis in East Timor and US Policy Toward Indonesia*, Hearings Before the Committee in Foreign Relations, Washington: US Government Printing Office.
van Klinken, Gerry (1999) 'How ABRI's militias in Timor are structured': <http://www.easttimor.com/html/notices2.htm>
van Walsum, Peter (2002) 'The East Timor Crisis and the doctrine of humanitarian intervention', Melbourne: Asialink:

<http://www.asialink.unimelb.edu.au/cpp/transcripts/vanwalsum200202.html>

Verrier, June R. (1976) 'Australia, Papua New Guinea and the West New Guinea question, 1949–1969', unpublished PhD thesis, Clayton: Monash University.

Viviani, Nancy (1976) 'Australians and the East Timor issue', *Australian Outlook*, 30, 3: 241–61; reprinted in James Cotton (ed.) (1999) *East Timor and Australia*, Canberra: ADSC/AIIA, 81–107.

—— (1997) 'The Whitlam Government's policy towards Asia', in David Lee and C. Waters (eds) *Evatt to Evans. The Labor Tradition in Australian Foreign Policy*, St Leonards: Allen & Unwin, 99–109.

Wain, Barry (1982) 'Military seen behind firm controlling Timor's coffee', *Asian Wall Street Journal*, 16 June.

Wallace, Alfred Russel (1869) *The Malay Archipelago*, 1869 edition, reprinted 1987, Singapore: Graham Brash.

Walsh, J.R. and Munster, G.J. (eds) (1980) *Documents on Australian Defence and Foreign Policy 1968–1975*, Hong Kong: Walsh and Munster.

—— (1982) *Secrets of State. A Detailed Assessment of the Book They Banned*, Hong Kong: Walsh and Munster.

Ward, Eilís and Carey, Peter (2001) 'The East Timor issue in the context of EU–Indonesian relations, 1975–99', *Indonesia and the Malay World*, 29, 83: 51–74.

Way, Wendy (ed.) (2000) *Australia and the Indonesian Incorporation of Portuguese Timor, 1974–1976*, Melbourne: Melbourne University Press/Department of Foreign Affairs and Trade.

Wensley, Penny (2000) 'East Timor and the United Nations', speech of 23 February, Australian Institute of International Affairs, Sydney.

Wheeldon, John (1984) 'The "Finlandisation" of Australia and the occupation of East Timor', *Quadrant*, 28, September: 24–5.

Wheeler, Nicholas J. and Dunne, Tim (2001) 'East Timor and the new humanitarian interventionism', *International Affairs*, 77, 4: 805–27.

Whitlam, E.G. (1963) *Australian Foreign Policy 1963*, Fourteenth Roy Milne Memorial Lecture, Armidale: AIIA.

Whitlam, Gough (1997) *Abiding Interests*, Brisbane: University of Queensland Press.

Willesee, Don (1999) 'Willesee: Whitlam reigned on East Timor', *The Australian*, 10 March.

Woolcott, Richard (2003) *The Hot Seat. Reflections on Diplomacy from Stalin's Death to September 11*, Sydney: HarperCollins.

World Bank (2002) *East Timor. Policy Challenges for a New Nation. Country Economic Memorandum*, May: <Inweb18.worldbank.org/eap/eap.nsf/Countries/East+Timor/>

Wright, Lincoln (2000) 'Aussie soldiers may face longer East Timor stay', *Canberra Times*, 13 May.

Other works

Acharya, Amitav (2001) *Constructing a Security Community in Southeast Asia. ASEAN and the Problem of Regional Order*, London: Routledge.

Alcorn, Gay (1999) 'Bill to cut all US aid to go before Congress', *Sydney Morning Herald*, 9 September.

Alcorn, Gay (2001) 'Powell puts Australia on Jakarta watch', *Sydney Morning Herald*, 19 January.

Anderson, Benedict (1998) *The Spectre of Comparisons*, London: Verso.

Anderson, Benedict and McVey, Ruth (1971) *A Preliminary Analysis of the October 1, 1965 Coup in Indonesia*, Ithaca: Modern Indonesia Project, Cornell University.

ASEAN (2000) 'Joint Communiqué of the 33rd ASEAN Ministerial Meeting, Bangkok, Thailand, 24–25 July': <http://www.aseansec.org/3659.htm>

ASEAN Regional Forum (1999) Chairman's Statement, the Sixth Meeting of the ASEAN Regional Forum', 26 July: <http://www.aseansec.org/3587.htm>

—— (2000) Chairman's Statement, the Seventh Meeting of the ASEAN Regional Forum', 27 July: <http://www.aseansec.org.3576.htm>

Asian Wall Street Journal (2002) 'Indonesia's timidity', 25 January.

Baehr, Peter (1997) 'Problems of aid conditionality: the Netherlands and Indonesia', *Third World Quarterly*, 18, 2: 363–76.

Baker, Mark (2002) 'Offensive behaviour', *Sydney Morning Hearld*, 7–8 December, 35.

Ball, Des and Kerr, Pauline (1996) *Presumptive Engagement: Australia's Asia-Pacific Security Policy in the 1990s*, Sydney: Allen & Unwin.

Ball, Des and Wilson, Helen (eds) (1991) *Strange Neighbours. The Australia–Indonesia Relationship*, Sydney: Allen & Unwin.

Becker, Elizabeth and Shenon, Philip (1999) 'US priority is to maintain good ties with Indonesia, officials indicate', *New York Times*, 9 September.

Boyle, Michael G. (2003) 'Policy making and pragmatism. Australia's management of security cooperation with Indonesia during the New Order Period', unpublished PhD thesis, University of New South Wales, Australian Defence Force Academy.

Brahimi, Lakhdar (2000) *Report of the Panel on United Nations Peace Operations*, 21 August: <http://www.un.org/peace/reports/peace_operations/report.htm>

Brenchley, Fred (1999) 'The Howard defence doctrine', *The Bulletin*, 28 September, Sydney.

Brown, Colin (1997) 'Indonesia', in Bernie Bishop and Deborah McNamara (eds) *The Asia–Australia Survey 1997–98* , Melbourne: Macmillan, 183–211.

Bull, Hedley (1977) *The Anarchical Society. A Study of Order in World Politics*, London: Macmillan.

Cameron, Clyde (1990) *The Cameron Diaries*, Sydney: Allen & Unwin.

Caplan, Richard (2002) *A New Trusteeship? The International Administration of War-torn Territories*, Adelphi Paper 341, London: IISS/Oxford University Press.

Catley, Bob and Dugis, Vinsenio (1998) *Australian Indonesian Relations since 1945. The Garuda and the Kangaroo*, Aldershot: Ashgate.

Chopra, Jarat (1999) *Peace-Maintenance: The Evolution of International Political Authority*, London: Routledge.

Clarke, Walter and Herbst, J. (eds) (1997) *Learning from Somalia*, Boulder: Westview.

Commonwealth of Australia 2000, *Budget Overview 2000–01*: <http://www.budget.gov.au/2000-01/highlhts/glossy.pdf>

Conboy, Ken (2003) *Kopassus. Inside Indonesia's Special Forces*, Jakarta: Equinox.

Cosgrove, Peter J. (2000) 'The ANZAC Lecture at Georgetown University', 4 April.

Cotton, James and Ravenhill, John (eds) (1997a) *Seeking Asian Engagement. Australia in World Affairs 1991–95*, Melbourne: Oxford University Press.

—— (1997b) 'Australia's "Engagement with Asia"', in James Cotton and John Ravenhill (eds) *Seeking Asian Engagement. Australian World Affairs 1991–95*, Melbourne: Oxford University Press, 1–16.

—— (eds) (2002) *The National Interest in a Global Era. Australia in World Affairs 1996–2000*, Melbourne: Oxford University Press.

Cribb, Robert (ed.) (1990) *The Indonesian Killings 1965–1966. Studies from Java and Bali*, Clayton: Monash Papers on Southeast Asia 21, Monash University.

Cronin, Patrick M. (1994) 'Coalition Warfare Facts, Fads and Challenges', *Strategic Review*, 22, 2.

Crouch, Harold (1992) 'An ageing President, an ageing regime', in Harold Crouch and Hal Hill (eds) *Indonesia Assessment 1992: Political Perspectives on the 1990s*, Canberra: Australian National University, Political and Social Change Monograph 17, 41–62.

Damrosch, Lori Fisler (ed.) (1993) *Enforcing Restraint. Collective Intervention in Internal Conflicts*, New York: Council on Foreign Relations Press.

Department of Defence (2000) *White Paper*, Department of Defence, Canberra.

Department of Foreign Affairs and Trade (1989) *Australia's Regional Security: Ministerial Statement*, Canberra: DFAT.

—— (1997) *In the National Interest. Australia's Foreign and Trade Policy*, Canberra: DFAT.

Department of National Defense, the Philippines (1998) *In Defense of the Philippines. 1998 Defense Policy Paper*, Manila: Department of National Defense.

Deutsch, Karl W., Burrell, S. A., Kann, R. A., Lee, M. Jr., Lichterman, M., Lindgren, R. E., Loewenheim, F. L. and Van Wagenen, R. W. (1968) *Political Community and the North Atlantic Area: International Organization in the Light of Historical Experience*, Princeton: Princeton University Press.

Downer, Alexander (1999) 'Australia and Asia – a new paradigm for the relationship', Speech to the Foreign Correspondents' Association, Sydney: 16 April, mimeo.

—— (2002) 'Prime Minister's Comments':
<http://www.dfat.gov.au/media/transcripts/2002/021204_fa_abcam.html>

Dupont, Alan (2001) *East Asia Imperilled. Transnational Threats to Security*, Cambridge: Cambridge University Press.

The Economist (1966) 'One million dead?', 20 August, 727–8.

Edwards, Peter, with Pemberton, Greg (1992) *Crises and Commitments: The Politics and Diplomacy of Australia's Involvement in Southeast Asian Conflicts 1948–1965*, Sydney: Allen & Unwin.

Elson, R.E. (2001) *Suharto: A Political Biography*, Cambridge: Cambridge University Press.

Evans, Gareth and Grant, Bruce (1991) *Australia's Foreign Relations in the World of the 1990s*, Melbourne: Melbourne University Press.

Financial Times, London: <www.ft.com>

Freudenberg, Graham (1993) 'Aspects of foreign policy', in Hugh Emy, O. Hughes and R. Mathews (eds) *Whitlam Re-Visited. Policy Development, Policies and Outcomes*, Sydney: Pluto.

Funston, John (1998) 'ASEAN: out of its depth?', *Contemporary Southeast Asia*, 20, 1: 22–37.

Garnaut, Ross (1989) *Australia and the Northeast Asian Ascendancy*, Canberra: AGPS.

Goldsworthy, David (2001) *Facing North. A Century of Australian Engagement with Asia*, vol. 1, Melbourne: Department of Foreign Affairs and Trade/Melbourne University Press.

Hardjono, Ratih (1992) *White Tribe of Asia. An Indonesian View of Australia*, Clayton: Monash Asia Institute, Monash University.

Hartcher, Peter (1996) 'How the enemy became an ally', *Australian Financial Review*, 4–5 July, 1: 18–19, 26–7.

Henningham, Stephen (1993) 'The uneasy peace: New Caledonia's Matignon Accords at mid-term', *Pacific Affairs*, 66, 4: 519–38.

Hill, Hall and Manning, Chris (1999) 'Indonesia–Australia ties – what went wrong', *The Jakarta Post*, Jakarta, 30 November: 4.

Hitchens, Christopher (2001) *The Trial of Henry Kissinger*, London: Verso.

Hoffmann, Stanley (1987) *Janus and Minerva. Essays in the Theory and Practice of International Politics*, Boulder: Westview.

Howard, John (2002) 'Transcript of the Prime Minister interview with Laurie Oakes':
<http://www.pm.gov.au/news/interviews/2002/interview2015.htm>

Ileto, Reynaldo C. (1979) *Pasyon and Revolution. Popular Movements in the Philippines, 1840–1910*, Manila: Ateneo de Manila University Press.

International Crisis Group (2002) 'How the *Jemaah Islamiyah* Terrorist Network Operates', Brussels: ICG:
<http://www.crisisweb.org/projects/asia/indonesia/reports/A400845_11122002.pdf>

Jackman, Simon (1998) 'Pauline Hanson, the mainstream, and political elites: the place of race in Australian political ideology', *Australian Journal of Political Science*, 33, 2: 167–84.

Japan Defense Agency (1999) *1999 Defense of Japan*, Tokyo: Urban Connections.

Jenkins, David (1986) 'Indonesia: government attitudes towards the domestic and foreign media', *Australian Outlook. The Australian Journal of International Affairs*, 40, 3: 153–61.

Jin, Linbo (2000) 'The principle of non-intervention in the Asia Pacific region: a Chinese perspective', in David Dickens and Guy Wilson-Roberts (eds) *Non-Intervention and State Sovereignty in the Asia-Pacific*, Wellington: Centre for Strategic Studies.

Jorgensen-Dahl, Arnfinn (1982) *Regional Organization and Order in South-East Asia*, New York: St Martin's Press.

Kahin, Audrey *et al.* (1992) 'Current data on the Indonesian military elite', *Indonesia*, 53: 93–136.

Kahin, George and Kahin, Audrey (1995) *Subversion as Foreign Policy: The Secret Eisenhower and Dulles Debacle in Indonesia*, New York: Norton.

Langford, Tonya (1999) 'Things fall apart: state failure and the politics of intervention', *International Studies Review*, 1, 1: 59–79.

Lee, David (1997) 'The Curtin and Chifley governments. Liberal internationalism and world organisation', in David Lee and C. Waters (eds) *Evatt to Evans. The Labor Tradition in Australian Foreign Policy*, Canberra, ACT: Allen & Unwin, 48–61.

Leifer, Michael (1983) *Indonesia's Foreign Policy*, London: Allen & Unwin/RIIA.

Lyons, John (1999a) 'The Howard doctrine', *The Bulletin*, 28 September, 22–4.

McAllister, Ian and Ravenhill, John (1998) 'Australian attitudes towards closer engagement with Asia', *The Pacific Review*, 11, 1: 119–41.

Mackie, Jamie (1974) 'Australia's relations with Indonesia: principles and policies I and II', *Australian Outlook. The Australian Journal of International Affairs*, 28, 1 & 2: 3–14, 168–78.

MacQueen, Norrie (1997) *The Decolonization of Portuguese Africa. Metropolitan Revolution and the Dissolution of Empire*, London: Longman.

Mahbubani, Kishore (1995) 'The Pacific Way', *Foreign Affairs*, 74, 1: 100–11.

Mak, Joon-Num (1999) 'The security environment in Southeast Asia', in Desmond Ball (ed.) *Maintaining the Strategic Edge: The Defence of Australia in 2015*, Canberra: Strategic and Defence Studies Centre.

Meredith, David and Dyster, Barrie (1999) *Australia in the Global Economy*, Cambridge: Cambridge University Press.

Ministry of Defence, Malaysia (1997) *Towards Defence Self-Reliance*, Kuala Lumpur: Ministry of Defence.

Ministry of Defence, Thailand (1996) *The Defence of Thailand 1996*, Bangkok: Ministry of Defence/Strategic Research Institute.

Ministry of National Defense, Republic of Korea (1999) *Defense White Paper 1998*, Seoul: Ministry of National Defense.

Moynihan, Daniel P. (1978) *A Dangerous Place*, Boston: Little Brown.

Murphy, Dan (1999) 'Up in Arms', *Far Eastern Economic Review*, 1 February, 24–5.

Murphy, Sean D. (1996) *Humanitarian Intervention. The United Nations in an Evolving World Order*, Philadelphia: University of Pennsylvania Press.

Myall, James (1996) *The New Interventionism, 1991–1994 : UN Experience in Cambodia, Former Yugoslavia, and Somalia*, New York : Cambridge University Press.

Narine, Shaun (2002) *Explaining ASEAN: Regionalism in Southeast Asia*, Boulder: Rienner.

New York Times, New York: <www.nytimes.com>

Newitt, Malyn (2002) 'Mozambique', in Patrick Chabal *et al. A History of Postcolonial Lusophone Africa*, Bloomington: Indiana University Press.

Noble, Gregory W. and Ravenhill, John (eds) (2000) *The Asian Financial Crisis and the Architecture of Global Finance*, Cambridge: Cambridge University Press.

Nye, Joseph S. (1971) *Peace in Parts. Integration and Conflict in Regional Organization*, Boston: Little Brown.

O'Rourke, Kevin (2002) *Reformasi. The Struggle for Power in Post-Soeharto Indonesia*, Crow's Nest: Allen & Unwin.

Parliament of the Commonwealth of Australia (1975) *Debates, House of Representatives*.

—— (1976) *Debates, House of Representatives*.

—— (1999) *Debates, House of Representatives*.

—— (2000) *Debates, House of Representatives*.

—— (2003) *Debates, Senate*.

—— (1993) Joint Standing Committee on Foreign Affairs, Defence and Trade, *Australia's Relations with Indonesia*, Canberra: Australian Government Publishing Service.

—— (2002) Joint Standing Committee on Treaties, 12 July, TR33.

Pemberton, Greg (1987) *All the Way: Australia's Road to Vietnam*, Sydney: Allen & Unwin.

Peou, Sorpong (2000) *Intervention and Change in Cambodia. Towards Democracy?*, Singapore: ISEAS.

Ramsbotham, Oliver and Woodhouse, Tom (1996) *Humanitarian Intervention in Contemporary Conflict*, Cambridge: Polity Press.

Renouf, Alan (1979) *The Frightened Country*, Melbourne: Macmillan.

Richardson, Michael (1978) 'Jakarta's tough sea boundary claim', *Australian Financial Review*, 20 December.

Robison, Richard (1986) *Indonesia: The Rise of Capital*, Sydney: Allen & Unwin.

Shawcross, William (2000) *Deliver us from Evil. Warlords & Peacekeepers in a World of Endless Conflict*, London: Bloomsbury.

Snitwongse, Kusuma (1998) 'Thirty years of ASEAN: achievements through political cooperation', *The Pacific Review*,11, 2: 184–94.

Sulaiman, Idris F., Sofyan, G. Hanafi, Smith, Shannon Luke (eds) (1998) *Bridging the Arafura Sea. Australia–Indonesia Relations in Prosperity and Adversity*, Canberra: National Centre for Development Studies.

Tang, James T.H. (ed.) (1995) *Human Rights and International Relations in the Asia Pacific*, London: Pinter.

Toohey, Brian and Pinwill, William (1990) *Oyster. The Story of the Australian Secret Intelligence Service*, Melbourne: Mandarin.

Toohey, Brian and Wilkinson, Marian (1987) *The Book of Leaks. Exposés in defence of the public's right to know*, North Ryde: Angus and Robertson

Tow, William T. (2001) *Asia-Pacific Strategic Relations: Seeking Convergent Security*, Cambridge: Cambridge University Press.

United Nations DPKO (1995) 'The Comprehensive Report on Lessons Learned from the UN Operations in Somalia (UNOSOM)':
<http://www.un.org/Depts/dpko/lessons/UNOSOM.pdf>

Walsh, Patrick (1999) *Military Coalition Building: A Structural and Normative Assessment of Coalition Architecture*, Ann Arbor: UMI.

Wanandi, Jusuf (2000) 'Asean's future at stake', *The Straits Times*, Singapore, 9 August.

Wesley, Michael (2002) 'Australia and the Asian financial crisis', in James Cotton and John Ravenhill (eds) *The National Interest in a Global Era. Australia in World Affairs 1996–2000*, Melbourne: Oxford University Press, 301–25.

Wheeler, Nicholas J. (2000) *Saving Strangers: Humanitarian Intervention in International Society*, London and New York : Oxford University Press.

Whitlam Documents (1999) *Sydney Morning Herald*, 8 March.

Winters, Jeffrey A. (1999) 'The determinant of financial crisis in Asia', in T. J. Pempel (ed.) *Politics of the Asian Economic Crisis*, Ithaca: Cornell University Press, 79–97.

Woodard, Garry (1998) 'Best practice in Australian foreign policy: Konfrontasi (1963–66)', *Australian Journal of Political Science*, 33, 1: 85–99.

Worsley, Peter (1970) *The Trumpet Shall Sound. A Study of Cargo Cults in Melanesia*, London: Paladin.

Index